THIRD EDITION

Understanding Race and Ethnic Relations

Vincent N. Parrillo
William Paterson University

PEARSON

Boston ■ New York ■ San Francisco
Mexico City ■ Montreal ■ Toronto ■ London ■ Madrid ■ Munich ■ Paris
Hong Kong ■ Singapore ■ Tokyo ■ Cape Town ■ Sydney

Senior Editor: *Jeff Lasser*
Series Editorial Assistant: *Lauren Houlihan*
Senior Marketing Manager: *Kelly May*
Production Editor: *Pat Torelli*
Editorial Production Service: *Modern Graphics, Inc.*
Composition Buyer: *Linda Cox*
Manufacturing Buyer: *Debbie Rossi*
Photo Researcher: *Annie Pickert*
Cover Administrator: *Kristina Mose-Libon*

For related titles and support materials, visit our online catalog at
www.ablongman.com.

Portions of this material appeared in *Strangers to These Shores: Race and
Ethnic Relations in the United States*, Eighth Edition, copyright © 2006 by
Pearson Education.

To obtain permission(s) to use material from this work, please submit a
written request to Allyn and Bacon, Permissions Department, 75 Arlington
Street, Boston, MA 02116 or fax your request to 617-848-7320.

Between the time website information is gathered and then published, it
is not unusual for some sites to have closed. Also, the transcription of
URLs can result in typographical errors. The publisher would appreciate
notification where these errors occur so that they may be corrected in
subsequent editions.

ISBN 0-205-53056-7

Printed in the United States of America

10 9 8 7 6 5 4 3 2 1   11 10 09 08 07

Photo credits appear on p. 212, which constitutes an extension of the copyright page.

CONTENTS

Preface   ix

1 **The Study of Minorities**   **1**

The Stranger as a Social Phenomenon   **3**
Similarity and Attraction   3
Social Distance   3
Perceptions   7
Interactions   8

A Sociological Perspective   **9**
Functional Theory   9
Conflict Theory   10
Interactionist Theory   12

Minority Groups   **13**
Development of a Definition   13
Minority-Group Characteristics   15

Racial and Ethnic Groups   **16**

Ethnocentrism   **18**
In the United States   20
In Other Times and Lands   20
Eurocentrism and Afrocentrism   22

Objectivity   **23**

The Dillingham Flaw   **24**

Personal Troubles and Public Issues   **26**

The Dynamics of Intergroup Relations   **27**

Retrospect   **28**

Key Terms   **29**

Review Questions   **29**

Suggested Readings   **30**

Internet Resources   **30**

2 **The Role of Culture** **31**

The Concept of Culture **31**
The Reality Construct 34

Cultural Change **38**
Cultural Diffusion 38
Subcultures 40

Theories of Minority Integration **42**
Assimilation (Majority-Conformity Theory) 42
Amalgamation (Melting-Pot Theory) 46
Accommodation (Pluralistic Theory) 49

Is There a White Culture? **52**

Retrospect **53**

Key Terms **54**

Review Questions **54**

Suggested Readings **54**

Internet Resources **55**

3 **Ethnic and Racial Stratification** **56**

Stratification **57**

Social Class **58**
Class Consciousness 59
Ethnicity and Social Class 59
Blaming the Poor or Society? 61

Intergroup Conflict **66**
Cultural Differentiation 67
Structural Differentiation 68

Ethnic Stratification **69**
The Power-Differential Theory 69
The Internal-Colonialism Theory 71
Origins of Ethnic Stratification 72

Retrospect **74**

Key Terms **75**

Review Questions   75

Suggested Readings   75

Internet Resources   76

4   Prejudice   77

The Psychology of Prejudice   79
Levels of Prejudice   79
Self-Justification   80
Personality   81
Frustration   83

The Sociology of Prejudice   85
Socialization   85
Economic Competition   86
Social Norms   88

Stereotyping   89
Ethnophaulisms   91
Ethnic Humor   93

The Influence of Television   93
Perpetuation of Stereotypes   94
Influencing of Attitudes   94
Ingroup and Outgroup Perceptions   96

The Influence of Advertising and Music   96
Advertising   96
Music   97

Can Prejudice Be Reduced?   98
Interaction   98
Information   99

Diversity Training   101

Retrospect   102

Key Terms   103

Review Questions   103

Suggested Readings   103

Internet Resources   104

5 **Discrimination**   **105**

Levels of Discrimination   **105**

Relationships between Prejudice and Discrimination   **106**

Social and Institutional Discrimination   **108**

The Affirmative-Action Controversy   **109**
  The Concepts of Justice, Liberty, and Equality   109
  Affirmative Action Begins   112
  Court Challenges and Rulings   113
  Has Affirmative Action Worked?   115
  Public Opinion   116

Racial Profiling   **117**

Retrospect   **118**

Key Terms   **119**

Review Questions   **119**

Suggested Readings   **119**

Internet Resources   **120**

6 **Dominant–Minority Relations**   **121**

Minority-Group Responses   **121**

Ethnic- and Racial-Group Identity   **122**
  Avoidance   124
  Deviance   125
  Defiance   127
  Acceptance   128

Consequences of Minority-Group Status   **129**
  Negative Self-Image   129
  The Vicious Circle   131
  Marginality   131
  Middleman Minorities   133

Dominant-Group Responses   **134**
  Legislative Controls   135
  Segregation   135
  Expulsion   137

Xenophobia   137
Annihilation   139
Hate Groups   141
Hate Crimes   142

Exploitation   143

Retrospect   146

Key Terms   147

Review Questions   147

Suggested Readings   147

Internet Resources   148

7   **Contemporary Patterns and Issues   149**

Ethnic Consciousness   150
Country of Origin as a Factor   150
The Three-Generation Hypothesis   152

The Changing Face of Ethnicity   154
Transnationalism   154
Social Capital   155
Segmented Assimilation   156
Naturalization   157
Ethnicity as a Social Process   158

Migration Patterns   159
Symbolic Ethnicity   162

Current Issues   163
Immigration Fears   163
Undocumented Migrants   167

Language Retention   169
Bilingual Education   171
The English-Only Movement   173
Multiculturalism   175

Racial and Ethnic Diversity in the Future   178
Indicators of Ethnoreligious Change   179
Beyond Tomorrow   181

Key Terms   182

Review Questions   182

Suggested Readings   183

Internet Resources   184

Notes   185

Appendix   205

PREFACE

Race and ethnic relations is an exciting, challenging, and dynamic field of study. It touches all of us, directly and indirectly, in many ways, and it does so on personal, regional, national, and even global levels. Each generation thinks it lives through a unique situation, as shaped by the times or the "peculiarities" of a group's characteristics. In truth, each generation is part of a larger process that includes behavioral patterns inherited from past generations, who also thought their situation was unique.

Intergroup relations change continually, through alternating periods of quiet and turmoil, of entry of new groups of immigrants or refugees, and of problems sporadically arising between native-born racial or ethnic groups within the country. Often, we can best understand these changes within the context of discernible, recurring patterns that are influenced by economic, political, psychological, and sociological factors. This is partly what C. Wright Mills meant when he spoke of the intricate connection between the patterns of individual lives and the larger historical context of society, a concept we discuss in Chapter 1.

To understand both the interpersonal dynamics and the larger context of changing intergroup relations—particularly the reality of historical repetitions of behavior—we must utilize social science theory, research, and analysis. This volume provides the framework for such understanding, as adapted from my more comprehensive book *Strangers to These Shores*. I am grateful for the widespread adoptions of that book and the favorable response to it from colleagues and students through the United States, Canada, and Europe. I am equally pleased with the many similar positive responses from other students and colleagues to this book, which is intended as a concise but thorough sociological introduction to race and ethnic relations.

Following a presentation of some introductory concepts in the first chapter—particularly that of the stranger as a social phenomenon and the concept of the Dillingham Flaw—the first group of chapters examines differences in culture, reality perceptions, social class, and power as reasons for intergroup conflict. These chapters also look at the dominant group's varying expectations about how minorities should "fit" into its society. Chapters 2 and 3 include coverage of some middle-range conflict and interactionist theories. Chapters 4 and 5 explore the dimensions and interrelationships of prejudice and discrimination, and Chapter 6 covers the dominant–minority response patterns so common across different groups and time periods. This chapter presents middle-range conflict theories about economic exploitation too.

Chapter 7 employs holistic sociological concepts in discussing ethnic consciousness; ethnicity as a social process; current racial and ethnic issues, fears, and reactions; and the various indicators of U.S. diversity in the twenty-first century.

Review questions, an annotated bibliography, and Internet resources appear at the end of each chapter, along with a list of key terms. At the end of the book, the reader will find an appendix giving immigration statistics for the period 1820–2004. I also encourage readers to visit the Web site for *Strangers to These Shores* at www.ablongman.com/parrillo8e to find links and exercises directly related to the chapters that have been adapted for this book.

What's New in the Third Edition

This new edition reflects a number of changes.

First, and most important, is the continuation of our policy to provide a thorough updating of all data and information, and the inclusion of the most recent and relevant studies not only in sociology but in many other related fields as well.

Second, to enhance the reader's understanding, I have expanded discussion on: the three main theories for understanding intergroup relations; the shaping of perceptions; social distance; the interconnection between the Dillingham Flaw and the Thomas Theorem; differences between race and ethnicity; the social construction of race; the culture of poverty; the link between concepts of justice and equality with affirmative action; and the role of employers in hiring immigrant labor.

Third, where appropriate, student-relevant examples have been added to bring the issues closer to the students' own experiences.

Fourth, because the last chapter deals with the contemporary scene, it has been extensively revised to reflect recent and current events. Added are new sections on transnationalism, social capital, segmented assimilation, naturalization, and language retention. Also, this chapter thoroughly examines the extensive debate and actions that have been occurring over legal immigration and undocumented migrants, enhanced by the use of graphics to further student understanding.

Fifth, new International Scene boxes on the 2005 French riots and the recent problems of undocumented migrants in Italy and Spain bring comparative relevance to our understanding of race and ethnic relations.

Finally, each chapter now ends with an Internet Resources section, giving links that enable students either to read more on certain subjects or explore interactive sites that offer directly pertinent insights.

Acknowledgments

I would like to thank the following reviewers for their helpful suggestions for this edition: Mary Ann Jacobs, San Diego State University; Yolanda Johnson, University of Nebraska, Lincoln; Roberta Osuyos, San Diego State University; and Nena Stracuzzi, University of New Hampshire.

I have also had the good fortune to work with a team at Allyn and Bacon whose competence, cooperation, and dedication have made the production of this concise volume a most satisfying project. My special thanks go to Jeff Lasser, Senior Editor, for signing the project and offering valuable input on the book's structure and features. Finally, I want to express my gratitute to my wife, Beth, and to my daughters Chrysti, Cara, Beverley, and Liz, for the joy they bring to my life and the constant support they provide in my writing endeavors.

Vincent N. Parrillo
William Paterson University
Wayne, New Jersey 07470
E-mail: parrillov@wpunj.edu

CHAPTER

1

The Study of Minorities

"We may have different religions, different languages, different colored skin, but we all belong to one human race. We all share the same basic values."
—Kofi Annan, former UN Secretary General

We pride ourselves on being a nation of immigrants. Many still call the United States a great melting pot where people of all races, religions, and nationalities come to be free and to improve their lives. Certainly, a great number of immigrants offer living testimony to that ideal; their enthusiasm for their adopted country is evident in countless interviews found in oral histories at Ellis Island and elsewhere. As college students, regardless of how recently or long ago your family emigrated to the United States, most of you also provide evidence of the American Dream of freedom of choice, economic opportunity, and upward mobility.

Yet beneath the Fourth of July speeches, the nation's absorption of diverse peoples over the years, and the numerous success stories lies a disquieting truth. Native-born Americans have not always welcomed newcomers with open arms; indeed, they have often responded with overt acts of discrimination, ranging from avoidance to violence and murder. The dominant group's treatment of native-born Blacks and Native Americans disturbingly illustrates the persistence of subjugation and entrenched inequality. Today, we continue to face serious problems in attitudes toward and treatment of Native Americans on reservations, poor Blacks in urban ghettos, large concentrations of recent Asian and Hispanic immigrants, and Arab and Muslim Americans struggling to gain acceptance. For some, the American Dream becomes a reality; for others, blocked opportunities create an American nightmare.

Interethnic tensions and hostilities within a nation's borders have been an unfortunate worldwide reality for thousands of years. Within any society, groupings of people by race, religion, tribe, culture, or lifestyle can

1

generate prejudices, tensions, and outbursts of violence. Sometimes the violence takes on epic proportions.

Since 2001, terrorist killings of innocent people have occurred in Afghanistan, England, India, Indonesia, Iraq, the Philippines, Spain, Turkey, and the United States. Tens of thousands of Africans have been slaughtered in the Darfur region of the Sudan. Religious factions in Africa, Asia, the Middle East, and Europe still harbor such animosity toward one another that violence continues to erupt sporadically.

Each decade, in fact, has its own sad history of large-scale interethnic and interracial killings. In the 1990s, thousands of Christians and Muslims fell victim to "ethnic cleansing" (expulsion, massacres) in Bosnia and Kosovo that became so widespread that it resulted in NATO military action and a still-continuing presence to prevent further violence. Elsewhere, in Rwanda, tribal warfare between the Hutu and Tutsi led to the massacre of hundreds of thousands of Tutsis, but no outside intervention.

The 1980s saw the longest conventional war of the twentieth century (1980–1988) between Iran and Iraq that resulted in one million casualties. Civil war in Ecuador and another war among tribes in Nigeria each resulted in thousands of casualties, human rights violations, and enormous suffering. Under Saddam Hussein, Iraq used poison gas to kill thousands of Kurds in Halabja, a town 150 miles northeast of Baghdad. Worst of all was the genocide in Cambodia in the 1970s that ended with the death of 1.7 million people.

On college campuses, which are microcosms of the larger society in which they exist, intergroup relations are thankfully not as horrific as anything just described, but on a different level, they can sometimes be rather tense and occasionally even worse. Dorm life and social events may be marred by a level of discomfort with unlike roommates or by arguments, complaints, fights, vandalism, and verbal abuse that erupt out of strained intercultural or interracial interactions. Most common, however, are the self-segregated cafeteria tables or the clustering of specific minority groups at other campus locales, both illustrative of the sociological axiom "like likes to be with like." This seemingly harmless situation is nevertheless an indicator of a less-than-cohesive college community where avoidance and limited social interaction may produce social isolation and reduced acceptance of unlike others as equals.

Individuals of the dominant group usually absolve themselves of blame for a minority group's low status and problems, ascribing these instead to specific flaws they perceive within the group itself (e.g., slowness in learning the main language of the country or supposed lack of the work ethic). Sociologists, however, note among different groups distinct patterns of interaction that transcend national boundaries, specific periods, or idiosyncrasies of particular groups. Opinions may vary as to the causes of these patterns of behavior, but a consensus does exist about their presence.

The Stranger as a Social Phenomenon

To understand intergroup relations, we must recognize that differences among various peoples cause each group to look on other groups as strangers. Among isolated peoples, the arrival of a stranger has always been a momentous occasion, often eliciting strong emotional responses. Reactions might range from warm hospitality to conciliatory or protective ceremonies to hostile acts. In an urbanized and mobile society, the stranger still evokes similar responses. From the Tiwi of northern Australia, who consistently killed intruders, to the nativists of any country or time, who continually strive to keep out "undesirable elements," the underlying premise is the same: The outsiders are not good enough to share the land and resources with the "chosen people" already there.

Similarity and Attraction

At least since Aristotle (384–322 BCE) commented, "We like those who resemble us, and are engaged in the same pursuits," social observers have been aware of the similarity-attraction relationship.[1] Numerous studies have explored the extent to which a person likes others because of similar attitudes, values, beliefs, social status, or physical appearance. Examining the development of attraction among people who are initially strangers to one another, an impressive number of these studies have found a positive relationship between the similarity of two people and their liking for each other. Most significantly, the findings show that people's perception of similarity between themselves is a more powerful determinant than actual similarity.[2] Cross-cultural studies also support this conclusion.[3] Considerable evidence exists showing greater human receptivity to strangers who are perceived as similar than to those who are perceived as different.

Social Distance

One excellent technique for evaluating how perceptions of similarity attract closer interaction patterns consists of ranking **social distance**. Devised by Emory Bogardus in 1926, this measurement device has been used repeatedly since then.[4] In five comparable studies spanning 50 years, researchers obtained responses from a fairly evenly divided group of undergraduate and graduate students aged 18 to 35, about 10 percent of whom were Black. The students selected the degree of social closeness or distance personally acceptable to members of a particular group.

These five national surveys measured the students' preferences among thirty groups, most of them Europeans but also including Native Americans, Canadians, Black Americans, and six Asian groups (Asian Indians,

Chinese, Filipinos, Japanese, Japanese Americans, and Koreans). Some fluctuation occurred over the 50-year span of these surveys, most notably Blacks moving upward from near the bottom to the middle. Generally, the distribution showed White Americans, Canadians, northern and western Europeans in the top third, with southern, central, and eastern Europeans in the middle third, and racial minorities in the bottom third.

With a few exceptions, the relatively consistent positioning of response patterns illustrates the similarity-attraction relationship. Italians have moved up steadily, becoming the first group not from northwest Europe to break into the top ten. The leap upward by Blacks was even more dramatic, from near bottom to the midpoint. International politics or war usually causes groups to drop: Germans, Italians, and Japanese in 1946 and Russians after 1946 (Cold War, McCarthyism, Vietnam).[5] However, the political changes Russia underwent in the 1990s enabled Russians to rise to fourteenth place in a smaller 1993 study.[6]

In 2001, this author updated both the wording of the choices and the list of groups.[7] I eliminated mostly homogenized groups (e.g., Armenians, Czechs, Finns, Norwegians, Scots, and Swedes) and added various Asian, Hispanic, and West Indian groups. In this new national study, the available choices were:

1. Would accept marrying into my family (1 point).
2. Would accept as a personal friend in my social circle (2 points).
3. Would accept as a neighbor on my street (3 points).
4. Would work in the same office (4 points).
5. Would only have as speaking acquaintances (5 points).
6. Would only have as visitors to my country (6 points).
7. Would bar from entering my country (7 points).

As expected, nonethnic Whites remained in the top position as the most accepted group, with other top-ten slots filled by Canadians, British, Irish, French, Germans, and Dutch, essentially continuing a 70-year pattern. What is particularly striking about the new listing, however, is the dramatic rise of African Americans. In placing ninth, they broke the racial barrier in entering the top sector and placing ahead of other White ethnic groups. The rise of Italians into the second position ahead of the previously dominating English, Canadians, and French, as well as the movement of Greeks into the seventh position, were other significant changes. However, only one-hundredth of a point separates a group from the next ranked group in positions 13 through 25. Therefore, in the middle part of the list in Table 1.1, the exact placement of a group in relation to those near it should not be given much importance, in view of the close scores, because these rankings may be the result of sampling variability.

Although this analysis is not directly comparable with the 1977 data in Table 1.1 because of changes in the list of groups, some comparisons are still

TABLE 1.1 **U.S. Social Distance Changes, 1977–2001**

1977		2001	
1. Americans (U.S. Whites)	1.25	1. Americans (U.S. Whites)	1.07
2. English	1.39	2. Italians	1.15
3. Canadians	1.42	3. Canadians	1.20
4. French	1.58	4. British	1.23
5. Italians	1.65	5. Irish	1.24
6. Swedish	1.68	6. French	1.28
7. Irish	1.69	7. Greeks	1.32
8. Hollanders	1.83	8. Germans	1.33
9. Scots	1.83	9. African Americans	1.34
10. Indians (American)	1.84	10. Dutch	1.35
11. Germans	1.87	11. Jews	1.38
12. Norwegians	1.93	12. Indians (American)	1.40
13. Spanish	1.98	13. Africans	1.43
14. Finns	2.00	14. Polish	1.44
15. Jews	2.01	15. Other Hispanic/Latino	1.45
16. Greeks	2.02	16. Filipinos	1.46
17. Negroes	2.03	17. Chinese	1.47
18. Poles	2.11	18. Puerto Ricans	1.48
19. Mexican Americans	2.17	19. Jamaicans	1.49
20. Japanese Americans	2.18	20. Russians	1.50
21. Armenians	2.20	21. Dominicans	1.51
22. Czechs	2.23	22. Japanese	1.52
23. Chinese	2.29	23. Cubans	1.53
24. Filipinos	2.31	24. Koreans	1.54
25. Japanese	2.38	25. Mexicans	1.55
26. Mexicans	2.40	26. Indians (from India)	1.60
27. Turks	2.55	27. Haitians	1.63
28. Indians (from India)	2.55	28. Vietnamese	1.69
29. Russians	2.57	29. Muslims	1.88
30. Koreans	2.63	30. Arabs	1.94
Arithmetic mean of 44,640		Arithmetic mean of 126,053	
Racial reactions	1.93	Racial reactions	1.44
Spread in distance	1.38	Spread in distance	0.87

Sources: Carolyn A. Owen, Howard C. Eisner, and Thomas R. McFaul, "A Half-Century of Social Distance Research: National Replication of the Bogardus Studies," *Sociology and Social Research* 66 (October 1981): 89; and Vincent N. Parrillo and Christopher Donoghue, "Updating the Bogardus Social Distance Studies: A New National Survey," *The Social Science Journal*, 42: 2 (2005): 257–71.

possible and the findings are encouraging in many ways. The spread in social distance—despite (1) increased diversity in society, (2) a revised list reflecting that demographic reality, and (3) increased diversity among respondents—continues to shrink. The 2001 overall mean score of 1.44 is significantly lower than the 1977 overall mean score of 1.93, as is the spread in social distance of 0.87 compared with 1.38. Despite the removal of more assimilated groups and the addition of less assimilated groups to the list, the downward trend in both indicators of social distance has continued. These results suggest a growing level of acceptance of diverse groups, even though many are recent arrivals, racial minorities, and/or from non-Western lands.

Remarkably, despite media reports of sporadic instances in the 9/11 aftermath of group blame and hate crimes against those identified (sometimes erroneously) as Arabs or Muslims, that mindset did not extend to most respondents in this survey. Although relegating Muslims and Arabs to the bottom, respondents nevertheless gave them lower (i.e., more socially acceptable) mean scores than those received by seventeen of the thirty groups in the 1977 study. Their distinction between the ethnicity of the terrorists and others who were Arabs and/or Muslims resulted in even lower scores than given to past low-ranked groups, which is indeed an impressive finding.

The ranking of Muslims and Arabs in the last two places is hardly surprising as a repercussion of the terrorist attacks, but how do we explain their comparatively low social distance nonetheless? Perhaps the answer is the same as for the strong findings for African Americans and other groups as well. This study may bear witness to a "unity syndrome," the coalescing of various groups against a common enemy who attacked us. Only time will tell how lasting this new spirit is, both in the bottom rankings of Muslims and Arabs and in the low social distance scores for all groups. This study only captures social acceptance of groups at a given moment in time, on the heels of 9/11. It is neither conclusive nor yet indicative of new patterns. Future social distance studies incorporating the new groups will ideally give a clearer picture of how tolerant Americans are in their ever-growing multiracial, multicultural society.

Sometimes the social distance maintained between minority groups is greater than that preserved between each minority and the dominant group. For example, a 1989 study of 708 Anglos, 249 Blacks, and 256 Mexican Americans in Texas found Blacks and Mexican Americans more accepting of Anglos than of each other. However, higher-status members (those having more education and higher incomes) and youths of all three groups were generally more accepting of contact with the outgroup minority than were lower-status group members.[8]

Social distance affects many types of choices and actions, one of which is living with diverse others, whether on a college campus or in a neighborhood. A 2005 study found that, despite a public university's efforts, no reduction of social distance regarding roommates or dating occurred as its students progressed toward degree completion. White students showed greater social distance with Blacks than with Hispanics, although cross-racial friendships did reduce the level of social distance.[9] Another 2005 study of the Toronto metropolitan area found that understanding social distance among groups proved more helpful in understanding residential segregation than just examining broad racial and pan-ethnic classifications.[10] Using simulation analyses, Mark Fossett (2006) reported that the persistence of segregation in recent decades results not just from discrimination, but also from social distance and status dynamics.[11]

Perceptions

By definition, the stranger is not only an outsider but also someone different and personally unknown. People perceive strangers primarily through **categoric knowing**—the classification of others on the basis of limited information obtained visually and perhaps verbally.[12] People make judgments and generalizations on the basis of scanty information, confusing an individual's characteristics with typical group-member characteristics. For instance, if a visiting Swede asks for tea rather than coffee, the host may incorrectly conclude that all Swedes dislike coffee.

Perceptions based on categoric knowing are often in part prompted or deepened by media portrayals. Throughout history, in fact, minority groups have complained that the media usually portrayed them unfavorably, thereby generating negative public impressions and fears. For example, since much of daily news reporting is about negative events and since the dominant group mostly controls what gets reported and how, these minority complaints may have some merit. The educated person needs to be constantly vigilant against undue influence resulting from one-sided, biased statements that may even appear in news reports.

Native-born Americans have in the past perceived immigrants—first-generation Americans of different racial and ethnic groups—as a particular kind of stranger: one who intends to stay. Eventually, the presence of immigrants became less of a novelty; then fear, suspicion, and distrust often replaced the natives' initial curiosity. The strangers remained strangers as each group sought its own kind for personal interaction.

The role of a stranger can be analyzed regardless of the particular period in history: Georg Simmel (1858–1918) theorized that strangers represent both *nearness*, because they are physically close, and *remoteness*, because they react differently to the immediate situation and have different values and ways of doing things.[13] The stranger is both inside and outside: physically present and participating but also outside the situation as a result of being from another place.

The natives perceive the stranger in an abstract, typified way. That is, the individual becomes the *totality*, or stereotype, of the group. The stranger, however, perceives the natives in concrete, individual terms. Simmel suggested that strangers have a higher degree of objectivity about the natives because the strangers' geographical mobility reflects mobility in their minds as well. The stranger is free from indigenous habit, piety, and precedent.

Furthermore, because strangers do not participate fully in society, they have a certain mental detachment, causing them to see things more objectively.

Interactions

Simmel approached the role of the stranger through an analysis of the formal structures of life. In contrast, Alfred Schutz (1899–1959)—himself an immigrant to the United States—analyzed the stranger as lacking "intersubjective understanding."[14] By this he meant that people from the same social world mutually "know" the language (including slang), customs, beliefs, symbols, and everyday behavior patterns that the stranger usually does not.

For the native, then, every social situation is a coming together not only of roles and identities but also of shared realities—the intersubjective structure of consciousness. What is taken for granted by the native is problematic to the stranger. In a familiar world, people live through the day by responding to daily routines without questions or reflection. To strangers, however, every situation is new and is therefore experienced as a crisis.

Strangers experience a "lack of historicity"—a lack of the shared memories of those with whom they live. Human beings who interact together over a period of time "grow old together"; strangers, however, are "young" because they are newcomers, and they experience at least an approximation of the freshness of childhood. They are aware of things that go unnoticed by the natives, such as the natives' customs, social institutions, appearance, and lifestyle.

Sometimes the stranger may be made the comical butt of jokes because of unfamiliarity with the everyday routine of life in the new setting. In time, however, strangers take on the natives' perspective; the strangers' consciousness lessens because the freshness of their perceptions is lost. Concurrently, the natives' **abstract typifications** about the strangers become more concrete through social interaction. As Schutz said, "The vacant frames become occupied by vivid experiences." As acculturation takes place, the native begins to view the stranger more concretely, and the stranger becomes less questioning about daily activities. Use of the term *naturalized citizen* takes on a curious connotation when examined from this perspective because it implies that people are in some way odd or unnatural until they have acquired the characteristics of the natives.

Many strangers have come—and are still coming—to the United States in search of a better life. Through an examination of sociological theory and the experiences of these many racial and ethnic groups, the story of how the stranger perceives the society and is received by it will continually be retold. The adjustment from stranger to neighbor may be viewed as movement along a continuum, but this continuum is not frictionless, and assimilation is not inevitable. Rather, it is the process of social interaction among different groups of people.

A Sociological Perspective

Sociology is the study of human relationships and patterns of behavior. Through scientific investigation, sociologists seek to determine the social forces that influence behavior as well as to identify recurring patterns that help them and others better understand that behavior.

Using historical documents, reports, surveys, ethnographies, journalistic materials, and direct observation, sociologists systematically gather empirical evidence about intergroup relations. The sociologist then analyzes these data in an effort to discover and describe the causes, functions, relationships, meanings, and consequences of intergroup harmony or tension. Ascertaining reasons for the beginning, continuance, intensification, or alleviation of readily observable patterns of behavior among different peoples is complex and difficult, and not all sociologists concur when interpreting the data. Different theories, ideas, concepts, and even ideologies and prejudices may influence a sociologist's conclusions too.

Disagreement among sociologists is no more unusual than in other areas of scientific investigation, where such matters as how the universe was created, what constitutes a mental disorder, or whether heredity or environment is more important in shaping behavior are discussed. Nonetheless, differing sociological theories have played an important role in influencing the pattern of relations and are grounded in the social scientists' values regarding those relations. In sociological investigation, three major perspectives shape analysis of the study of minorities: functional theory, conflict theory, and interactionist theory. Each has a contribution to make, for each acts as a different lens providing a distinct focus on the subject.

Functional Theory

Proponents of **functional theory** emphasize that the various parts of society have functions, or positive effects, that promote solidarity and maintain the stability of the whole. Sometimes called the *structural-functional paradigm* or model, it represents the core tradition of sociology, inspired by the writings of Auguste Comte (1798–1857), Herbert Spencer (1829–1905), and Emile Durkheim (1858–1917) in Europe, and developed further in the United States by Talcott Parsons (1902–1979) and Robert Merton (1910–2003).

This perspective emphasizes that society is a structure of beliefs and traditional ways of doing things. A society contains values (competition, honesty, success), **status positions** (occupation, class structure, gender roles), and institutions (family, education, religion, economics, and governance). Each of these parts plays a role in keeping the society going, although few people actually realize all the various functions of their society. Thus, functionalists organize their sociological analyses through identifying these many structures of society and investigating how well or poorly their functions operate.

Some components of the social structure have **manifest functions** (obvious and intended results), but they often have **latent functions** (hidden and unexpected results). For example, the obvious functions of the tourist visa program are to attract foreign visitors to build goodwill and to stimulate local economies at places they visit, thereby increasing the gross domestic product (GDP). One unintended result is thousands of visitors not returning after their visas expire and remaining here as illegal aliens.

Functionalists maintain that all the elements of a society should function together to maintain order and stability. Under ideal conditions, a society would be in a state of balance, with all its parts interacting harmoniously. Problems arise when parts of the social system become dysfunctional, upsetting the society's equilibrium. This system disorganization can occur for many reasons, but the most frequent cause is rapid social change. Changes in one part of the system necessitate compensatory adjustments elsewhere, but these usually do not occur fast enough, resulting in tensions and conflict.

Functionalists view dysfunctions as temporary maladjustments to an otherwise interdependent and relatively harmonious society. Because this perspective focuses on societal stability, the key issue in this analysis of social disorganization is whether to restore the equilibrium to its predisturbance state or to seek a new and different equilibrium. For example, how do we overcome the problem of undocumented aliens? Do we expel them to eliminate their exploitation, their alleged depression of regional wage scales, and their high costs to taxpayers in the form of health, education, and welfare benefits? Or do we grant them amnesty, help them enter the economic mainstream, and seal our borders against further undocumented entries? Whatever the solution—and these two suggestions do not exhaust the possibilities—functionalists emphasize that all problems regarding minorities can be resolved through adjustments to the social system that restore it to a state of equilibrium. Instead of major changes in the society, they prefer smaller corrections in the already functioning society.

Critics argue that this theoretical viewpoint focuses on order and stability and thus ignores the inequalities of gender, race, and social class that often generate tension and conflict. Those who see structural-functionalism as too conservative often favor the conflict perspective.

Conflict Theory

Proponents of **conflict theory**, influenced by Karl Marx's socioeconomic view of an elite exploiting the masses, see society as being continually engaged in a series of disagreements, tensions, and clashes as different groups compete for limited resources. They argue that social structure fails to promote the society as a whole, as evidenced by existing social patterns benefiting some people while depriving others.

Rejecting the functionalist model of societal parts that usually work harmoniously, conflict theorists see disequilibrium and change as the norm. They examine the ongoing conflict between the dominant and subordinate groups in society, such as between Whites and people of color, between men and women, or between native born and foreign born. Regardless of the category studied, say conflict analysts, the pattern is usually that of those with power seeking to protect their privileges and those lower on the socioeconomic level struggling to gain a greater share than they have.

Conflict analysts focus on the inequalities that generate racial and ethnic antagonisms between groups. To explain why discrimination persists, conflict theorists ask this question: Who benefits? Those already in power—employers and holders of wealth and property—exploit the powerless, seeking additional profits at the expense of unassimilated minorities. Because lower wages allow higher profits, ethnic discrimination serves the interests of investors and owners by weakening workers' bargaining power.

By putting economics into perspective, Marxist analysis offers penetrating insight into intergroup relations, but John Solomos and Les Back argue that this methodology does not provide a substantial explanation for contemporary racism and problems associated with it.[15] Conflict theorists counter that racism has much to do with maintaining power and controlling resources. Racism is an **ideology**—a set of generalized beliefs used to explain and justify the interests of those who hold them.

In this sense, **false consciousness**—holding attitudes that do not accurately reflect the objective facts of the situation—exists, impelling workers to adopt attitudes that run counter to their own real interests. If workers believe that the economic gains by workers of other groups would adversely affect their own living standards, they will not support actions to end discriminatory practices. If workers struggling to improve their situation believe other groups entrenched in better job positions are holding them back, they will view their own gains as possible only at the expense of the better established groups. In both cases, the wealthy and powerful benefit by pitting exploited workers of different racial and ethnic groups against each other, causing each to have strong negative feelings about the others. This distorted view foments conflict and occasional outbursts of violence between groups, preventing workers from recognizing their common bond of joint oppression and uniting to overcome it.[16]

Critics contend that this theoretical viewpoint focuses too much on inequality and thus ignores the achieved unity of a society through the social cement of shared values and mutual interdependence among its members. Those who see conflict theory as too radical often favor the functionalist perspective. Still other critics reject both of these macrosocial theories as too broad and favor instead an entirely different approach, as explained in the next section.

Interactionist Theory

A third theoretical approach, **interactionist theory**, examines the microsocial world of personal interaction patterns in everyday life (e.g., social distance when talking, individual use of commonly understood terms) rather than the macro social aspects of social institutions and their harmony or conflict. **Symbolic interaction**—the shared symbols and definitions people use when communicating with one another—provides the focus for understanding how individuals create and interpret the life situations they experience. Symbols—our spoken language, expressions, body language, tone of voice, appearance, and images of television and other mass media—are what constitute our social worlds.[17] By means of these symbols, we communicate, create impressions, and develop understandings of the surrounding world. Symbolic interaction theories are useful in understanding race and ethnic relations because they assume that minority groups are responsive and creative rather than passive.[18]

Essential to this perspective, according to Peter L. Berger and Thomas Luckmann, is how people define their reality through a process they called the **social construction of reality**.[19] Individuals create a background against which to understand their separate actions and interactions with others. In a continuing social situation, the participants' interactions create a shared history resulting in **reciprocal typifications**—mutual categorizations—of one another. Taken-for-granted routines emerge on the basis of shared expectations. Participants see this socially constructed world as legitimate by virtue of its "objective" existence. When problems arise, specific "universe maintenance" procedures often become necessary to preserve stability. Conceptual machineries such as mythology, theology, philosophy, and science may be used for this purpose. In short, people create cultural products: material artifacts, social institutions, ideologies, and so on (externalization). Over time, they lose awareness of having created their own social and cultural environment (objectification), and subsequently, they learn these supposedly objective facts of reality through the socialization process (internalization).

The interactionist perspective can be particularly helpful in understanding some of the false perceptions that occur in dominant-minority relations. As we will discuss shortly, racism is a good example of the social construction of reality. Another dimension of this viewpoint lies in misunderstandings between different groups rather than the shared understandings of members of the same group. One example is the oft-heard complaint that today's immigrants don't want to learn English or assimilate. Those who so believe offer as evidence the presence of foreign-language media programs or signs in stores and other public places, or they cite overheard conversations in languages other than English and/or differences in dress, or they point to residential ethnic clusters where "non-American" customs and practices, along with language, seemingly perpetuate nonassimilation. Critics often link such complaints with a comparison to previous immigrants, typically European, who were not like this and who chose to assimilate rather than remain apart from the rest of society.

In reality, these **nativists** (people who advocate a policy of protecting the interests of native inhabitants against those of immigrants) fail to realize that they are simply witnessing a new version of a common pattern among all immigrants who come to the United States. They create in their minds a reality about the newcomers' subculture as permanent instead of temporary, whereas their positive role model of past immigrant groups assimilating was actually seen by other nativists back then as also not assimilating, for the same reasons cited today. Interactionists would thus examine this reality that people create, the meaning they attach to that subjective reality, and how it affects their interactions with one another.

Critics complain that this focus on everyday interactions neglects the important roles played by culture and social structure, and the critical elements of class, gender, and race. Interactionists say they do not ignore the macroelements of society but that, by definition, a society is a structure in which people interact, and why and how they do that needs investigation and explanation.

Perhaps it would be most helpful if you viewed all three theoretical perspectives as different camera lenses looking at the same reality. Whether a wide-angle lens (a macrosocial view) or a telephoto lens (a microsocial view), each has something to reveal, and together they offer a more complete understanding of society. Figure 1.1 summarizes the three sociological perspectives just discussed.

Minority Groups

Sociologists use the term *group* to refer to collectivities of different sizes. Often, a **group** connotes a small, closely interacting set of persons. A **secondary group** consists of people who interact on an impersonal or limited emotional basis for some practical or specific purpose. Larger still, a group such as a *minority* can refer to an aggregate of millions of people. Throughout this book, I will use the term *group* in this broad sense when referring to minorities because groups and group identity are important components of racial and ethnic relations.

Development of a Definition

Sociologists use the term **minority group** to indicate a group's relative power and status in a society, not to designate its numerical representation. The term was first used in the World War I peace treaties to protect

FIGURE 1.1   **Sociological Perspectives**

Functional Theory
- A stable, cooperative social system in which everything has a function and provides the basis of a harmonious society.
- Societal elements function together to maintain order, stability, and equilibrium.
- Social problems, or dysfunctions, result from temporary disorganization or maladjustment.
- Rapid social change is the most frequent cause of loss of societal equilibrium.
- Necessary adjustments will restore the social system to a state of equilibrium.

Conflict Theory
- Society is continually engaged in a series of disagreements, tensions, and clashes.
- Conflict is inevitable because new elites form, even after the previously oppressed group "wins."
- Disequilibrium and change are the norm because of societal inequalities.

- If we know who benefits from exploitation, we understand why discrimination persists.
- False consciousness is a technique by which a ruling elite maintains power and control of resources.
- Group cohesiveness and struggle against oppression are necessary to effect social change.

Interactionist Theory
- This theory focuses on the microsocial world of personal interaction patterns in everyday life.
- Shared symbols and definitions provide the basis for interpreting life experiences.
- A social construction of reality becomes internalized, making it seem to those who adopt it as if it were objective fact.
- Shared expectations and understandings, or the absence of these, explain intergroup relations.
- Better communication and intercultural awareness improve majority–minority interaction patterns.

approximately 22 million of 110 million people in east central Europe, but it was most frequently used as a description of biological features or national traits. Donald Young in 1932 thus observed that Americans make distinctions among people according to race and national origin.[20]

Louis Wirth expanded Young's original conception of minority groups to include the consequences of those distinctions: group consciousness and differential treatment.[21] Wirth's contribution marked two important turning points in sociological inquiry. First, by broadening the definition of minority group to encompass any physical or cultural trait instead of just race or national origin, Wirth enlarged the range of variables to include also the aged, people with disabilities, members of various religions or sects, and groups with unconventional lifestyles. Second, his emphasis on the social consequences of minority status leads to a focus on prejudice, discrimination, and oppression. Not everyone agrees with this approach. Richard

Schermerhorn, for example, notes that this "victimological" approach does not adequately explain the similarities and differences among groups or analyze relationships between majority and minority groups.[22]

A third attempt to define minority groups rests on examining relationships between groups in terms of each group's position in the social hierarchy.[23] This approach stresses a group's social power, which may vary from one country to another as, for example, does that of the Jews in Russia and in Israel. The emphasis on stratification instead of population size explains situations in which a relatively small group subjugates a larger number of people (e.g., the European colonization of African and Asian populations). Schermerhorn adopts a variation on this viewpoint. He also viewed social power as an important variable in determining a group's position in the hierarchy, but he believes that other factors are equally important. Size (a minority group must be less than one half the population), ethnicity (as defined by Wirth's physical and cultural traits), and group consciousness also help define a minority group.[24]

Minority-Group Characteristics

As social scientists reached some consensus on a definition of minority groups, anthropologists Charles Wagley and Marvin Harris identified five characteristics shared by minorities worldwide:

1. The group receives unequal treatment as a group.
2. The group is easily identifiable because of distinguishing physical or cultural characteristics that are held in low esteem.
3. The group feels a sense of peoplehood—that each of them shares something in common with other members.
4. Membership in the minority group has **ascribed status:** One is born into it.
5. Group members practice **endogamy:** They tend to marry within their group, either by choice or by necessity because of their social isolation.[25]

In our discussion of racial and ethnic minorities, these five features provide helpful guidelines. However, we should also understand that the last two characteristics do not apply to certain other types of minority groups: Women constitute a minority group, whether married or not, as do the aged or people with disabilities. One is not born old, and people with disabilities are not always born that way.

Because our discussion of various minority groups rests on their subordination to a more powerful, although not necessarily larger group, we will use the term **dominant group** when referring to a minority group's relationships with the rest of society. Another consideration is that a person may be a member of both dominant and minority groups in different categories. For example, an American Roman Catholic who is White belongs to a prominent religious minority group but also is a member of the racially dominant group.

Racial and Ethnic Groups

Race is a categorization in which a large number of people sharing visible biological characteristics regard themselves or are regarded by others as a single group on that basis. Race may seem at first glance an easy way to group people, but it is not. The more than 6 billion humans inhabiting this planet exhibit a wide range of physical differences in body build, hair texture, facial features, and skin color. Centuries of migration, conquest, intermarriage, and evolutionary physical adaptation to the environment have caused these varieties. Anthropologists have attempted racial categorizations, ranging from three to more than a hundred. Some, such as Ashley Montagu, even argue that only one race exists—the human race.[26] Just as anthropologists apply different interpretations to biological groupings, so do most people. It is by examining these social interpretations that sociologists attempt to analyze and explain racial prejudice.

The social construction of race varies by culture and in history. The United States, for example, has had a rigid racial classification ("White" and "non-White"), unlike Latin America, which acknowledges various gradations of race, reflecting the multiracial heritage of the people. U.S. purists have even subscribed to the "one-drop theory," that someone with even a tiny portion of nonwhite ancestry should be classified as Black. However, it's not just outsider classification. Sometimes people will identify as, say, Black or Native American, when their DNA reveals higher percentage of a different race. Racial classifications are thus often arbitrary, with individuals or society placing undue emphasis on race. Indeed, some geneticists argue that race is a meaningless concept, that far more genetic variation exists within races than between them, and that many racial traits overlap without distinct boundaries.[27] Furthermore, with more than 3 million people of mixed racial parentage living in the United States, many social scientists have called for the "deconstruction of race," arguing against the artificial boundaries that promote racial prejudice.[28]

Racism may be defined as linking the biological conditions of a human organism with alleged sociocultural capabilities and behavior to assert the superiority of one race. When people believe that one race is superior to another because of economic advantages or specific achievements, racist thinking prevails. The subordinate group experiences prejudice and discrimination, which the dominant group justifies by reference to such invidious perceptions. In addition to Blacks and Native Americans, Asians,

Hispanics, and even White southern Europeans have encountered hostility because of social categorizations of their abilities based simply on their physical appearance.

While *race* deals with visible physical characteristics, **ethnicity** goes beyond a simple racial similarity to encompass shared cultural traits and/or national origin. People may be of the same race but different in language and cultural practices, such as Africans, Haitians, and Jamaicans. Conversely, people may be of different races, but members of the same ethnic group, such as Hispanics. The complexities of social groupings by ethnicity don't stop there. People may be members of the same race and large ethnic group, such as the Belgians, but speak different languages (Dutch, French, or German) and so also be members of different subcultural ethnic groups. Moreover, if we add the element of social class, we will find even more differences within even these subcultural ethnic groups.

Religion is another determinant of ethnic group composition. Sometimes religion and national origin seem like dual attributes of ethnicity, such as Irish and Italian Catholics (although not all Irish or Italians are Catholic). Sometimes, too, what appear to be these dual attributes—Arab Muslims, for example—are not so; for example, the majority of Arabs in the United States are Christians, with one-third of the total Arab American population Catholic.[29] Religion most commonly links with other elements of ethnicity—national origin, culture, language—among immigrant groups. Even here, though, we should refrain from generalizing about all members of any national origin group (or any racial group), because of the extensive differences within such groups.

The word *race* often is incorrectly used as a social rather than a biological concept. Thus, the British and Japanese are frequently classified as races, as are Hindus, Latins, Aryans, Gypsies, Arabs, Native Americans, Basques, and Jews.[30] Many people—even sociologists, anthropologists, and psychologists—use race in a general sense that includes racial and ethnic groups, thereby giving the term both a biological and a social meaning. *Ethnic group* is now commonly used to include the three elements of race, religion, and national origin.[31] Such varied use of these terms results in endless confusion because racial distinctions are socially defined categories based on physical distinctions. Some groups, such as African Americans, were once defined on racial grounds but emerged as ethnocultural groups. Various ethnic groups often get lumped together in much broader racial categories—for example, Asians and Native Americans.

In this book, the word *race* will refer to the common social distinctions made on the basis of physical appearance. The term *ethnic group* will refer only to social groupings that the dominant group considers unique because of religious, linguistic, or cultural characteristics. Both terms will be used in discussing groups whose racial and ethnic characteristics overlap.

Ethnocentrism

Understanding the concept of the stranger is important to understanding **ethnocentrism**—a "view of things in which one's own group is the center of everything, and all others are scaled and rated with reference to it."[32] Ethnocentrism thus refers to people's tendency to identify with their own ethnic or national group as a means of fulfilling their needs for group belongingness and security. (The word is derived from two Greek words: *ethnos*, meaning "people," and *kentron*, meaning "center.") As a result of ethnocentrism, people usually view their own cultural values as somehow more real than, and therefore superior to, those of other groups, and they prefer their own way of doing things. Unfortunately for human relations, such ethnocentric thought is often extended until it negatively affects attitudes toward and emotions about those who are perceived as different.

Sociologists define an **ingroup** as a group to which individuals belong and feel loyal; thus, everyone—whether a member of a majority group or a minority group—is part of an ingroup. An **outgroup** is defined, in relation to ingroups, as groups consisting of all people who are not members of one's ingroup. Studying majority groups as ingroups helps us understand their reactions to strangers of another race or culture entering their society. Conversely, considering minority groups as ingroups enables us to understand their efforts to maintain their ethnic identity and solidarity in the midst of the dominant culture.

From European social psychologists comes one of the more promising explanations for ingroup favoritism. **Social identity theory** holds that ingroup members almost automatically think of their group as being better than outgroups because doing so enhances their own social status or social identity and thus raises the value of their personal identity or self-image.[33]

There is ample evidence about people from past civilizations who have regarded other cultures as inferior, incorrect, or immoral. This assumption that *we* are better than *they* are generally results in outgroups becoming objects of ridicule, contempt, or hatred. Such attitudes may lead to stereotyping, prejudice, discrimination, and even violence. What actually occurs depends on many factors, including structural and economic conditions; these factors will be discussed in subsequent chapters.

Despite its ethnocentric beliefs, the ingroup does not always view the outgroup as inferior. In numerous documented cases, groups have retained their values and standards while recognizing the superiority of another group in specific areas.[34] Moreover, countless people reject their own ingroup by becoming "voluntary exiles, expatriates, outgroup emulators, social climbers, renegades, and traitors."[35] An outgroup may become a positive **reference group**—that is, it may serve as an exemplary model—if members of the ingroup perceive it as having a conspicuous advantage over them in terms of survival or adaptation to the environment, success in warfare, a stronger political structure, greater wealth, or a higher occupational status.[36]

Ethnocentrism is an important factor in determining minority-group status in society, but because of many variations in intergroup relations, it alone cannot explain the causes of prejudice. For example, majority-group members may view minority groups with suspicion, but not all minority groups become the targets of extreme prejudice and discrimination.

Some social-conflict theorists argue that when the ingroup perceives the outgroup as a serious threat competing for scarce resources, the ingroup reacts with increased solidarity and ethnocentrism—and concomitant prejudice, discrimination, and hostility toward the outgroup.[37] According to this view, the degree of this hostility depends on several economic and geographic considerations. It would thus appear that ethnocentrism leads to negative consequences when the ingroup feels threatened. One counterargument to this view is that ethnocentric attitudes—thinking that because

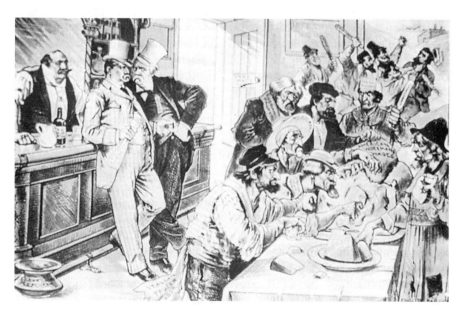

"Free Trade Lunch"

The immigrant laborer often was seen as an economic threat. Here English, Italian, Mexican, Russian, and German immigrants are shown devouring meat, symbolizing American workingmen's wages, and bread, symbolizing prosperity. In the background, immigrants are shown preventing the American laborer from entering the restaurant to get his share of the free lunch. This cartoon appeared in *Judge* on July 28, 1888.

others are different, they are thus a threat—initially caused the problem. The primary difficulty with this approach, however, is that it does not explain variations in the frequency, type, or intensity of intergroup conflict from one society to the next or between different immigrant groups and the ingroup.

In the United States

Often, an ethnocentric attitude is not deliberate but rather an outgrowth of growing up and living within a familiar environment. Even so, if recognized for the bias it is, it can be overcome. Consider, for example, that Americans have labeled their Major League Baseball championship games a *World Series*, although until recently not even Canadian teams were included in an otherwise exclusively U.S. professional sports program. *American* is another word we use—even in this book—to identify ourselves to the exclusion of people in other parts of North, Central, and South America. The Organization of American States (OAS), which consists of countries in North, Central, and South America, should remind us that others are equally entitled to call themselves Americans.

At one point in this country's history, many state and national leaders identified their expansionist goals as Manifest Destiny, as if divine providence had ordained specific boundaries for the United States. Indeed, many members of the clergy over the years preached fiery sermons regarding God's special plans for this country, and all presidents have invoked the deity in their inaugural addresses for special assistance to this country.

In Other Times and Lands

Throughout history, people of many cultures have demonstrated an ethnocentric view of the world. For example, British Victorians, believing their way of life superior to all others, felt obliged to carry the "white man's burden" of cultural and intellectual superiority in colonizing and "civilizing" the non-Western world. Yet 2,000 years earlier, the Romans had thought natives of Britain were an especially inferior people, as indicated in this excerpt from a letter written by the orator Cicero to his friend Atticus: "Do not obtain your slaves from Britain because they are so stupid and so utterly incapable of being taught that they are not fit to form a part of the household of Athens."

The Greeks, whose civilization predated the Roman Empire, considered all those around them—Persians, Egyptians, Macedonians, and others—distinctly inferior and called them barbarians. (*Barbarikos*, a Greek word, described those who did not speak Greek as making noises that sounded like *bar-bar*.)

Religious chauvinism blended with ethnocentrism in the Middle Ages when the Crusaders, spurred on by their beliefs, considered it their duty to free the Holy Land from the control of the "infidels." They traveled a great distance by land and sea, taking with them horses, armor, and armaments, to wrest control from the native inhabitants because the "infidels" had the audacity to follow the teachings of Muhammad rather than Jesus. On their journey across Europe, the Crusaders slaughtered Jews (whom they falsely labeled "Christ killers"), regardless of whether they were men, women, or children, all in the name of the Prince of Peace. The Crusaders saw both Muslims and Jews not only as inferior peoples but also as enemies.

In the following passage, Brewton Berry offers several other examples of ethnocentric thinking in past times:

> Some writers have attributed the superiority of their people to favorable geographical influences, but others incline to a biological explanation. The Roman, Vitruvius, maintained that those who live in southern climates have the keener intelligence, due to the rarity of the atmosphere, whereas "northern nations, being enveloped in a dense atmosphere, and chilled by moisture from the obstructing air, have a sluggish intelligence." . . . Ibn Khaldun argued that the Arabians were the superior people, because their country, although in a warm zone, was surrounded by water, which exerted a cooling effect. Bodin, in the sixteenth century, found an astrological explanation for ethnic group differences. The planets, he thought, exerted their combined and best influence upon that section of the globe occupied by France, and the French, accordingly, were destined by nature to be the masters of the world. Needless to say, Ibn Khaldun was an Arab, and Bodin a Frenchman. The Italian, Sergi, regarded the Mediterranean peoples as the true bearers of civilization and insisted that Germans and Asiatics only destroy what the Mediterraneans create. In like manner, the superiority of Nordics, Alpines, Teutons, Aryans, and others has been asserted by those who were members of each of these groups, or thought they were.[38]

Anthropologists examining the cultures of other peoples have identified countless instances of ethnocentric attitudes. One frequent practice has been in geographic reference and mapmaking. For example, some commercially prepared Australian world maps depicted that continent in the center in relation to the rest of the world.

> There is nothing unusual about this type of thinking: the Chinese, who called their country the Middle Kingdom, were convinced that China was the center of the world, and similar beliefs were held by other nations—and are still held. The British drew the Prime Meridian of longitude to run through Greenwich, near London. Europeans drew maps of the world with Europe at the center, Americans with the New World at the center.[39]

But beyond providing a group-centered approach to living, ethnocentrism is of utmost significance in understanding motivation, attitudes, and behavior when members of racially or ethnically distinct groups interact, for it often helps explain misunderstandings, prejudice, and discrimination.

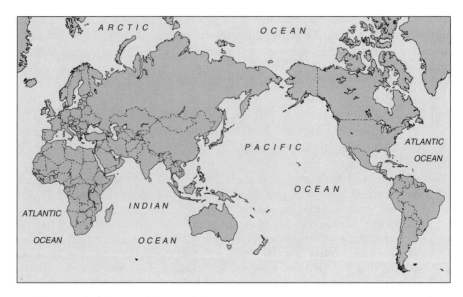

Unlike most U.S. maps of the world showing the American continents on the left side, this map—a common one in many Asian countries—puts the Americas on the right. The effect is to place these countries (such as Japan) in the center and not the edge, thus emphasizing the pacific Rim rather than the Atlantic. Such repositioning is a form of ethnocentrism, shaping perceptions of the rest of the world.

Eurocentrism and Afrocentrism

In recent years, many scholars and minority leaders have criticized the underrepresentation of non-European curriculum materials in the schools and colleges, calling this approach Eurocentric. **Eurocentrism** is a variation of ethnocentrism in which the content, emphasis, or both in history, literature, and other humanities primarily, if not exclusively, concern Western culture. Critics argue that this focus, ranging from the ancient civilizations of Greece and Rome to the writings of Shakespeare, Dickens, and other English poets and authors, ignores the accomplishments and importance of other peoples.

One counterforce to Eurocentrism is **Afrocentrism**, a viewpoint emphasizing African culture and its influence on Western civilization and the behavior of American Blacks. In its moderate form, Afrocentrism is an effort to counterbalance Eurocentrism and the suppression of the African influence in American culture by teaching African heritage as well.[40] In its bolder form, Afrocentrism becomes another variation of ethnocentrism. For example, a New York professor of African American Studies, Leon Jeffries, became embroiled in controversy when he asserted the superiority of African "sun people" over European "ice people." Others who argue that Western civilization merely reflects the Black African influence on Egyptian civilization find critics who charge them with excessively distorting history.[41]

For most advocates of pluralism, however, ethnocentrism in any form produces erroneous views. What is needed is a balanced approach that is inclusive, not exclusive, of the cultures, civilizations, and contributions of all peoples, both in our curriculum and in our thinking (see the accompanying International Scene box for an example from abroad).

Objectivity

When we are talking about people, usually those who differ from us, we commonly offer our own assumptions and opinions more readily than when we are discussing some other area, such as statistics or biology. But if we are to undertake a sociological study of ethnicity, we must question our assumptions and opinions—everything we have always believed without question. How can we scientifically investigate a problem if we have already reached a conclusion?

Sociologists attempt to examine group relationships objectively, but it is impossible to exclude their own subjectivity altogether. All human be-

Children and adults in this Afrocentric school in Akron, Ohio, begin their morning Haramabe ceremony. This Swahili word means "working together through unity," and is one small part of an emphasis on teaching students about their heritage. Advocates say such schools enhance educational achievement, motivation, and self-esteem.

ings have **values**—socially shared conceptions of what is good, desirable, and proper, or bad, undesirable, and improper. Because we are human, we cannot be completely objective because these values influence our orientations, actions, reactions, and interpretations. For example, selecting intergroup relations as an area of interest and concern, emphasizing the sociological perspective of this subject, and organizing the material in this book thematically all represent value judgments regarding priorities.

In fact, **value neutrality** may be impossible to attain because we are all members of groups and have been influenced by many others in our perceptions and experiences. It is nevertheless important to try conscientiously to maintain an open mind to examine this subject as objectively as possible. You must be aware of your own strong feelings about these matters and be willing to examine new concepts, even if they challenge previously held beliefs. To study this subject properly, you should attempt to be a stranger in your familiar world. Look at everything as if you were seeing it for the first time, trying to understand how and why it is rather than just taking it for granted. In addition, you should recognize that all of us are members of groups; consequently, the debate about and study of intergroup relations are themselves part of what we are studying. As part of an ingroup, we find all other outgroup members unlike our reference group; for this reason, our judgments about these "outsiders" are not as fully informed as the ones we make about known "insiders."

Trying to be *objective* about race and ethnic relations presents a strong challenge. People tend to use selective perception, accepting only information that agrees with their values or interpreting data in a way that confirms their attitudes about other groups. Many variables in life influence people's subjectivity about minority relations. Some views may be based on personal or emotional considerations or even on false premises. Sometimes, however, reasonable and responsible people disagree on the matter in an unemotional way. Whatever the situation, the study of minority-group relations poses a challenge for objective examination.

The subject of race and ethnic relations is complex and touches our lives in many ways. As members of the groups we are studying, all readers of this book come to this subject with preconceived notions. Because many individuals have a strong tendency to tune out disagreeable information, you must make a continual effort to remain open-minded and receptive to new data.

The Dillingham Flaw

Part of the problem with complaints about today's foreign-born presence in the United States lies in the critics' mistaken belief that they are reaching their judgments objectively. In comparing the supposedly nonassimilating newcomers to past immigrants, many detractors fall victim to a fallacy of thinking that I call the **Dillingham Flaw.**[42]

The International Scene
Overcoming German Ethnocentrism

CDS International, an organization that runs exchange programs, distributed a pamphlet, "An Information Guide for Germans on American Culture," to Germans working as interns in U.S. companies during the 1990s. The pamphlet was based on previous German interns' experiences and on their interviews with other colleagues; its intent was to provide insights into U.S. culture and to overcome ethnocentric reactions.

- Americans say "Hello" or "How are you?" when they see each other. "How are you?" is like "Hello." A long answer is not expected; just answer "Thank you, fine. How are you?"
- Using deodorant is a must.
- American women usually shave their legs and under their arms. Women who don't like to do this should consider wearing clothes that cover these areas.
- Expect to be treated like all other Americans. You won't receive special treatment because you are a German. Try not to talk with other Germans in German if Americans are around; this could make them feel uncomfortable.
- Please consider the differences in verbal communication styles between Americans and Germans. The typical German speaking style sounds abrupt and rude to Americans. Keep this in mind when talking to Americans.
- Be polite. Use words like "please" and "thank you." It is better to use these too often than not enough. Also, be conscious of your voice and the expression on your face. Your voice should be friendly, and you should wear a smile. Don't be confused by the friendliness and easygoing, nonexcitable nature of the people. They are deliberate, think independently, and do things their own way. Americans are proud of their independence.
- Keep yourself out of any discussions at work about race, sex, religion, or politics. Be open-minded; don't make judgments based on past experiences in Germany.
- Be aware that there are a lot of different cultures in the United States. There are also many different churches, which mean a great deal to their members. Don't be quick to judge these cultures; this could hurt people's feelings.
- Do it the American way and try to intermingle with the Americans. Think positive.

Critical thinking question: What guidelines for avoiding ethnocentrism should Americans follow when traveling to or working in other countries?

Senator William P. Dillingham chaired a congressional commission on immigration that conducted extensive hearings between 1907 and 1911 on the massive immigration then occurring. In issuing its forty-one-volume report, the commission erred in its interpretation of the data by using simplis-

tic categories and unfair comparisons of past and present immigrants by ignoring three important factors: (1) differences of technological evolution in
the immigrants' countries of origin; (2) the longer interval during which past
immigrants had time to acculturate; and (3) changed structural conditions in
the United States wrought by industrialization and urbanization.[43]

The Dillingham Flaw thus refers to any inaccurate comparison based
on simplistic categorizations and anachronistic judgments. This also occurs
any time we apply modern classifications or sensibilities to an earlier time,
when either they did not exist or, if they did, they had a different form or
meaning. To avoid the Dillingham Flaw, we must resist the temptation to use
modern perceptions to explain a past that contemporaneous people viewed
quite differently.

Here is an illustration of this concept. Anyone who criticizes today's
immigrants as being slower to Americanize, learn English, and become a cohesive part of American society than past immigrants is overlooking the reality of the past. Previous immigrant groups went through the same gradual
acculturation process and encountered the same complaints. Ethnic groups
that are now held up as role models and as studies in contrast to today's immigrants were themselves once the objects of scorn and condemnation.

To understand what is happening today, we need to view the present
in a larger context—from a sociohistorical perspective. That is in part the approach taken in this book. By understanding past patterns in intergroup relations, we will better comprehend what is occurring in our times, and we
will avoid becoming judgmental victims of the Dillingham Flaw.

Personal Troubles and Public Issues

Both ethnocentrism and subjectivity are commonplace in problems involving intergroup relations. In *The Sociological Imagination*, C. Wright Mills explained that an intricate connection exists between the patterns of individual
lives and the larger historical context of society. Ordinary people do not realize this, however, and so view their personal troubles as private matters.
Their awareness is limited to their "immediate relations with others" and
"the social setting that is directly open to personal experience and to some
extent [their] willful activity." Personal troubles occur when individuals believe their values are threatened.

However, said Mills, what we experience in diverse and distinct social
settings is often traceable to structural changes and institutional contradic-
tions. The public issues of the social structure transcend these local environments of the individual; many local settings "overlap and interpenetrate to
form the larger structure of social and historical life." An issue is a public
matter concerning segments of the public who believe that one of their cherished values is being threatened.[44]

To illustrate, if a handful of undocumented aliens are smuggled into the United States and placed in a sweatshop in virtual slavery, that is their personal trouble, and we look for a resolution of that particular problem. But if large-scale smuggling of undocumented aliens into the country occurs, resulting in an underground economy of illegal sweatshops in many locales (as indeed happens), we need "to consider the economic and political institutions of the society, not just the personal situation and character of a scatter of individuals."[45]

Similarly, if a few urban African American or Hispanic American youths drop out of school, the personal problems leading to their quitting and the means by which they secure economic stability in their lives become the focus of our attention. But if their dropout rate in most U.S. cities is consistently far greater than the national average (and it is), we must examine the economic, educational, and political issues that confront our urban institutions. These are larger issues, and we cannot resolve them by improving motivation, discipline, and opportunities for a few individuals.

Throughout this book, and particularly in Chapters 2 and 3, we will examine this interplay of culture and social structure, ethnicity and social class. What often passes for assigned or assumed group characteristics— or for individual character flaws or troubles—needs to be understood within the larger context of public issues involving the social structure and interaction patterns.

Mills also wrote, "All sociology worthy of the name is 'historical' sociology."[46] Therefore, we should place all groups we study within a sociohistorical perspective so we can understand both historical and contemporary social structures that affect intergroup relations.

The Dynamics of Intergroup Relations

The study of intergroup relations is both fascinating and challenging because relationships continually change. The patterns of relating may change for many reasons: industrialization, urbanization, shifts in migration patterns, social movements, upward or downward economic trends, and so on. However, sometimes the changing relationships also reflect changing attitudes as, for example, in the interaction between Whites and Native Americans. Whites continually changed the emphasis: exploitation; extermination; isolation; segregation; paternalism; forced assimilation; and more recently, tolerance for pluralism and restoration of certain (but not all) Native American ways. Similarly, African Americans, Asian Americans, Jews, Catholics, and other minority groups have all had varying relations with the host society.

Some recent world events also illustrate changing dominant-group orientations toward minority groups, such as Arabs and Muslims after 9/11.

The large migrations of diverse peoples into Belgium, Denmark, France, Germany, the Netherlands, Sweden, and the United Kingdom triggered a backlash in each of those countries. Strict new laws enacted in most of these nations in 1993–1994 resulted in a marked increase in deportations. **Ethnoviolence**—hostile behavior against people solely because of their race, religion, ethnicity, or sexual orientation—also flared up, particularly in Germany and Italy, where neo-Nazi youths assaulted foreigners and firebombed their residences.

Elsewhere, intergroup relations fluctuate, as between Blacks and Whites in South Africa, Hindus and Muslims in India, Muslims and Christians in Lebanon, Arabs and Jews in the Middle East, Catholics and Protestants in Northern Ireland, and many other groups. All go through varying periods of tumult and calm in their dealings with one another.

The field of race and ethnic relations is rife with theoreticians and investigators examining changing events and migration patterns. Each year, a vast outpouring of information from papers presented at meetings and from articles, books, and other sources adds to our knowledge. New insights, new concepts, and new interpretations of old knowledge inundate the interested observer. What both the sociologist and the student must attempt to understand, therefore, is not a fixed and static phenomenon but a dynamic, ever-changing one, about which more is being learned all the time.

Retrospect

Human beings follow certain patterns when responding to strangers. Their perceptions of newcomers reflect categoric knowing; if they perceive that the newcomers are similar, people are more receptive to their presence. What makes interaction with strangers difficult is the varying perceptions of each to the other, occasioned by a lack of shared understandings and perceptions of reality.

In sociological investigation of minorities, three perspectives shape analysis: Functional theory stresses the orderly interdependence of a society and the adjustments needed to restore equilibrium when dysfunctions occur. Conflict theory emphasizes the tensions and conflicts that result from exploitation and competition for limited resources. Interactionist theory concentrates on everyday interaction patterns operating within a socially constructed perception of reality.

By definition, minority groups—regardless of their size—receive unequal treatment, possess identifying physical or cultural characteristics held in low esteem, are conscious of their shared ascribed status, and tend to practice endogamy. Racial groups are biologically similar groups, and ethnic groups are groups that share a learned cultural heritage. Intergroup relations are dynamic and continually changing.

Ethnocentrism—the tendency to identify with one's own group—is a universal human condition that contributes to potential problems in relating to outgroups. Examples of ethnocentric thinking and actions can be found in all countries throughout history. Eurocentrism and Afrocentrism are views emphasizing one culture or civilization over others.

The study of minorities presents a difficult challenge because our value orientations and life experiences can impair our objectivity. Even trained sociologists, being human, encounter difficulty in maintaining value neutrality. Indeed, some people argue that sociologists should take sides and not attempt a sterile approach to the subject. The Dillingham Flaw—using an inaccurate comparison based on simplistic categorizations and anachronistic judgments—seriously undermines the scientific worth of supposedly objective evaluations. Both ethnocentrism and subjectivity are commonplace in problems involving intergroup relations.

KEY TERMS

Abstract typifications
Afrocentrism
Ascribed status
Categoric knowing
Conflict theory
Dillingham Flaw
Dominant group
Endogamy
Ethnicity
Ethnocentrism
Ethnoviolence
Eurocentrism
False consciousness
Functional theory
Group
Ideology
Ingroup
Interactionist theory

Latent functions
Manifest functions
Minority group
Nativists
Outgroup
Race
Racism
Reciprocal typifications
Reference group
Secondary group
Social construction of reality
Social distance
Social identity theory
Status positions
Symbolic interaction
Value neutrality
Values

REVIEW QUESTIONS

1. What is ethnocentrism? Why is it important in relations between dominant and minority groups?

2. Why is objective study of racial and ethnic minorities difficult?

3. Explain the Dillingham Flaw and offer some examples.

4. What are the focal points of the functional, conflict, and interactionist theories?

5. How does a minority group differ from an ethnic group? How does a race differ from an ethnic group?

SUGGESTED READINGS

Asante, Molefi K. *The Afrocentric Idea*, rev. ed. Philadelphia: Temple University Press, 1998.

Presents the provocative thesis that African culture permeates Western civilization and American Black behavior.

Berger, Peter L., and Thomas Luckmann. *The Social Construction of Reality*. Garden City, N.Y.: Doubleday, 1967.

Highly influential work discussing how people define their reality and interact on the basis of shared expectations.

Doob, Christopher B. *Racism: An American Caldron*. New York: HarperCollins, 1993.

Examination of the economic, political, and social forces that create racism and their functions and consequences today.

Gilroy, Paul. *Against Race: Imagining Political Culture Beyond the Color Line*. Cambridge, Mass.: Belknap Press, 2002.

A provocative book that is both factual and utopian in its premise that humanity should not be divided into groups based on skin color.

Parrillo, Vincent N. *Diversity in America*, 2d ed. Thousand Oaks, Calif.: Pine Forge Press, 2005.

Explains the Dillingham Flaw and examines multiculturalism throughout U.S. history.

Schutz, Alfred. "The Stranger," *American Sociological Review* 69 (May 1944): 449–507.

Early, influential essay, still highly pertinent today, explaining the interaction problems of a stranger.

Simmel, Georg. "The Stranger," in Kurt H. Wolff (ed.), *The Sociology of Georg Simmel*. New York: Free Press, 1950.

Classic analysis of the role of the stranger made through an analysis of the formal structures of life.

Waters, Mary. *Ethnic Options: Choosing Identity in America*. Berkeley: University of California Press, 1990.

Informative discussion of the role ethnicity plays in the pluralistic society of the United States and the evolution of group identity politics.

INTERNET RESOURCES

To learn more about the social construction of race, go to http://raceandgenomics .ssrc.org/ for "Is Race 'Real'?," a forum on the subject sponsored by the Social Science Research Council.

2 The Role of Culture

"No culture can live, if it attempts to be exclusive."
—Mahatma Gandhi

Understanding what makes people receptive to some, but not all, strangers requires knowledge of how culture affects perceptions and response patterns. Culture provides the guidelines for people's interpretations of situations they encounter and for the responses they consider appropriate. The distinctions and interplay between cultures are important to the assimilation process as well. For example, cultural orientations of both minority and dominant groups shape expectations about how a minority group should fit into the society.

This chapter first examines the various aspects of culture that affect dominant–minority relations, followed by an examination of varying cultural expectations about minority integration.

The Concept of Culture

Human beings both create and grow out of their own social worlds. Adapting to the environment, to new knowledge, and to technology, we learn a way of life within our society. We invent and share rules and patterns of behavior that shape our lives and the way we experience the world about us. The shared products of society that we call *culture*, whether material or immaterial, make social life possible and give our lives meaning. **Material culture** consists of all physical objects created by members of a society and the meanings/significance attached to them (e.g., cars, cell phones, iPods, hightop sneakers, or clothing). **Nonmaterial culture** consists of abstract human creations and their meanings/significance in life (e.g., beliefs, customs, ideas, languages, norms, social institutions, and values). **Culture**, then, consists of physical or material objects as well as the nonmaterial attitudes, beliefs, customs, lifestyle, and values shared by members of a society and transmitted to the next generation.

These cultural attributes provide a sense of peoplehood and common bonds through which members of a society can relate (see Figure 2.1). Most social scientists therefore emphasize the impact of culture in shaping behavior.[1] Through language and other forms of symbolic interaction, the members of a society learn the thought and behavior patterns that constitute their commonality as a people.[2] In this sense, culture is the social cement that binds a society together.

Shared cultural norms encourage solidarity and orient the behavior of members of the ingroup. **Norms** are a culture's rules of conduct—internalized by the members—embodying the society's fundamental expectations. Through norms, ingroup members (majority or minority) know how to react toward the acts of outgroup members that surprise, shock, or annoy them or in any way go against their shared expectations. Anything contrary to this "normal" state is seen as negative or deviant. When minority-group members "act uppity" or "don't know their place," majority-group members often get upset and sometimes act out their anger. Violations of norms usually trigger strong reactions because they appear to threaten the social fabric of a community or society. Eventually, most minority groups adapt their distinctive cultural traits to those of the host society through a process called **acculturation**. Intragroup variations remain, though, because ethnic-group members use different reference groups as role models.

An important component of intragroup cultural variations, seldom a part of the acculturation process, is religion. Not only does religion have strong links to the immigrant experience in the United States, as well as to African American slavery and pacification efforts toward Native Americans, but it also has many other connections to prejudice and social conflict. Indeed, the Catholic and Jewish faiths of past European immigrants provoked many manifestations (some quite violent and vicious) of Protestant nativism. Similarly, recent immigrants who are believers of such religions as Hinduism, Islam, Rastafarianism, or Santería often experience prejudice and conflict of their faith, as have the Amish, Mormons, Quakers, and many others in the United States in past years. Religious conflict is a sad reality in many parts of the world—the Balkans, India, the Middle East, and Northern Ireland, to mention just a few.

Professional sports are another part of culture, which also provide an area for the study of prejudice and racism. Historically, sports have favored males, a practice fostered by the mistaken belief that females lacked the strength and stamina to be athletes or would be "less feminine" if they were. Long excluded from major league sports, people of color now are prominent participants in baseball, basketball, boxing, football, and track. In fact, African Americans (13 percent of the U.S. population) account for 69 percent

FIGURE 2.1   **Basic U.S. Values**

Within the United States' diverse society of racial, ethnic, and religious groups, each with a distinctive set of values, exists a common core of values. Sociologist Robin Williams, after decades of study, identified fifteen value orientations—the foundation of our beliefs, behaviors, definitions of social goals, and life expectations. Some are contradictory—freedom and individualism but external conformity; democracy and equality but racism and group superiority; nationalism but individualism—and these may spark divisions among people. Although other societies may subscribe to many of these values as well, this particular combination of values—virtually present from the nation's founding—have had and continue to have enormous impact in shaping our society.

1. **Achievement and success.** Competition-oriented, our society places much value on gaining power, prestige, and wealth.
2. **Activity and work.** We firmly believe that everyone should work, and we condemn as lazy those who do not work.
3. **Moral orientation.** We tend to moralize, seeing the world in absolutes of right and wrong.
4. **Humanitarian mores.** Through charitable and crisis aid, we lean toward helping the less fortunate and the underdog.
5. **Efficiency and practicality.** We try to solve problems by the quickest, least costly means.
6. **Progress.** We think technology can solve all problems, and we hold an optimistic outlook toward the future.
7. **Material comfort.** We share the American Dream of a high standard of living and owning many material goods.
8. **Equality.** We believe in the abstract ideal of equality, relating to one another informally as equals.
9. **Freedom.** We cherish individual freedom from domination by others.
10. **External conformity.** Despite our professed belief in individualism, we tend to join, conform, and go along; and we are suspicious of those who do not.
11. **Science and rationality.** We believe that through science we can gain mastery over our environment and secure a better lifestyle.
12. **Nationalism.** We think the American way of life is the best and distrust "un-American" behavior.
13. **Democracy.** We believe that everyone has the right of political participation, that our government is highly democratic.
14. **Individualism.** We emphasize personal rights and responsibilities, giving the individual priority over the group.
15. **Racism and group superiority themes.** Through our attitudes and actions, we favor some racial, religious, and ethnic groups over others.

Source: Robin M. Williams, Jr., *American Society: A Sociological Interpretation*, 3d ed. (New York: Knopf, 1970).

of National Football League (NFL) players and 76 percent of National Basketball Association (NBA) players. Nevertheless, the vast majority of owners, managers, and head coaches in all sports are White, and in some sports, such as football, one's race and position on the field are closely linked: Whites dominate in offensive slots and Blacks dominate defensive positions, with Whites more likely to play leadership roles on both sides of the line.[3] Still, many Blacks and Hispanics, and an increasing number of Asians, excel in athletics, serving as a source of racial and/or ethnic pride for many of their fellow group members.

The Reality Construct

Our perception of reality is related to our culture: Through our culture, we learn how to perceive the world about us. Cultural definitions help us interpret the sensory stimuli from our environment and tell us how to respond to them. Thus, "culture is something that intervenes between the human organism and its environment to produce actions."[4] It is the screen through which we "see," and we cannot get rid of it (Figure 2.2).

Language and Other Symbols.   Culture is learned behavior, acquired chiefly through verbal communication, or language. A word is nothing more than a symbol—something that stands for something else. Whether it is tan-

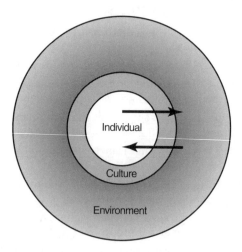

FIGURE 2.2   Cultural Reality

Each *individual* observes the world through *sense perceptions*, which are evaluated in terms of *culture*—values, attitudes, customs, and beliefs.

gible (*chair*) or intangible (*honesty*), the word represents a mental concept that is based on empirical reality. Words reflect culture, however, and one word may have different meanings in different cultures. If you are *carrying the torch* in England, you are holding a flashlight, not yearning for a lost love; if you could use a *lift*, you want an elevator, not a ride or a boost to your spirits. Because words symbolically interpret the world to us, the **linguistic relativity** of language may connote both intended and unintended prejudicial meanings. For example, *black* is the symbol for darkness (in the sense of lightlessness) or evil, and *white* symbolizes cleanliness or goodness, and a society may subtly (or not so subtly) transfer these meanings to Black and White people.

Walter Lippmann, a prominent political columnist, once remarked, "First we look, then we name, and only then do we see." He meant that until we learn the symbols of our world, we cannot understand the world. A popular pastime in the early 1950s, called "Droodles," illustrates Lippmann's point. The object was to interpret drawings such as those in Figure 2.3. Many people were unable to see the meaning of the drawings until it was explained. They looked but did not see until they knew the "names." Can you guess what these drawings depict?[5]

Interpreting symbols is not merely an amusing game; it is significant in real life. Human beings do not respond to stimuli but to their definitions of those stimuli as mediated by their culture.[6] The definition of beauty is one example. Beyond the realm of personal taste, definitions of beauty have cultural variations. For instance, in different times and places, societies have based their appraisal of a woman's beauty on her having distended lips, scar markings, tattoos, or beauty marks or on how plump or thin she was.

Nonverbal communication—or body language—is highly important too. Body movements, gestures, physical proximity, facial expressions (there are between 100 and 136 facial expressions, each of which conveys a distinct meaning[7]), and **paralinguistic signals** (sounds but not words, such as a sigh, a kiss-puckering sound, or the *m-m-m* sound of tasting something good) all convey information to the observer-listener. Body language is important in intergroup relations too, whether in conversation, interaction, or perception.

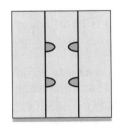 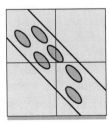 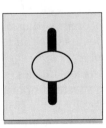 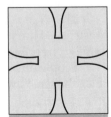

FIGURE 2.3   "Droodles"

Body language may support or belie one's words; it may suggest friendliness, aloofness, or deference.

Although some forms of body language are fairly universal (e.g., most facial expressions), many cultural variations exist in body language itself and in the interpretation of its meanings. Body movements such as posture, bearing, and gait vary from culture to culture. The degree of formality in a person's environment (both past and present) and other cultural factors influence such forms of nonverbal communication. Consider the different meanings one could attach to a student's being unwilling to look directly into the eyes of a teacher. The teacher may assume that this behavior reflects embarrassment, guilt, shyness, inattention, or even disrespect. Yet, if the student is Asian or Hispanic, such demeanor is a mark of respect. The symbol's definition, in this case the teacher's interpretation of what the student's body language means, determines the meaning the observer ascribes to it.

A person who is foreign to a culture must learn both its language and the rest of its symbol system, as the members of the culture did through socialization. Certain gestures may be signs of friendliness in one culture but obscene or vengeful symbols in another. For example, in the United States, placing thumb and forefinger in a circle with the other fingers upraised indicates that everything is fine, but in Japan, this sign refers to money, and in Greece, it is an insulting anal expression.[8] Kisses, tears, dances, emblems, silence, open displays of emotions, and thousands of other symbols can and often do have divergent meanings in different cultures. Symbols, including language, help an ingroup construct a reality that may be unknown to or altogether different for an outgroup. Members of one group may then select, reject, ignore, or distort their sensory input regarding the other group because of cultural definitions.

The Thomas Theorem.   William I. Thomas once observed that, if people define situations as real, those situations become real in their consequences.[9] His statement, known as the **Thomas theorem**, relates directly to the *Dillingham Flaw*, discussed in the first chapter. Whereas Thomas emphasized how definitions lead to actions that produce consequences to conform to the original, ill-founded definition, the Dillingham Flaw suggests the misguided thought process that may result in that definition in the first place.

The Thomas theorem is thus further testimony to the truth of reality constructs: Human beings respond to their definitions of stimuli rather than to the stimuli themselves.

People often associate images (e.g., "Yellow peril," "Indian menace," or "illegal aliens") with specific minority groups. They then behave according to the meaning they assign to the situation, and the consequences of their behavior serve to reaffirm the meaning; the definition becomes a self-fulfilling prophecy. For example, when Whites define Blacks as inferior and then offer them fewer opportunities because of that alleged inferiority, Blacks are disadvantaged, which in turn supports the initial definition.

Several variables contribute to the initial definition, but culture is one of the most important of these. Culture establishes the framework through which an individual perceives others, classifies them into groups, and assigns certain general characteristics to them. Because ethnocentrism leads people to consider their way of life as the best and most natural, their culturally defined perceptions of others often lead to suspicion and differential treatment of other groups. In effect, each group constructs myths about other groups and supports those myths through ingroup solidarity and outgroup hostility. As each group's attitudes and actions toward other groups continue, the **vicious-circle phenomenon** plays out.[10] In such instances, people create a culturally determined world of reality, and their actions reinforce their beliefs. Social interaction or social change may counteract such situations, however, leading to their redefinition.

Gregory Razran conducted a study illustrating how cultural definitions can influence perception.[11] Twice within a 2-month interval, he showed the same set of thirty pictures of unknown young women to the same group of one hundred male college students and fifty noncollege men. Using a five-point scale, the subjects rated each woman's beauty, character, intelligence, ambition, and general likableness. At the first presentation, the pictures had no ethnic identification, but at the second presentation, they were labeled with Irish, Italian, Jewish, and old American (English) surnames. All women were rated equally on the first presentation, but when the names were given, the ratings changed. The "Jewish" women received higher ratings in ambition and intelligence. Both "Jewish" and "Italian" women suffered a large decline in general likableness and a slight decline in beauty and character evaluations. This study is one of many illustrating how cultural definitions affect judgments about others.

Through **cultural transmission**, each generation transmits its culture to the next generation, which learns those cultural definitions at an early age. This fact is dramatically expressed in the Rodgers and Hammerstein musical *South Pacific*. The tragic subplot is the touching romance between Lieutenant Cable and the young Tonkinese woman Liat. Although Cable and Liat are sincerely in love, Cable's friends remind him that the couple's life would not be the same in the United States. Their differences in race and culture would work against a happy marriage for them and his own acceptance in Philadelphia high society. Miserable because of the choice his cultural values force him to make, he sings "Carefully Taught," a poignant song about how prejudice is taught to children. The lyrics tell how one must be continually taught to hate and fear people whose eyes are "oddly made" or "whose skin is a different shade." Other lines tell how this teaching must occur before it's too late, that before a child turns eight, he or she must learn to hate all the people one's relatives hate.

These lyrics reinforce the reality construct discussed earlier and illustrated in Figure 2.2. From family, friends, school, mass media, and all other sources of informational input, we learn our values, attitudes, and beliefs.

Some of our learning reflects the prejudices of others, which we may incorporate in our own attitudes and actions.

Cultural Change

Culture continually changes. Discoveries, inventions, technological advances, innovations, and natural disasters alter the customs, values, attitudes, and beliefs of a society. This section focuses on two common processes of cultural change: cultural diffusion within a whole society and changes within a particular subculture of that society.

Cultural Diffusion

Paradoxically, although the members of a dominant culture wish to keep their society untainted by contact with foreign elements, cultures are inevitably influenced by other cultures—a phenomenon termed **cultural diffusion**. Ideas, inventions, and practices spread from one culture to another, albeit at different rates of diffusion. Negative attitudes and a large distance between groups can pose formidable barriers, and sometimes cultural diffusion occurs only under temporarily favorable conditions. Sometimes ideas are modified or reinterpreted before being accepted, such as when some Latin Native American tribes of the early twentieth century showed a fondness for automobile tires: They used them to make sandals, for they neither owned nor drove cars.

Borrowed Elements.   U.S. anthropologist Ralph Linton calculated that any given culture contains about 90 percent borrowed elements. To demonstrate both the enormity and the subtlety of cultural diffusion, he offered a classic portrait of the "100 percent American" male:

> Our solid American citizen awakens in a bed built on a pattern which originated in the Near East but which was modified in Northern Europe before it was transmitted to America. He throws back covers made from cotton, domesticated in India, or linen, domesticated in the Near East, or wool, from sheep, also domesticated in the Near East, or silk, the use of which was discovered in China. All of these materials have been spun or woven by processes invented in the Near East. He slips into his moccasins, invented by the Indians of the Eastern woodlands, and goes to the bathroom, whose fixtures are a mixture of European and American inventions, both of recent date. He takes off his pajamas, a garment invented in India, and washes with soap, invented by the ancient Gauls. He then shaves, a masochistic rite which seems to have been derived from either Sumer or ancient Egypt.
>   Returning to the bedroom, he removes his clothes from a chair of southern European type and proceeds to dress. He puts on garments whose

form originally derived from the skin clothing of the nomads of the Asiatic steppes, puts on shoes made from skins tanned by a process invented in ancient Egypt and cut to a pattern derived from the classical civilizations of the Mediterranean, and ties around his neck a strip of bright-colored cloth which is a vestigial survival of the shoulder shawls worn by the seventeenth-century Croatians. Before going out for breakfast he glances through the window, made of glass invented in Egypt, and if it is raining puts on overshoes made of rubber discovered by the Central American Indians and takes an umbrella, invented in southeastern Asia. Upon his head he puts a hat made of felt, a material invented in the Asiatic steppes.

On his way to breakfast he stops to buy a paper, paying for it with coins, an ancient Lydian invention. At the restaurant a whole new series of borrowed elements confronts him. His plate is made of a form of pottery invented in China. His knife is of steel, an alloy first made in southern India, his fork a medieval Italian invention, and his spoon a derivative of a Roman original. He begins breakfast with an orange, from the eastern Mediterranean, a cantaloupe from Persia, or perhaps a piece of African watermelon. With this he has coffee, an Abyssinian plant, with cream and sugar. Both the domestication of cows and the idea of milking them originated in the Near East, while sugar was first made in India. After his fruit and first coffee, he goes on to waffles, cakes made by a Scandinavian technique from wheat domesticated in Asia Minor. Over these he pours maple syrup, invented by the Indians of the Eastern woodlands. As a side dish he may have the egg of a species of bird domesticated in Indo-China, or thin strips of the flesh of an animal domesticated in Eastern Asia which have been salted and smoked by a process developed in northern Europe.

When our friend has finished eating he settles back to smoke, an American Indian habit, consuming a plant domesticated in Brazil in either a pipe, derived from the Indians of Virginia, or a cigarette, derived from Mexico. If he is hardy enough he may even attempt a cigar, transmitted to us from the Antilles by way of Spain. While smoking he reads the news of the day, imprinted in characters invented by the ancient Semites upon a material invented in China by a process invented in Germany. As he absorbs the accounts of foreign troubles he will, if he is a good conservative citizen, thank a Hebrew deity in an Indo-European language that he is 100 percent American.*

Cultural diffusion is also an important element in ethnic relations within our pluralistic society. It can take many forms, including widened food preferences such as tacos or burritos, or use within U.S. corporations of Japanese management techniques such as employee participation in setting work goals. Whatever the form, cultural diffusion is an ongoing process, influencing various aspects of our culture and sometimes altering our views of the cultures of other peoples.

*Ralph Linton, *The Study of Man* (1936), 326–27. Reprinted by permission of Prentice Hall Inc., Upper Saddle River, N.J.

Cultural Contact.   Culture can also undergo change through people of different cultures coming into contact with one another. Because people tend to take their own culture for granted, it operates at a subconscious level in forming their expectations. When people's assumptions are jolted through contact with an unfamiliar culture that supports different expectations, they often experience **culture shock**, which is characterized by feelings of disorientation and anxiety and a sense of being threatened.

Culture shock does not always occur. When people of two different cultures interact, many possible patterns can emerge. The two groups may peacefully coexist, with a gradual cultural diffusion occurring. History offers some excellent examples of connections between migrations and innovations, wherein geographical conditions and native attitudes have determined the extent to which a group has resisted cultural innovations, despite invasions, settlements, or missionary work. The persistent pastoralism of Bedouin tribes and the long-sustained resistance to industrialization of Native Americans are two examples. Stanley Lieberson, however, suggests that power alone determines the outcome, causing one group to become dominant and the other subservient.[12] If the subordinate group proves to be the nonmigratory group, the changes to its social organization can be devastating. No longer possessing the flexibility and autonomy it once enjoyed, it may suffer material deprivation and find its institutions undermined.

If the migratory group finds itself in the subordinate position, it must adapt to its new environment to survive. Most commonly, the minority group draws from its familiar world as it attempts to cope with the prevailing conditions. Group members form a subculture with unique behavior and interests—neither those of the larger society nor those of their old culture. For example, both Catholicism and Judaism have undergone significant changes in form and expression since taking root in the United States. U.S. ethnic subcultures blend elements of homeland and dominant U.S. cultures once group members adapt to their new environment.

Subcultures

Usually, immigrants follow a pattern of **chain migration**, settling in an area already containing family, friends, or compatriots who located there earlier. An ethnic community evolves, providing an emotional support system to these strangers in a strange land as they strive to forge a better life for themselves. Part of this process of cultural insulation among others like themselves is the re-creation in miniature of the world they left behind. Thus, **parallel social institutions**—their own clubs, organizations, newspapers, stores, churches, and schools duplicating those of the host society—appear, creating cohesiveness within the minority subculture, whether it is an immigrant or native-born grouping.

As **ethnic subcultures** among immigrants in the United States evolve in response to conditions within the host society, the immigrants sometimes develop a group consciousness unknown in their old countries. Many first-generation Americans possess a village orientation toward their homeland rather than a national identity. They may speak different dialects, feud with other regions, and have different values. But their common experience in the United States causes them to coalesce into a national grouping. One example is Italian Americans, who initially identified with their cities of origin: Calabria, Palermo, Naples, Genoa, Salerno, and so on. Within a generation, many came to view themselves as Italians, partly because the host society classified them as such.

Yet, even as a newly arrived group forges its community and subculture, a process called **ethnogenesis** occurs.[13] Shaped partly by the core culture in selectively absorbing some elements and modifying others, the group also retains, modifies, or drops elements from its cultural heritage as it adapts to its new country. The result is a distinctive new ethnic group unlike others in the host country, dominant or minority, but also somewhat different from the people who still live in the group's homeland. For example, first-generation German Americans differ from other ethnic groups and from native-born U.S. citizens, but they also possess cultural traits and values that distinguish them from nonmigrating Germans.

Convergent Subcultures.   Some ethnic subcultures are **convergent subcultures**; that is, they tend toward assimilation with the dominant society. Although recognizable by residential clustering and adherence to the language, dress, and cultural norms of their native land, these ethnic groups are nonetheless becoming assimilated. As the years pass—possibly across several generations—the distinctions between the dominant culture and the convergent subculture gradually lessen. Eventually, this form of subculture becomes completely integrated into the dominant culture.

Because the subculture is undergoing change, its members may experience problems of **marginality**—living under stress in two cultures simultaneously. The older generation may seek to preserve its traditions and heritage while the younger generation may be impatient to achieve full acceptance within the dominant society. Because of the impetus toward assimilation, time obviously favors the younger generation. The Dutch, German, and Irish subcultures are examples of once-prevalent ethnic subcultures that are barely visible today. Italian, Polish, and Slovak subcultures have also begun to converge more fully. These nationality groups still exhibit ethnic pride in many ways, but for the most part, they are no longer set apart by place of residence or subcultural behavior. Because of their multigenerational length of residence, these nationality groups are less likely to live in clustered housing arrangements or to display behavior patterns such as conflict, deviance, or endogamy to any greater degree than the rest of the majority group.

Persistent Subcultures.   Not all subcultures assimilate. Some do not even desire to do so, and others, particularly non-White groups, face difficulties

Some religious groups, such as the Amish, are persistent subcultures, remaining re-markably constant in a radically changing dominant society. Their communities are highly integrated because their social institutions—family, school, church, and eco-nomic endeavors—are complementary and consistent in values and expectations. Young and old live similar lives, sharing the same lifestyle and restrictions, accept-ing them as the will of God.

in assimilating. These unassimilated subcultures are known as **persistent subcultures**. Some adhere as much as possible to their own way of life and resist absorption into the dominant culture. Religious groups such as the Amish, some Hutterites, and Hasidic Jews reject modernity and insist on maintaining their traditional ways of life; they may represent the purest form of a persistent subculture in U.S. society. Other ethnic groups adopt a few aspects of the dominant culture but adamantly preserve their own way of life; examples are most Native Americans who live on reservations and many *Hispanos* (Spanish Americans) in the Southwest. Chinatowns also sup-port preservation of the Chinese way of life in many ways.

A minority group's insistence on the right to be different has not usu-ally been well received among dominant-group members. This clash of wills sometimes leads to conflict; at the very least, it invites stereotyping and prej-udice on both sides (see the accompanying International Scene example).

Just as convergent subcultures illustrate assimilation, persistent sub-cultures illustrate pluralism. We next examine these two forms of minority integration, as well as a third.

Theories of Minority Integration

More than 70 million immigrants have come to the United States since its founding as a nation. Over the course of this extensive migration, three different theories have emerged regarding how these ethnically different peoples either should or did fit into U.S. society. These theories are (1) assimilation, or majority-conformity, theory; (2) amalgamation, or melting-pot, theory; and (3) accommodation, or pluralistic, theory.

The type of interaction between minority peoples and those of the dominant culture has depended partly on which ideology was then accepted by those already established in the community and partly on the ideology of the minority groups. People formulate attitudes and expectations based on the values they hold. If those values include a clear image of how an "American" should look, talk, and act, people who differ from that model will find their adjustment to and acceptance by others more difficult. Conversely, if those values allow for diversity, a greater possibility exists that harmonious relationships will evolve.

Assimilation (Majority-Conformity) Theory

Generally speaking, **assimilation (majority-conformity) theory** refers to the functioning within a society of racial or ethnic minority-group members who lack any marked cultural, social, or personal differences from the people of the majority group. Physical or racial differences may persist, but they do not serve as the basis for group prejudice or discrimination. In effect, members of the minority groups no longer appear to be strangers because they have abandoned their own cultural traditions and successfully imitated the dominant group. Assimilation may thus be described as $A + B + C = A$.[14]

Anglo-Conformity.   Because most of the people in power in the United States during the eighteenth century were of English descent, English influence on the new nation's culture was enormous—in language, institutional forms, values, and attitudes. By the first quarter of the nineteenth century, a distinct national consciousness had emerged, and many U.S. citizens wanted to deemphasize their English origins and influences. However, when migration patterns changed the composition of the U.S. population in the 1880s, the "Yankees" reestablished the Anglo-Saxon as the superior archetype.[15] Anglo-Saxonism remained dominant well into the twentieth century as the mold into which newcomers must fit.

To preserve their Anglo-Saxon heritage, people in the United States have often attempted, sometimes with success, to curtail the large numbers of non–Anglo-Saxon immigrants. Social pressures demanded that new

The International Scene
Attempts to Eliminate a Persistent Subculture

The 20 million Kurds are an ethnic group with their own language. They live mostly in the bordering lands of Iran, Iraq, and Turkey—a region known as Kurdistan, or "Land of the Kurds." After World War I, this territory was partitioned among Turkey, Syria, and Iraq. Once a nomadic people who followed the seasonal migrations of their sheep and goat herds, the Kurds were thus compelled to abandon their traditional ways for village life and settled farming.

In the Kurdistan region, the Kurds remain a persistent subculture, whereas those living in urban areas are at least nominally assimilated. Marriages are typically endogamous, with a strong extended family network. The Kurds were once a tribal people under the firm leadership of a sheikh or an aga; however, that aspect of societal life is now felt (to a much smaller degree) only in the villages.

In 1924, the Turkish government engaged in cultural repression by renaming Kurds "Mountain Turks," outlawing their language, and forbidding their wearing the distinctive Kurdish costume in or near major cities. The government also encouraged many to migrate to the urbanized portion of western Turkey to dilute their population concentration. Uprisings in 1925, 1927–1930, and 1937–1938 were crushed; hundreds of thousands of Kurds were killed or expelled from the area.

Saddam Hussein's killing of thousands of Iraqi Kurds in 1988 with chemical weapons brought these relatively unknown people to the attention of Western cultures. Then came the Kurds' dramatic flight from Hussein's military forces in the spring of 1991 across snowclad mountains. Encouraged by the UN coalition's Gulf War victory, the Kurds rebelled against the repressive Baghdad regime, only to have Hussein's remaining forces drive them out. Iran let 1 million refugees cross its border to safety, but Turkey closed its border to about 500,000, trapping the Kurds in the mountains under harsh weather conditions. After two months, the coalition enticed the Kurds back into Iraq into an area designated as a "safe haven."

In 2003, these Kurds fought with U.S. troops against the Iraqi government and hope for a better life under the new government, in which they have representation.

Today, Kurds remain divided between assimilationist and nationalist goals. Facing varying degrees of government repression and tolerance, they continue to face an uncertain future.

Critical thinking questions: What other persistent subcultures have faced harsh repressive actions? Are there common reasons for these government-endorsed actions?

---

arrivals shed their native culture and attachments as quickly as possible and be remade into "Americans" along cherished Anglo-Saxon lines. The schools served as an important socializing agent in promoting the shedding of cultural differences.

Sometimes insistence on assimilation reached feverish heights, as evidenced by the **Americanization movement** during World War I. The arrival of a large number of "inferior" people in the preceding 30 years and the participation of the United States in a European conflict raised questions about nationals who were not "100 percent American." Government agencies at all levels, together with many private organizations, acted to encourage more immediate adoption by foreigners of U.S. practices: citizenship, reverence for U.S. institutions, and use of the English language.[16] Because this policy required that all minority groups divest themselves of their distinctive ethnic characteristics and adopt those of the dominant group, George R. Stewart suggested (some decades later) that assimilation be called the "transmuting pot" theory.[17]

Other assimilation efforts have not been very successful—for example, with people whose ancestral history in an area predates the nation's expansion into that territory. Most Native American tribes throughout the United States as well as the Hispanos of the Southwest have resisted this cultural hegemony.

Types of Assimilation.   Milton Gordon suggested assimilation has several phases.[18] One important phase is **cultural assimilation (acculturation)**—the change of cultural patterns to match those of the host society. **Marital assimilation (amalgamation)**—large-scale intermarriage with members of the majority society—and **structural assimilation**—large-scale entrance into the cliques, clubs, and institutions of the host society on a primary-group level—best reveal the extent of acceptance of minority groups in the larger society.

Other types of assimilation are *identificational assimilation,* the development of a sense of peoplehood or ethnicity based exclusively on the host society and not on one's homeland; *attitude-receptional assimilation,* reaching the point of encountering no prejudiced attitudes; *behavior-receptional assimilation,* reaching the point of encountering no discriminatory behavior; and *civic assimilation,* the absence of value and power conflicts with the native-born population.

Gordon states, "Once structural assimilation has occurred, either simultaneously with or subsequent to acculturation, all other types of assimilation will naturally follow."[19] Other sociologists disagree, claiming that cultural assimilation does not necessarily result from structural assimilation. Studies show that descendants of European immigrants have attained a significant level of structural assimilation. Descendants of non-European immigrants, even those beginning at the bottom of the socioeconomic ladder, have also been gaining some degree of structural assimilation, but at a much slower rate than earlier Europeans.[20]

Louis Wirth maintained that situational variables are important in the assimilation of minority groups.[21] Wirth distinguished among pluralism, assimilation, secession, and militancy as successive orientations by minorities in response to majority-group prejudice and discrimination. As groups begin to gain some power, they generally attempt to gain social tolerance of the group's differences (*pluralism*) and then become absorbed by the dominant society (*assimilation*). Those groups who are prevented from assimilating eventually withdraw from the societal mainstream (*secession*), but if conflict then ensues, they seek more extreme remedies (*militancy*).

Assimilation may be both a majority-group and a minority-group goal, but one or both may view assimilation as undesirable in some cases. Accordingly, the preceding typologies are not always helpful when examining dominant–minority relationships. Gordon shows the complexity of the assimilation process; Wirth suggests that the dynamics of the situation shape the evolution of dominant–minority relations throughout the assimilation process. The larger question of whether the assimilation process is linear remains in all cases. Not all groups seek assimilation, and not all groups who seek assimilation attain it.

Assimilation as a belief, goal, or pattern helps explain many aspects of dominant–minority relations, particularly acceptance and adjustment. For many members of the dominant society, assimilation of minorities has meant their absorption into the mold, reflecting what Barbara Solomon calls "the Anglo Saxon complex."[22] For physically or culturally distinct groups (e.g., Blacks, Native Americans, Asians, or Muslims), this concept has raised a seemingly insurmountable barrier. Even without the Anglo-Saxon role model, assimilation is preceded by a transitional period in which the newcomer gradually blends in with majority-group members. In doing so, the individual acquires a new behavioral identity, perhaps at some personal cost.

Amalgamation (Melting-Pot) Theory

The democratic experiment in the United States fired many an imagination. A new society was being shaped, peopled by immigrants from different European nations and not slavishly dependent on the customs and traditions of the past. This set of circumstances generated a romantic notion of the United States as a melting pot. The **amalgamation (melting-pot) theory** states that all the diverse peoples blend their biological and cultural differences into an altogether new breed—the American. This concept may be expressed as $A + B + C = D$.[23]

Advocates.   J. Hector St. John de Crèvecoeur, a French settler in New York, first popularized the idea of a melting pot. Envisioning the United States as more than just a land of opportunity, Crèvecoeur in 1782 spoke of a new breed of humanity emerging from the new society. That he included only White Europeans partly explains the weakness of this approach to minority integration:

What is an American? He is either a European, or the descendant of a European; hence that strange mixture of blood which you will find in no other country. I could point out to you a man whose grandfather was an Englishman, whose wife was Dutch, whose son married a French woman, and whose present four sons have now four wives of different nations. He is an American, who, leaving behind him all his ancient prejudices and manners, receives new ones from the new mode of life he has embraced, the new government he obeys and the new rank he holds. . . . Here individuals of all nations are melted into a new race of men, whose labors and posterity will one day cause great changes in the world.[24]

This idealistic concept found many advocates over the years. In 1893, Frederick Jackson Turner updated it with his frontier thesis, a notion that greatly influenced historical scholarship for half a century. Turner believed that the challenge of frontier life was the catalyst that fused immigrants into a composite new national stock within an evolving social order:

Thus the Middle West was teaching the lesson of national cross-fertilization instead of national enmities, the possibility of a newer and richer civilization, not by preserving unmodified or isolated the old component elements, but by breaking down the line-fences, by merging the individual life in the common product—a new product, which held the promise of world brotherhood.[25]

In 1908, the play *The Melting-Pot* by English author Israel Zangwill enthusiastically etched a permanent symbol on the assimilationist ideal:

There she lies, the great melting pot. Listen! Can't you hear the roaring and the bubbling? There gapes her mouth—the harbor where a thousand mammoth feeders come from the ends of the world to pour in their human freight. Ah, what a stirring and a seething—Celt and Latin, Slav and Teuton, Greek and Syrian. America is God's Crucible, the great Melting Pot where all the races of Europe are melting and reforming!—Here you stand good folk, think I, when I see you at Ellis Island, here you stand, in your fifty groups, with your fifty languages and histories, and your fifty hatreds and rivalries. But you won't be long like that, brothers, for these are the fires of God you come to—these are the fires of God! . . . Germans and Frenchmen, Irishmen and English, Jews and Russians, into the Crucible with you all! God is making the American! . . . the real American has not yet arrived . . . He will be the fusion of all races, perhaps the coming superman. . . . Ah, Vera, what is the glory of Rome and Jerusalem, where all races and nations come to worship and look back, compared with the glory of America, where all races and nations come to labor and look forward.[26]

Both the frontier thesis and the melting-pot concept have since come under heavy criticism. Although many commentators still pay homage to the melting-pot concept, few social scientists accept this explanation of minority integration into society. Nevertheless, many people in the United

States hold this view. The "English-only" movement, arguments against bilingual education, and exclusive emphasis on Western heritage are examples of some U.S. citizens' rejecting multiple cultures and wanting others to "blend in," although they really mean that they want people of ethnic subgroups to assimilate.

Did We Melt?   Over several generations, intermarriages have occurred frequently between people of different nationalities, less frequently between people of different religions, and still less frequently between people of different races. One could thus argue that a biological merging of previously distinct ethnic stocks, and to a lesser extent of different races, has taken place.[27] However, the melting-pot theory spoke not only of intermarriages among the different groups but also of a distinct new national culture evolving from elements of all other cultures. Here the theory has proved to be unrealistic. From its founding, the United States has been dominated by an Anglo-Saxon population and thus by the English language and Anglo-Saxon institutional forms. Rather than various cultural patterns melting into a new U.S. culture, elements of minority cultures have metamorphosed into the Anglo-Saxon mold.

Milton Gordon suggested that only in the institution of religion did minority groups alter the national culture.[28] From a mostly Protestant nation in its early history, the United States has become a land of four major faiths: Protestant, Catholic, Jewish, and Muslim. In the mid-twentieth century, some social observers viewed the United States as a **triple melting pot**. From her studies in New Haven, Connecticut, Ruby Jo Reeves Kennedy reported on extensive intermarriage between various nationalities but only within the then three major religious groupings (Protestant, Catholic, Jew).[29] Will Herberg echoed this analysis, arguing that ethnic differences were disappearing as religious groupings became the primary foci of identity and interaction.[30] Today, the high religious intermarriage rate and the increasing numbers of U.S. believers in Islam, Hinduism, and other non-Western religions render the concept of a triple melting pot obsolete.

In other areas, the entry of diverse minority groups into U.S. society has not produced new social structures or institutional forms in the larger society. Instead, subcultural social structures and institutions have evolved to meet group needs, and the dominant culture has benefited from the labors and certain cultural aspects of minority groups within the already existing dominant culture. For example, minority influences are found in word usage, place names, cuisine, architecture, art, recreational activities, and music.

Sociologist Henry Pratt Fairchild offered a physiological analogy to describe how the absorption of various cultural components or peoples produces assimilation and not amalgamation. An organism consumes food and is somewhat affected (nourished) by it; the food, though, is assimilated in the sense that it becomes an integral part of the organism, retaining none of its original characteristics. This is a one-way process. In a similar manner, U.S. culture has remained basically unchanged, though strengthened, despite the influx of many minority groups.[31]

Most social scientists now believe that the melting-pot theory is a myth. Its idealistic rhetoric continues to attract many followers, however. In reality, the melting meant **Anglo-conformity**—being remade according to the idealized Anglo-Saxon mold, as Herberg observed:

> But it would be a mistake to infer from this that the American's image of himself—and that means the ethnic group member's image of himself as he becomes American—is a composite or synthesis of the ethnic elements that have gone into the making of the American. It is nothing of the kind; the American's image of himself is still the Anglo-American ideal it was at the beginning of our independent existence. The "national type" as ideal has always been, and remains, pretty well fixed. It is the *Mayflower*, John Smith, Davy Crockett, George Washington, and Abraham Lincoln that define the American's self-image, and this is true whether the American in question is a descendant of the Pilgrims or the grandson of an immigrant from southeastern Europe.[32]

The rejection of the melting-pot theory by many people, coupled with an ethnic consciousness, spawned a third ideology: the accommodation (pluralistic) theory.

Accommodation (Pluralistic) Theory

The **accommodation (pluralistic) theory** recognizes the persistence of racial and ethnic diversity, as in Canada, where the government has adopted multiculturalism as official policy. Pluralist theorists argue that minorities can maintain their distinctive subcultures and simultaneously interact with relative equality in the larger society. In countries such as Switzerland and the United States, this combination of diversity and togetherness is possible to varying degrees because the people agree on certain basic values (refer to Figure 2.1). At the same time, minorities may interact mostly among themselves, live within well-defined communities, have their own forms of organizations, work in similar occupations, and marry within their own group. Applying our descriptive equation, pluralism would be $A + B + C = A + B + C$.[33]

Early Analysis.   Horace Kallen is generally recognized as the first exponent of cultural pluralism. In 1915, he published "Democracy Versus the Melting Pot," in which he rejected the assimilation and amalgamation theories.[34] Not only did each group tend to preserve its own language, institutions, and cultural heritage, he maintained, but democracy gave each group the right to do so. To be sure, minority groups learned the English language and participated in U.S. institutions, but what the United States really had become was a "cooperation of cultural diversities." Seeing Americanization movements as a threat to minority groups and the melting-pot notion as unrealistic, Kallen believed that cultural pluralism could be the basis for a great democratic commonwealth. A philosopher, not a sociologist, Kallen nonetheless directed sociological attention to a long-standing U.S. pattern.

Pluralistic Reality.   From its colonial beginnings, the United States has been a pluralistic country. Early settlements were small ethnic enclaves, each peopled by different nationalities or religious groups. New Amsterdam and Philadelphia were exceptions; both were heavily pluralistic within their boundaries. Chain-migration patterns resulted in immigrants settling in clusters. Germans and Scandinavians in the Midwest, Poles in Chicago, Irish in New York and Boston, French in Louisiana, Asians in California, Cubans in Miami, and many others illustrate how groups ease their adjustment to a new country by re-creating in miniature the world they left behind. Current immigrant groups and remnants of past immigrant groups are testimony to the pluralism in U.S. society.

   Cultural pluralism—two or more culturally distinct groups living in the same society in relative harmony—has been the more noticeable form of pluralism. **Structural pluralism**—the coexistence of racial and ethnic groups in subsocieties within social-class and regional boundaries—is less noticeable.

   As Gordon observes, "Cultural pluralism was a fact in American society before it became a theory—at least a theory with explicit relevance for the nation as a whole and articulated and discussed in the general English-speaking circles of American intellectual life."[35] Many minority groups lose their visibility when they acculturate. They may, however, identify with and take pride in their heritage and maintain primary relationships mostly with members of their ethnic group. Despite this pluralistic reality, intolerance of such diversity remains a problem within U.S. society.

Dual Realities.   Although Americans give lip service to the concept of a melting pot, they typically expect foreigners to assimilate as quickly as possible. Mainstream Americans often tolerate pluralism only as a short-term phenomenon, for many believe sustained pluralism is the enemy of assimilation, a threat to the cohesiveness of U.S. society.

   Assimilation and pluralism are not mutually exclusive however; nor are they necessarily enemies. In fact, they have always existed simultaneously among different groups, at different levels. Whether as persistent subcultures or as convergent ones that gradually merge into the dominant culture over several generations, culturally distinct groups have always existed. And even when their numbers have been great, they have never threatened the core cultures, as we will see. Assimilation remains a powerful force affecting most minority groups, despite the assertions of anti-immigration fearmongers and radical multiculturalists. Although propo-

"Uncle Sam's Troublesome Bedfellows"

This cartoon pictures Uncle Sam annoyed by groups that were seen as unassimilable. Both racial differences (Blacks, Chinese, and Native Americans) and religious differences (Catholics and Mormons) were cause for being kicked out of the symbolic bed. This cartoon appeared in a San Francisco illustrated weekly, *The Wasp*, on February 8, 1879.

nents of one position may decry the other, pluralism and assimilation have always been dual realities within U.S. society.

As Richard D. Alba reminds us, assimilation occurs in different ways and to different degrees, and it does not necessarily mean the obliteration of all traces of ethnic origins. It can occur even as ethnic communities continue to exist in numerous cities and as many individuals continue to identify with their ethnic ancestry.

> [*Assimilation*] refers, above all, to long-term processes that have whittled away at the social foundations for ethnic distinctions. These processes have brought about a rough parity of opportunities to attain such socioeconomic goods as educational credentials and prestigious jobs, loosened the ties between ethnicity and specific economic niches, diminished cultural differences that serve to signal ethnic membership to others and to sustain ethnic solidarity, shifted residence away from central-city ethnic neighborhoods to

ethnically intermixed suburbs, and finally, fostered relatively easy social intermixing across ethnic lines, resulting ultimately in high rates of ethnic intermarriage and ethnically mixed ancestry.[36]

Herbert Gans suggests that a reconciliation between assimilation and pluralism may be found by recalling the distinction between acculturation and assimilation. Acculturation has always proceeded more quickly than assimilation, providing evidence in support of both traditional assimilationist theory and recent pluralist—or ethnic retention—theory. Moreover, researchers of past and present immigrations have studied different generations of newcomers and have approached their research with "outsider" and "insider" values, respectively.[37] Richard D. Alba and Victor Nee add that the evidence shows that assimilation is occurring among recent arrivals, albeit unevenly, and suggest that some fine-tuning of assimilationist theory to address these variances in settlement, language acquisition, and mobility patterns may improve our understanding of the contemporary ethnic and racial scene.[38]

Finally, we should note that several other positive models of pluralism exist elsewhere in the world. Switzerland, mentioned earlier, is actually a confederation with three official languages and proportional minority representation in the national legislature. Belgium also has three official languages, and its constitution gives formal recognition and autonomy to the Dutch-speaking Fleming region in the north and the French-speaking Walloon region in the south. In the northern regions of Scandinavia (Finland, Norway, and Sweden) live the Sami, one of the largest indigenous groups in Europe (about 85,000), about half of whom live in Norway. To make up for past efforts to force assimilation of the people once known as Laplanders (a term no longer socially acceptable), the three national governments actively work to promote Sami culture and language, support the authority of democratically elected Sami Parliament, and officially recognize February 6 as Sami National Day. Newspapers, radio programs, and daily news bulletins on national TV—all in the Sami language—plus education with Sami as the first language—are other measures to preserve their language and culture.

Is There a White Culture?

In the mid-1990s, interest in White studies rose significantly. White studies essentially focuses on how whiteness has led to racial domination and hegemony, in which White American culture is simply called "American," thereby presuming that Black, Native American, Asian, or Hispanic cultures are not "American" but instead racial and/or ethnic subcultures. The idea that a White culture also exists is difficult for many people to grasp, say the

White studies advocates, much like a fish is unaware of water until out of it, because of its environmental universality.

The premise for a White culture existing independent of an "American" culture is that all racial groups have large social/cultural characteristics that change over time. These White values, attitudes, shared understandings, and behavior patterns—like many aspects of culture—are often unrealized by group members because they are part of a taken-for-granted world. Yet even though White culture may not be identifiable among its members, it is nonetheless real and easily recognizable by non-Whites. For example, says Jeff Hitchcock in *Lifting the White Veil*, in Black culture feelings take precedence over sensibilities. He explains that when a feeling comes upon a person, Black culture says it is appropriate to express it, but White culture

> works hard to keep the volume down, least we all go crazy from the demands we place on each other's capacity for self-control. Experience in the culture helps. We learn how not to step on toes, hurt other people's "feelings," to not make a scene, and all the other little social rules and practices of a lifetime. We rein it in, and trade spontaneity . . . for an orderly demeanor and generally predictable and controlled everyday existence.[39]

Lacking an understanding of the existence of White culture, say its proponents, results in the dominant group misinterpreting alternative cultural experiences as racial or else as the personal failings of someone of color. Recognizing its existence could be a first step toward building a truly multiracial society.

Retrospect

Culture provides the normative definitions by which members of a society perceive and interpret the world about them. Language and other forms of symbolic interaction provide the means by which this accumulated knowledge is transmitted. Becoming acculturated requires learning both the language and the symbol system of the new society. Sometimes, though, situations become real in their consequences because people earlier defined them as real (the Thomas theorem). Unless it is isolated from the rest of the world, a society undergoes change through cultural contact and the diffusion of ideas, inventions, and practices. Within large societies, subcultures usually exist. They may gradually be assimilated (convergent subcultures), or they may remain distinct (persistent subcultures).

Three theories of minority integration have emerged. Assimilation, or majority-conformity, became a goal of many, both native-born and foreign-born; yet not all sought this goal or were able to achieve it. The romantic notion of amalgamation, or a melting pot, in which a new breed of people with a distinct culture would emerge, proved unrealistic. Finally, accommodation, or pluralism, arose as a school of thought recognizing the persistence of ethnic diversity in a society with a commonly shared core culture. Assimilation and pluralism are not mutually exclusive; both have always existed simultaneously, with assimilation exerting a constant, powerful force.

KEY TERMS

Accommodation (pluralistic) theory
Acculturation
Amalgamation (melting-pot) theory
Americanization movement
Anglo-conformity
Assimilation (majority-conformity) theory
Chain migration
Convergent subcultures
Cultural assimilation (acculturation)
Cultural diffusion
Cultural pluralism
Cultural transmission
Culture
Culture shock
Ethnic subcultures

Ethnogenesis
Linguistic relativity
Marginality
Marital assimilation (amalgamation)
Material culture
Nonmaterial culture
Norms
Paralinguistic signals
Parallel social institutions
Persistent subcultures
Structural assimilation
Structural pluralism
Thomas theorem
Triple melting pot
Vicious-circle phenomenon

REVIEW QUESTIONS

1. What is the relationship among culture, reality, and intergroup relations?

2. How does language affect our perception of reality?

3. How does the Thomas theorem help us understand problems in intergroup relations?

4. How would you answer someone who claims foreigners are changing American culture?

5. What are subcultures? What forms do they take? What significance do these forms have for intergroup relations?

6. Discuss the major theories of minority integration.

SUGGESTED READINGS

Gordon, Milton M. *Assimilation in American Life*. New York: Oxford University Press, 1964.
    A highly influential and still pertinent book offering an analysis of the role of race and ethnicity in American life.

Griswold, Wendy. *Cultures and Societies in a Changing World,* 2d ed. Thousand Oaks, Calif.: Pine Forge Press, 2003.

A thorough examination of the elements and dynamics of culture and the cultural diffusion spread by technology and the global economy.

Hall, Edward T. *Understanding Cultural Differences.* Yarmouth, Me.: Intercultural Press, 1990.

Focuses on national cultural contrasts between France, Germany, and the United States through an examination of business and management practices.

Harrison, Lawrence E., and Samuel P. Huntington (eds.). *Culture Matters: How Values Shape Human Progress.* New York: Basic Books, 2001.

A collection of essays by leading social scientists that examine how culture affects prosperity, democracy, and social justice among both countries and immigrants.

Hitchcock, Jeff. *Lifting the White Veil: An Exploration of White Culture in a Multiracial Context.* Roselle, N.J.: Crandall Dostie & Douglass Books, 2003.

An overview of the history of Whiteness in U.S. society, with a personal, provocative argument on the need to recognize the existence of White culture and to "decenter" it.

Ritzer, George. *The McDonaldization of Society,* 4th ed. Thousand Oaks, Calif.: Pine Forge Press, 2004.

Fine use of sociological imagination to show cultural diffusion in the organization of work throughout the world.

INTERNET RESOURCES

To learn more about the Sami in northern Scandinavia, go to www.google.com/top /society/ethnicity/sami.

For further information on white culture, visit the website of the Center for the Study of White American Culture at www.euroamerican.org/.

CHAPTER

3 Ethnic and Racial Stratification

"Poverty is a veil that obscures the face of greatness."
—Khalil Gibran

Relations between dominant and minority groups are influenced as much by structural conditions as by difference in culture. **Social structure**—the organized patterns of behavior among the basic components of a social system—establishes relatively predictable social relationships among the different peoples in a society.

The nature of the social structure influences not only the distribution of power resources (economic, political, and social) but also the accessibility of those resources to groups who seek upward mobility. An expanding economy and an open social system create increased opportunities for minority-group members, thereby reducing the likelihood that tensions will arise. In contrast, a stagnant or contracting economy thwarts many efforts to improve status and antagonizes those who feel most threatened by another group's competition for scarce resources. Such a situation may serve as a breeding ground for conflicts among minority groups even more than between majority and minority groups because the group next highest on the socioeconomic ladder may perceive a threat from below more quickly and react negatively.

The state of the economy is just one important structural factor influencing the opportunities for upward mobility. Another is the degree of change between a minority group's old society and the new one. A traditional or agrarian society typically has a much more stable social structure than a society undergoing transformation through industrialization. The latter society offers dramatic changes in opportunities and lifestyles, not all of them for the better. A migrating minority group's compatibility with the social structure of the new land depends on the degree of similarity between the new country's structural conditions and those of its homeland. A person who leaves an agrarian society for an industrial one is poorly prepared to enter any but the lowest social stratum in a low-paying position. Opportunities for upward mobility may exist, however, if the new land's economy is growing rapidly. In this sense, the structural conditions in the United States during the period from 1880 to 1920 were better for unskilled immigrants than are conditions today. Low-skill jobs are less plentiful today, and an unskilled worker's desire to support a family through hard work may not be matched by the opportunity to do so.

Meanwhile, technological advances have made the world smaller. Rapid transportation and communications (radios, televisions, telephones, computers, the Internet, fax machines, and overnight deliveries) permit ties to other parts of the world to remain stronger than in the past.[1] Accessibility to their homeland, friends, or relatives may make people less interested in becoming fully assimilated in a new land. Befriending strangers in the new country becomes less necessary. In addition, people's greater knowledge of the world, the rising social consciousness of a society, and structural opportunities for mobility all help to create a more hospitable environment for minority-group members.

Stratification

Social stratification is the hierarchical classification of the members of society based on the unequal distribution of resources, power, and prestige. The word *resources* refers to such factors as income, property, and borrowing capacity. *Power*, usually reflected by the stratified layers, represents the ability to influence or control others. *Prestige* relates to status, either *ascribed* (based on age, sex, race, or family background) or *achieved* (based on individual accomplishments).

The process of stratification may either moderate or exacerbate any strains or conflicts between groups depending on the form that the stratification takes. The form can range from rigid and explicit to flexible and subtle; from the overt rigidity of slavery, caste, and forced labor to implicit class distinctions and discrimination based on race or ethnic group. Whether racial and ethnic groups face insurmountable barriers or minor obstacles in achieving upward mobility depends on the form of stratification. The more rigid the stratification, the more likely is the emergence of racial, religious, or other ideologies justifying the existing arrangements—as happened with the rise of racism during slavery in the United States.

The form of stratification affects how groups within the various strata of society view one another. Some people confuse structural differentiation with cultural differentiation. For example, they may believe that a group's low socioeconomic status is due to its values and attitudes rather than to such structural conditions as racism, economic stagnation, and high urban unemployment. The form of stratification is an important determinant of the potential for intergroup conflict. In the United States, both the possibility of upward mobility and structural obstacles to that possibility have existed. When the disparity between the perception of the American Dream and the reality of the difficulty of achieving it grows too great, the possibility of conflict increases.

Social Class

Social class is one categorization sociologists use to designate people's place in the stratification hierarchy; people in a particular social class have a similar level of income, amount of property, degree of power, status, and type of lifestyle. Many factors help determine a person's social class, including the individual's membership in particular racial, religious, and status groups. Although no clearly defined boundaries exist between class groupings in the United States, people have a tendency to cluster together according to certain socioeconomic similarities. The concept or image of social-class reality can be traced to sociopsychological distinctions people make about one another on the basis of such variables as where they live and what they own as well as to interactions that occur because of those distinctions.

In the 1930s, W. Lloyd Warner headed a classic study of social-class differentiation in the United States.[2] Using the **reputational method**—asking people how they thought others compared to them—Warner found a well-formulated class system in place. In Newburyport, Massachusetts, a small town of about 17,000 that he called "Yankee City," Warner identified six classes: upper-upper, lower-upper, upper-middle, lower-middle, upper-lower, and lower-lower.

Although Warner reached several faulty conclusions because he failed to take a sociohistorical approach, as Stephan Thernstrom points out, some of his findings have validity to our focus here.[3] When he and his associates examined the distribution of ethnic groups among the various classes, certain factors emerged. First, a significant relationship existed between an ethnic group's length of residence and class status; the more recent arrivals tended to be in the lower classes. In addition, an ethnic group tended to be less assimilated and less upwardly mobile if its population in the community was relatively large, if its homeland was close (e.g., in the case of immigrant French Canadians), if its members had a sojourner rather than a permanent-settler orientation, and if limited opportunities for advancement existed in the community.[4]

Social class becomes important in intergroup relations because it provides a basis for expectations. As Alan Kerckhoff states, social class provides a particular setting for the interplay between the formative experiences of a child, others' expectations of the child, and what kind of adult the child be-comes.[5] Beyond this significant aspect, social class also serves as a point of reference in others' responses and in one's self-perception. As a result, social class helps shape an individual's world of reality and influences group in-teractions. Attitudes and behavior formed within a social-class framework are not immutable, however; they can change if circumstances change.

Class Consciousness

Just how important are the ethnic factors that Warner and others reported in shaping an awareness of social class? The significance of ethnic factors de-pends on numerous variables, including economic conditions, mobility pat-terns, and prevailing attitudes. John Leggett found that class consciousness depends on the ethnic factor: The lower a group's ethnic status in the soci-ety, the higher the level of class consciousness.[6] Other studies have shown that working-class ethnic groups tend to view their class as hostile to, and under the political control of, the higher-status classes.[7]

Because ethnic minorities are disproportionately represented among the lower classes and because middle-class values dominate in the United States, it seems reasonable to suppose that at least some of the attitudes of each group result from people's value judgments about social class. That is to say, the dominant group's criticism and stereotyping of the minority group probably rests in part on class distinctions.

Social-class status plays an important role in determining a minority group's adjustment to and acceptance by society. For example, because the first waves of Cuban (1960s) and Vietnamese (1970s) refugees who arrived in the United States possessed the education and occupational experience of the middle class, they succeeded in overcoming early native concerns and did not encounter the same degree of negativism as had earlier groups. On the other hand, when unskilled and often illiterate peasants enter the lower-class positions in U.S. society, many U.S. citizens belittle, avoid, and discriminate against them because of their supposedly inferior ways. Frequently, these at-titudes and actions reflect an awareness of class differences as well as cultural differences. Because the dominant group usually occupies a higher stratum in the social-class hierarchy, differences in social-class values and lifestyles—in addition to ethnic cultural differences—can be sources of friction.

Ethnicity and Social Class

Differences in stratification among various groups cannot be explained by a single cause, although many observers have tried to do so. For example, in his influential book *The Ethnic Myth*, Stephen Steinberg stressed the importance of social structure and minimized cultural factors.[8] For him, the success of Jews in the United States resulted more from their occupational skills in the urbanized country than from their values. Conversely, Thomas Sowell wrote in *Ethnic America* that the compatibility of a group's cultural characteristics with those of the dominant culture determines the level of a group's economic success.[9] Actually, structural and cultural elements intertwine. Emphasizing only social structure ignores such important cultural variables as values about education. Emphasizing only culture can lead to blaming people who do not succeed.

Colin Greer criticized those who overemphasize ethnic-centered analyses and ignore the larger question of class:

> This kind of ethnic reductionism forces us to accept as predetermined what society defines as truth. Only through ethnicity can identity be securely achieved. The result is that ethnic questions which could, in fact, further our understanding of the relationship of individuals to social structures are always raised in a way that serves to reconcile us to a common heritage of miserable inequities. Instead of realizing that the lack of a well-defined stratification structure, linked to a legitimated aristocratic tradition, led Americans to employ the language of ethnic pluralism in exchange for direct divisions by social class, we continue to ignore the real factors of class in our society.... What we must ultimately talk about is class. The cues of felt ethnicity turn out to be the recognizable characteristics of class position in this society: to feel black, Irish, Italian, Jewish has meant to learn to live in accommodation with that part of your heritage that is compatible with the needs and opportunities in America upon arrival and soon thereafter.[10]

In 1964, 10 years before Greer's observations, Milton Gordon first suggested that dominant–minority relations be examined within the larger context of the social structure.[11] This proposition marked an important turning point in racial and ethnic studies.[12] Although he believed that all groups would eventually become assimilated, Gordon offered an explanation of the present pluralistic society. His central thesis was that four factors, or social categories, play a part in forming subsocieties within the nation: ethnicity (by which Gordon also meant race), social class, rural or urban residence, and regionalism.[13] These factors unite in various combinations to create a number of **ethclasses**—subsocieties resulting from the intersection of stratifications of race and ethnic group with stratifications of social class. Additional determinants are the rural or urban setting and the particular region of the country in which a group lives. Examples of ethclasses are lower-middle-class White Catholics in a northeastern city, lower-class Black Baptists in the rural South, and upper-class White Jews in a western urban area.

Numerous studies support the concept that race and ethnicity, together with social class, are important in social structures and intergroup conflicts.[14]

For example, social scientists such as Thomas Pettigrew and Charles Willie argue that recognizing the intersection of race and class is a key element in understanding the continued existence of Black poverty.[15] Not only do eth-class groupings exist, but people tend to interact within them for their intimate primary relationships. To the extent that this is true, multiple allegiances and conflicts are inevitable. According to this view, both cultural and structural pluralism currently exist; numerous groups presently coexist in separate subsocieties based on social class and cultural distinctions. Even people whose families have been in the United States for several generations are affiliated with, and participate in, subsocieties. Nonetheless, Gordon views assimilation as a linear process in which even structural assimilation will eventually occur.

Blaming the Poor or Society?

In 1932, E. Franklin Frazier formulated his conception of a disorganized and pathological lower-class culture. This thesis served as the inspiration for the controversial **culture of poverty** viewpoint that emerged in the 1960s.[16] The writings of two men—Daniel P. Moynihan and Oscar Lewis—sparked an intense debate that continues to resonate today. In his 1965 government report, "The Negro Family: The Case for National Action," Moynihan used Frazier's observations as a springboard for arguing that a "tangle of pathology" so pervaded the Black community that it perpetuated a cycle of poverty and deprivation that only outside (government) intervention could overcome.[17]

Family Disintegration.   Moynihan argued that family deterioration was a core cause of the problems of high unemployment, welfare dependence, illegitimacy, low achievement, juvenile delinquency, and adult crime:

> At the heart of the deterioration of the fabric of Negro society is the deterioration of the Negro family. It is the fundamental source of weakness of the Negro community at the present time. . . . The white family has achieved a high degree of stability and is maintaining that stability. By contrast, the family structure of the lower class Negroes is highly unstable, and in many urban centers is approaching complete breakdown.[18]

Moynihan described Black males as occupying an unstable place in the economy, which prevented them from functioning as strong fathers and husbands. This environment, he said, served as a breeding ground for a continuing vicious circle: The women often not only raised the children but also earned the family income. Consequently, the children grew up in a poorly supervised, unstable environment; they often performed poorly or dropped out of school; they could secure only low-paying jobs—and so the cycle began anew.[19] The Moynihan Report called for federal action to create, among other things, jobs for Black male heads of household in the inner city:

> At the center of the tangle of pathology is the weakness of the family structure. Once or twice removed, it will be found to be the principal source of most of the aberrant, inadequate, or anti-social behavior that did not establish but now serves to perpetuate the cycle of poverty and deprivation. . . .
> What then is the problem? We feel that the answer is clear enough. Three centuries of injustice have brought about deep-seated structural distortions in the life of the Negro American. At this point, the present tangle of pathology is capable of perpetuating itself without assistance from the white world. The cycle can be broken only if these distortions are set right.[20]

In a controversial 1986 television documentary, Bill Moyers echoed Moynihan's view that a link existed between specific cultural values and deteriorating conditions in lower-class Black family life.[21] Then, in 1990, Moynihan reaffirmed his position, citing further social deterioration since the 1960s and noting in particular the startling rise in out-of-wedlock births from 3 percent of White births and 24 percent of Black births in 1963 to 16 percent and 63 percent, respectively, in 1987.[22] These distressing statistics led Moynihan to repeat a statement from his 1965 report:

> From the wild Irish slums of the nineteenth-century Eastern seaboard, to the riot-torn suburbs of Los Angeles, there is one unmistakable lesson in American history: a community that allows a large number of young men to grow up in broken families, dominated by women, never acquiring a stable relationship to male authority, never acquiring any set of rational expectations about the future—that community asks for and gets chaos. Crime, violence, unrest, disorder—most particularly the furious, unrestrained lashing out at the whole social structure—that is not only to be expected; it is very near to inevitable.[23]

Perpetuation of Poverty.   Moynihan's position shared the same premises as Oscar Lewis's theory about a subculture of poverty, detailed in *The Children of Sanchez* (1961) and *La Vida* (1966):[24]

> The culture of poverty, however, is not only an adaptation to a set of objective conditions of the larger society. Once it comes into existence it tends to perpetuate itself from generation to generation because of its effect on the children. By the time slum children are age six or seven they have usually absorbed the basic values and attitudes of their subculture and are not psychologically geared to take full advantage of changing conditions or increased opportunities which may occur in their lifetime.[25]

Politically, Lewis was a leftist, and he did not blame the poor as some critics misinterpreted. Rather, he emphasized the institutionalized tenacity of their poverty, arguing that the system damaged them.[26] Edward Banfield, a conservative, recast Lewis's position to assert that poverty continues because of subcultural patterns. Whereas Lewis held that the mechanics of capitalist production for profit caused poverty, Banfield found its cause in the folkways of its victims. Banfield argued that good jobs, good housing, tripled welfare payments, new schools, quality education, and armies of police officers would not stop the problem. He added:

> If, however, the lower classes were to disappear—if, say, their members were overnight to acquire the attitudes, motivations, and habits of the working class—the most serious and intractable problems of the city would all disappear. . . . The lower-class forms of all problems are at bottom a single problem: the existence of an outlook and style of life which is radically present-oriented and which therefore attaches no value to work, sacrifice, self-improvement, or service to family, friends, or community.[27]

Most Americans continue to think that the poor are responsible for their own poverty. National polls in 1972 and 1986 found the majority of people responding that economic opportunity exists for all who work hard and that individuals are responsible for their own position in society and deserve the income they get.[28] In a 2001 poll, 70 percent said drug abuse was a major cause of poverty, and more than half also thought that medical bills and a decline in moral values were important causes as well, but not a shortage of jobs.[29] Since drug abuse and moral values translate to individual causes in contrast to the structural cause of a job shortage, Americans still blame the poor for their circumstances.

Another form of the "blame game" occurs during the political wrangling that goes on whenever welfare measures are considered. For example, when Congress passed the welfare reform act in 1996, its title was the Personal Responsibility and Work Opportunity Act, a not-too-subtle implication that the poor must change their ways if they want to escape poverty. The act's key provisions were a time limit on welfare payments and a requirement that welfare recipients, after two years, must work. No doubt some lazy people preferred living off a government handout than working, but that was only an extremely small percentage of the welfare recipients. Then, as now, the heavy majority of those living in poverty *do* work, but their limited education and job skills restrict them to low-paying, often unstable, work.[30]

Criticism. Although they were not saying the same thing, Moynihan, Lewis, and Banfield all came under heavy criticism during the 1960s and 1970s—the height of the civil-rights movement—from commentators who felt that they were blaming the victim. Critics argued that intergenerational poverty results from discrimination, structural conditions, or stratification rigidity. Fatalism, apathy, low aspirations, and other similar orientations found in lower-class culture are thus situational responses within each generation and not the result of cultural deficiencies transmitted from parents to children.

To William Ryan, blaming the victim results in misdirected social programs. If we rationalize away the socially acquired stigma of poverty as being the expression of a subcultural trait, we ignore the continuing effect of current victimizing social forces. As a result, we focus on helping the "disorganized" Black family instead of on overcoming racism, or we strive to develop "better" attitudes and skills in low-income children rather than revamping the poor-quality schools they attend.[31]

Charles A. Valentine led an emotional attack on the culture of poverty thesis and on Lewis himself.[32] He argued that many of Lewis's "class distinctive traits" of the poor are either "externally imposed conditions" (unemployment, crowded and deteriorated housing, and lack of education) or "unavoidable matters of situational expediency" (hostility toward social institutions and low expectations and self-image).[33] Only by changing the total social structure and the resources available to the poor can we alter any subcultural traits of survival.

Yet Lewis was also saying this.[34] Michael Harrington, whose *The Other America* (1963) helped spark the federal government's "War on Poverty" program, defended Lewis.[35] Harrington—like Lewis—said that society was to blame for the culture of poverty: "The real explanation of why the poor are where they are is that they made the mistake of being born to the wrong parents, in the wrong section of the country, in the wrong industry, or in the wrong racial or ethnic group."[36]

Like Lewis, Valentine, and Harrington, others argued that all people would desire the same things and cherish the same values if they were in an economic position to do so. Because they are not, they adopt an alternative set of values to survive.[37] Eliot Liebow, in a participant-observer study of lower-class Black males, concluded that they try to achieve many of the goals of the larger society but fail for many of the same reasons their fathers did: discrimination, unpreparedness, lack of job skills, and self-doubt.[38] The similarities between generations are due not to cultural transmission but to the sons' independent experience of the same failures. What appears to be a self-sustaining cultural process is actually a secondary adaptation to an adult inability to overcome structural constraints.

In a similar vein, Hyman Rodman suggested that all social classes share the general values of a society but that the lower class, while not rejecting those values, adopts additional values representing realistic levels of attainment. The lower class does not reject the less attainable values of the majority society but adopts a **value-stretch approach**, which encompasses a wider range of values:

> Lower-class persons . . . do not maintain a strong commitment to middle-class values that they cannot attain, and they do not continue to respond to

This single, homeless mother of four children works as an administrative assistant for a high-tech company in California, but the family lives in a church-supported shelter because of her limited income. Living in a homeless shelter not only can be stressful on both the children and mother, but also may lead to multi-generational poverty.

others in a rewarding or punishing way simply on the basis of whether these others are living up to the middle-class values. A change takes place. They come to tolerate and eventually to evaluate favorably certain deviations from the middle-class values. In this way they need not be continually frustrated by their failure to live up to unattainable values. The resultant is a stretched value system.[39]

L. Richard Della Fave adds that the poor adopt this value-stretch approach when the gap between ideal value preference and achievement expectations becomes too great.[40] In other words, the poor do not have different values but have different behaviors that reflect pragmatic coping mechanisms. Since they expect less, they learn to be satisfied with less.

The debate over whether the culture of poverty results from **economic determinism** (structural barriers and discrimination) or from **cultural**

determinism (transmission of cultural inadequacies) continues.[41] Whatever the cause, most people's attitudes toward welfare and the urban poor (who are predominantly racial and ethnic minorities) reflect a belief in one position or the other. Interestingly, both viewpoints share a belief that determinism of some kind decides the fate of the poor, thereby reflecting the "free-will" thesis popular in Western thought—the notion that every individual "makes" his or her own luck. The two sociological viewpoints also support increased employment and educational opportunities to overcome the persistence of poverty.

However, functionalist explanations for inequality and the conditions of poverty differ significantly from conflict perspectives. Is poverty the result of personal deficiencies? Does long-term poverty result in the development of negative values passed from one generation to the next? Are personal characteristics of the poor the result of long-term poverty, or are they simply adjustments to conditions of poverty? Such questions of blaming the poor and/or existing socioeconomic systems for the existence of poverty, particularly among minority groups, evoke different analytical answers from the two perspectives. What if we used both perspectives instead of one over the other? How would we then answer this question: Is inequality an inevitable part of society?

Intergroup Conflict

Is conflict inevitable when culturally distinct groups interact? Do structural conditions encourage or reduce the probability of conflict? Robert E. Park argued that a universal, irreversible, possibly slowly evolving cycle of events made conflict and subsequent resolution by assimilation inevitable. This "race relations cycle" had four stages: (1) contact between the groups; (2) competition; (3) adjustment or accommodation; and (4) assimilation and amalgamation. (In Park's day, the term *race* referred to racial and ethnic groups, and his comments should be understood in this broader sense.) According to Park:

> The race relations cycle which takes the form, to state it abstractly, of contact, competition, accommodation, and eventual assimilation, is apparently progressive and irreversible. Customs regulations, immigration restrictions, and racial barriers may slacken the tempo of the movement; may perhaps halt it altogether for a time; but cannot change its direction, cannot, at any rate, reverse it. . . . It does not follow that because the tendencies to the assimilation and eventual amalgamation of races exist, they should not be resisted and, if possible, altogether inhibited. . . . Rising tides of color and oriental exclusion laws are merely incidental evidences of this diminishing distance. . . . In the Hawaiian Islands, where all the races of the Pacific meet and mingle . . . , the

native races are disappearing and new peoples are coming into existence. Races and cultures die—it has always been so—but civilization lives on.[42]

Park's theory fit nicely into the prevailing assimilationist thinking of his time, but his race relations cycle has several problems. By its very nature, the claim that all instances of interaction between subgroups in a society must end in assimilation is not testable because any instance of nonassimilation can be explained away as a case in which the cycle is not yet complete.[43] Indeed, Park never cited any example where his cycle had reached completion; but instead of seeing such negative data as refuting the theory, Park and other cyclical theorists attributed the lack of assimilation to temporary obstacles or interference. Such tautological reasoning, argues Stanford M. Lyman, leaves this theory deficient in an essential element of empirical science: It cannot be proved or disproved.[44] Perhaps, though, we might consider one example to be the interaction between Anglo-Saxon residents and Norman-French invaders, both of whom gradually disappeared as the "English" emerged.

Meanwhile, the supposed universality of the stages identified in Park's cyclical theory is refuted by counterexamples in which conflict and competition did not occur when different groups came into contact. Brazil and Hawaii are just two places where relatively peaceful and harmonious interactions have existed among different, unassimilated peoples. In many other instances of intergroup relations, however, some form of stress, tension, or conflict does occur. In this chapter, we will examine the major factors that may underlie such conflict: cultural differentiation and structural differentiation.

Cultural Differentiation

When similarities between the arriving minority group and the indigenous group exist, the relationship tends to be relatively harmonious and assimilation is likely to occur eventually.[45] Conversely, the greater and more visible the **cultural differentiation**, the greater the likelihood that conflict will occur. When large numbers of German and Irish Catholics came to the United States in the mid-nineteenth century, Protestants grew uneasy. As priests and nuns arrived and Catholics built churches, convents, and schools, Protestants became alarmed at what they feared was a papal conspiracy to gain control of the country. Emotions ran high, resulting in civil unrest and violence.

Religion has often been a basis for cultural conflict in the United States as is demonstrated by the history of discriminatory treatment suffered by Mormons, Jews, and Quakers. Yet many other aspects of cultural visibility also can serve as sources of contention. Cultural differences may range from clothing (e.g., Sikh turbans and Hindu saris) to leisure activities (e.g., Hispanic cockfights). Americans once condemned the Chinese as opium smokers, even though the British had introduced opium smoking into China, promoted it among the lower-class Chinese population, and even fought wars against the Chinese government to maintain the lucrative trade.

Cultural differentiation does not necessarily cause intergroup conflict. A partial explanation of variances in relations between culturally distinct groups comes from interactionist theory, which holds that the extent of shared symbols and definitions between intercommunicating groups determines the nature of their interaction patterns. Although actual differences may support conflict, interactionists state the key to harmonious or disharmonious relations lies in the definitions or interpretations of those differences. Tolerance or intolerance—acceptance or rejection of others—thus depends on whether others are perceived as threatening or nonthreatening, assimilable or nonassimilable, worthy or unworthy.

Structural Differentiation

Because they offer macrosocial analyses of a society, both functionalist theory and conflict theory provide bases for understanding how structural conditions (**structural differentiation**) affect intergroup relations. Functionalists seek explanations in the adjustments needed in the social system to compensate for other changes. Conflict theorists emphasize the conscious, purposeful actions of dominant groups to maintain systems of inequality.

Functionalists explain how sometimes economic and technological conditions facilitate minority integration. When the economy is healthy and jobs are plentiful, newcomers find it easier to get established and work their way up the socioeconomic ladder. In the United States today, however, technological progress has reduced the number of low-status, blue-collar jobs and increased the number of high-status, white-collar jobs, which require more highly skilled and educated workers. As a result, fewer jobs are available for unskilled, foreign, marginal, or unassimilated people.

Perhaps because of the importance of a job as a source of economic security and status, **occupational mobility**—the ability of individuals to improve their job position—seems to be an important factor in determining whether prejudice will increase or decrease. A number of studies have shown that downward social mobility increases ethnic hostility. One study of U.S. workers found that a perceived threat to either the cultural norms or economic well-being led to more negative attitudes toward immigrants.[46] Other researchers found that worsening economic circumstances intensify prejudicial stereotypes and attitudes about immigration.[47] In addition, upwardly mobile people are generally more tolerant than nonmobile individuals. It would appear that loss of status and prestige increases hostility toward outgroups, whereas upward gains enable people to feel more benevolent toward others.

Ethnic Stratification

If one group becomes dominant and another becomes subservient, obviously one group has more power than the other. Social-class status partly reflects this unequal distribution of power, which also may fall along racial or ethnic lines. **Ethnic stratification** is the structured inequality of different groups with different access to social rewards as a result of their status in the social hierarchy. Because most Americans associate ethnicity with anything different from the mainstream, they don't realize that ethnicity also exists at the top. Ashley W. Doane, Jr., reminds us that dominant group ethnicity lies "hidden" because its status results in the taken-for-granted nature of dominant group identity.[48]

Stratification is a normal component of all societies, but it typically falls along racial and ethnic lines in diverse societies. How does ethnic stratification continue in a democracy where supposedly all have an equal opportunity for upward mobility? Functionalists suggest that the ethnocentrism of those in the societal mainstream leads to discrimination against those in outgroups, as determined by their racial or cultural differences. Conflict analysts instead stress the subordination of minorities by the dominant group because they benefit from such ethnic stratification. Two middle-range conflict theories offer helpful insights into this perspective. The power-differential theory helps explain the initial phases of domination and conflict, whereas the internal-colonialism theory examines the continuation of such subordination.

The Power-Differential Theory

Stanley Lieberson suggested a **power-differential theory** in which intergroup relations depend on the relative power of the migrant group and the indigenous group.[49] Because the two groups usually do not share the same culture, each strives to maintain its own institutions. Which group becomes *superordinate* (superior in rank, class, or status) and which becomes *subordinate* (inferior in rank, class, or status) govern subsequent relations.

If the newcomers possess superior technology (particularly weapons) and social organization, conflict may occur at an early stage, with a consequent population decline due to warfare, disease, or disruption of sustenance activities. Finding their institutions undermined or co-opted, the local inhabitants may eventually participate in the institutions of the dominant group. In time, a group consciousness may arise, and sometimes the indigenous group even succeeds in ousting the superordinate migrant group.

When this happened, interethnic fighting in many former African colonies and in Southeast Asia among the many indigenous groups led to new forms of superordination and subordination within countries (as was the case with the Hutu and Tutsi peoples in Burundi and Rwanda).

Lieberson maintained that neither conflict nor assimilation is an inevitable outcome of racial and ethnic contact. Instead, the particular relationship between the two groups involved determines which alternative will occur. Conflict between a superordinate migrant group and a subordinate indigenous group can be immediate and violent. If the relationship is the reverse, and the indigenous group is superordinate, conflict will be limited and sporadic, and the host society will exert a great deal of pressure on the subordinate migrant group to assimilate, acquiesce, or leave.

In addition, a superordinate indigenous group can limit the numbers and groups entering to reduce the threat of demographic or institutional imbalance. Restrictive U.S. immigration laws against the Chinese in 1882 and against all but northern and western Europeans in 1921 and 1924 illustrate this process. Violent union attempts to remove Asian workers, labor union hostility toward African Americans, and efforts to expel foreigners (e.g., Indians, Japanese, and Filipinos) or to revolutionize the social order (Native American boarding schools and the Americanization movement) illustrate the use of institutional power against minority groups.

Another sociologist, William J. Wilson, has suggested that power relations between superordinate and subordinate groups differ in paternalistic and competitive systems.[50] With **paternalism** (the system that once governed South Africa and the Old South), the dominant group exercises almost absolute control over the subordinate group and can direct virtually unlimited coercion to maintain societal order. In a competitive system (e.g., the United States today), some degree of power reciprocity exists, so the dominant group in society is somewhat vulnerable to political pressures and economic boycotts.

Rapid social change—industrialization, unionization, urbanization, migration, and political change—usually loosens the social structure, leading to new tensions as both groups seek new power resources. If the minority group increases its power resources, through protective laws and improved economic opportunities, it may foresee even greater improvement in its condition. This heightened awareness is likely to lead to conflict unless additional gains are forthcoming. For example, the civil-rights movement of the mid-1960s brought about legislation ensuring minority rights and opportunities in jobs, housing, education, and other aspects of life, but this led to new tensions. The 1960s were marked by urban riots and burnings, protest demonstrations and human barricades to stop construction of low-income housing sites, school-busing controversies, and challenges to labor discrimination.

The Internal-Colonialism Theory

In analyzing the Black militancy of the late 1960s, Robert Blauner attempted to integrate the factors of caste and racism, ethnicity, culture, and economic exploitation.[51] His major point was that U.S. treatment of its Black population resembled past European subjugation and exploitation of non-Western peoples in their own lands. Although he focused on Black–White relations in the United States, he suggested that Mexican Americans might also fit his **internal-colonialism theory** and that Native Americans could be added as another suitable example:

> Of course many ethnic groups in America have lived in ghettoes. What makes the Black ghettoes an expression of colonized status are three special features. First, the ethnic ghettoes arose more from voluntary choice, both in the sense of the choice to immigrate to America and the decision to live among one's fellow ethnics. Second, the immigrant ghettoes tended to be a one- and two-generation phenomenon; they were actually way-stations in the process of acculturation and assimilation. When they continue to persist as in the case of San Francisco's Chinatown, it is because they are big business for the ethnics themselves and there is a new stream of immigrants. The Black ghetto on the other hand has been a more permanent phenomenon, although some individuals do escape it. But most relevant is the third point. European ethnic groups like the Poles, Italians and Jews generally only experienced a brief period, often less than a generation, during which their residential buildings, commercial stores, and other enterprises were owned by outsiders. The Chinese and Japanese faced handicaps of color prejudice that were almost as strong as the Blacks faced, but very soon gained control of their internal communities, because their traditional ethnic culture and social organization had not been destroyed by slavery and internal colonization. But Afro-Americans are distinct in the extent to which their segregated communities have remained controlled economically, politically, and administratively from the outside.[52]

Several of these statements need to be modified. Chinatowns long persisted not because of any business advantage but because of racial discrimination. In proportion to the Chinatown population, only a few Chinese benefit from the tourist trade. Also, the Chinese and Japanese *always* had "control of their internal communities," although they differ greatly from each other in their structure and cohesiveness.

Blauner considers the exploitation phase that was temporary for other groups to be more nearly permanent for Blacks and possibly Chicanos. He believes that conflict and confrontation, as well as real or apparent chaos and disorder, will continue because this may be the only way an internally colonized group can deal with the dominant society. This conflict orientation suggests that the multigenerational exploitation of certain groups creates a unique situation and a basis for the often violent conflict that sporadically flares up in our cities.

Origins of Ethnic Stratification

For ethnicity to become a basis for stratification, several factors seem necessary:

> Ethnic stratification will emerge when distinct ethnic groups are brought into sustained contact only if the groups are characterized by a high degree of ethnocentrism, competition, *and* differential power. Competition provides the motivation for stratification; ethnocentrism channels the competition along ethnic lines; and the power differential determines whether either group will be able to subordinate the other.[53]

This **power differential** is of enormous importance in race and ethnic relations. If the stratification system is rigid, as in a slave or caste system, so that people have no hope or means of improving their status, intergroup relations may remain stable despite perhaps being far from mutually satisfactory. Dominant power, whether expressed in legalized ways or through structural discrimination, intimidation, or coercion, maintains the social system.

Challenges to the Status Quo.   Even if the stratification system allows for upward mobility, some members of the dominant group may believe that the lower-class racial and ethnic groups are challenging the social order as they strive for their share of the "good life." If the dominant group does not feel threatened, the change will be peaceful. If the minority group meets resistance but retains hope and a sense of belonging to the larger society, the struggle for more power will occur within the system (e.g., by means of demonstrations, boycotts, voter-registration drives, or lobbying) rather than through violence.[54] The late-nineteenth-century race-baiting riots on the West Coast against Chinese and Japanese workers and the 1919 Chicago race riots against Blacks attempting to enter the meat-packing industry illustrate violent responses of a dominant group against a minority group over power resources. Similarly, the Black–Korean violence in several urban neighborhoods during the past decade, as well as the 1992 Los Angeles riots and the violence between Blacks and Cubans in Miami in 1988, typify minority-group clashes over limited resources.

Social-Class Antagonisms.   Conflict theorists, such as Ralf Dahrendorf, argue that social class is an important variable affecting conflict. Dahrendorf sees a correlation between a group's economic position and the intensity of its conflict with the dominant society. The greater the deprivation in eco-

In this ESL class these Latino immigrants, like many other newcomers, seek to master English to ease their entry into the societal mainstream. Nationwide, there is a shortage of such classes in this important step in the acculturation process that helps reduce cultural differentiation and enhances opportunities for occupational mobility.

nomic resources, social status, and social power, the likelier the weaker group is to resort to intense and violent conflict to achieve gains in any of these three areas. As the social-class position of a group increases, intergroup conflict becomes less intense and less violent.[55]

Years earlier, Max Weber argued that, when economic resources become more evenly distributed among classes, relative status will become the issue of conflict, if conflict occurs at all.[56] Conflict occurs not only because a lower-class group seeks an end to deprivation but also because the group next higher on the socioeconomic ladder feels threatened. Often, the working-class group displays the greatest hostility and prejudice of all established groups in the society toward the upward-striving minority group. Other factors may be at work as well, but status competition is a significant source of conflict.

Social-class antagonisms influence people's perceptions of racial and ethnic groups too.[57] Some social scientists maintain that the problem of

Black–White relations is more a problem of social class than of racism. James M. O'Kane illustrates this view:

> The gap exists between the classes, not the races; it is between the white and black middle classes on the one hand, and the white and black lower classes on the other. Skin color and the history of servitude do little to explain the present polarization of the classes. . . . Class differentials, not racial differentials, explain the presence and persistence of poverty in the ranks of the urban Negro.[58]

O'Kane suggests several parallels between Irish, Italian, and Polish immigrants and southern Blacks who migrated to northern cities (the Chinese, some of the Japanese, and others also fit this model). All emigrated from agrarian poverty to urban industrial slums. Encountering prejudice and discrimination, some sought alternative routes to material success: crime, ethnic politics, or stable but unskilled employment.[59] Other social scientists, however, argue that the Black experience does not equate with that of European immigrants. They hold, as did the Kerner Commission investigating the urban riots of the late 1960s, that the dominant society's practice of internal colonialism toward Blacks deprived them of the strong social organizations that other groups had. Moreover, they believe that today's labor market offers fewer unskilled jobs for Blacks than it offered other immigrant groups in earlier times, thereby depriving Blacks of a means to begin moving upward.[60]

This debate over whether race or social class is the primary factor in assessing full integration of Blacks in the United States continues to rage, particularly among Black social scientists.

Retrospect

Structural conditions influence people's perceptions of the world whether they live in an industrialized or agrarian society, a closed or open social system, a growing or contracting economy, a friendly or unfriendly environment, and whether their homeland, friends, and relatives are accessible or remote. Distribution of power resources and compatibility with the existing social structure greatly influence majority–minority relations as well. Interactionists concentrate on perceptions of cultural differences as they affect intergroup relations. Functionalists and conflict theorists emphasize structural conditions.

The interplay between the variables of race, ethnic group, and social class is important for understanding how some problems and conflicts arise. A feature interpreted as an attribute of a race or ethnic group may in fact be a broader aspect of social class. Because many attitudes and values are situational responses to socioeconomic status, a change in status or opportunities will bring about a change in those attitudes and values. Investigative studies have not supported the culture-of-poverty hypothesis of family disintegration and a self-perpetuating poverty value orientation.

KEY TERMS

Cultural determinism
Cultural differentiation
Culture of poverty
Economic determinism
Ethclasses
Ethnic stratification
Internal-colonialism theory
Occupational mobility
Paternalism

Power differential
Power-differential theory
Reputational method
Social class
Social stratification
Social structure
Structural differentiation
Value-stretch approach

REVIEW QUESTIONS

1. What economic factors can affect intergroup relations?

2. Does social class awareness affect ethnic self-consciousness?

3. What is the relationship between ethnicity and social class?

4. What is meant by the *culture of poverty*? What criticisms exist about this thinking?

5. What is the difference between cultural differentiation and structural differentiation?

6. How do the functional and conflict perspectives approach the factors likely to contribute to intergroup conflict?

SUGGESTED READINGS

Anderson, Elijah, and Douglas S. Massey, (eds.). *Problem of the Century: Racial Stratification in the United States*. New York: Russell Sage Foundation, 2004.

Offers sixteen essays on racial differentiation as measured by various demographic, economic, and educational indicators.

hooks, bell. *Where We Stand: Class Matters*. New York: Routledge, 2000.

An incisive examination of how the dilemmas of race and class are intertwined and how everyday interactions reproduce class hierarchy while simultaneously denying its existence.

Mangum, Garth L., Stephen L. Mangum, and Andrew M. Sum. *The Persistence of Poverty in the United States*. Baltimore: Johns Hopkins University Press, 2003.

A concise and coherent discussion of the causes and magnitude of poverty, with some strategic suggestions to alleviate the problem.

Reitz, Jeffrey G. *Warmth of the Welcome: The Social Causes of Economic Success for Immigrants in Different Nations and Cities*. Boulder, Colo.: Westview Press, 1999.

Compares trends in immigrant inequality in Australia, Canada, and the United States through a social institutional approach and analysis of social structure.

Russell, James W. *After the Fifth Sun: Class and Race in North America*. Upper Saddle River, N.J.: Prentice Hall, 1994.

Explores how different patterns of class and racial inequality developed in Canada, Mexico, and the United States, leading to different definitions of the significance of race.

Steinberg, Stephen. *The Ethnic Myth: Race, Ethnicity, and Class in America*, 3d ed. New York: Scribner, 2001.

Argues that traits considered as "ethnic" may be more directly related to class, locality, and other social conditions.

INTERNET RESOURCES

For a wide range of readings on class and stratification, go to the Sociosite readings at www.sociosite.net/topics/inequality.php#CLASS.

CHAPTER
4 Prejudice

"Prejudices are what fools use for reason."

—Voltaire

When strangers from different groups come into contact with one another, their interaction patterns may take many forms. So far, we have discussed the roles that ethnocentrism, social distance, culture, and social structure play in shaping perceptions of any outgroup. Prejudice and discrimination also emerge as major considerations in understanding intergroup relations. Why do they exist? Why do they persist? Why do certain groups become targets more frequently? How can we eliminate prejudicial attitudes?

The word *prejudice* is derived from the Latin word *praejudicium* and originally meant "prejudgment." Thus, some scholars defined a prejudiced person as one who hastily reached a conclusion before examining the facts.[1] This definition proved inadequate, however, because social scientists discovered that prejudice often arose *after* groups came into contact and had at least some knowledge of one another. For that reason, Louis Wirth described prejudice as "an attitude with an emotional bias."[2]

Because feelings shape our attitudes, they reduce our receptivity to additional information that may alter those attitudes. Ralph Rosnow had this fact in mind when he broadened the definition of prejudice to encompass "any unreasonable attitude that is unusually resistant to rational influence."[3] In fact, a deeply prejudiced person is almost totally immune to information. Gordon Allport offers a classic example of such an individual in the following dialogue:

MR. X: The trouble with the Jews is that they only take care of their own group.

MR. Y: But the record of the Community Chest campaign shows that they gave more generously, in proportion to their numbers, to the general charities of the community, than did non-Jews.

MR. X: That shows they are always trying to buy favor and intrude into Christian affairs. They think of nothing but money; that is why there are so many Jewish bankers.

MR. Y: But a recent study shows that the percentage of Jews in the banking business is negligible, far smaller than the percentage of non-Jews.

MR. X: That's just it; they don't go in for respectable business; they are only in the movie business or run night clubs.*

It is almost as if Mr. X is saying, "My mind is made up; don't confuse me with the facts." He does not refute the argument; rather, he ignores each bit of new and contradictory information and moves on to a new area in which he distorts other facts to support his prejudice against Jews.

Prejudicial attitudes may be either positive or negative. Sociologists primarily study the latter, however, because only negative attitudes can lead to turbulent social relations between dominant and minority groups. Numerous writers, therefore, have defined prejudice as an attitudinal "system of negative beliefs, feelings, and action-orientations regarding a certain group or groups of people."[4] The status of the strangers is an important factor in the development of a negative attitude. Prejudicial attitudes exist among members of both dominant and minority groups. Thus, in the relations between dominant and minority groups, the antipathy felt by one group for another is quite often reciprocated.

Psychological perspectives on prejudice—whether behaviorist, cognitive, or psychoanalytic—focus on the subjective states of mind of individuals. In these perspectives, a person's prejudicial attitudes may result from imitation or conditioning (behaviorist), perceived similarity–dissimilarity of beliefs (cognitive), or specific personality characteristics (psychoanalytic). In contrast, sociological perspectives focus on the objective conditions of society as the social forces behind prejudicial attitudes and behind racial and ethnic relations. Individuals do not live in a vacuum; social reality affects their states of mind.

Both perspectives are necessary to understand prejudice. As psychologist Gordon Allport argued, besides needing a close study of habits, perceptions, motivation, and personality, we need an analysis of social settings, situational forces, demographic and ecological variables, and legal and economic trends.[5] Psychological and sociological perspectives complement each other in providing a fuller explanation of intergroup relations.

---

*Gordon W. Allport, *The Nature of Prejudice* (Reading, Mass.: Addison-Wesley, 1954), pp. 13–14.

The Psychology of Prejudice

We can understand more about prejudice among individuals by focusing on four areas of study: levels of prejudice, self-justification, personality, and frustration.

Levels of Prejudice

Bernard Kramer suggested that prejudice exists on three levels: cognitive, emotional, and action orientation.[6] The **cognitive level of prejudice** encompasses a person's beliefs and perceptions of a group as threatening or non-threatening, inferior or equal (e.g., in terms of intellect, status, or biological composition), seclusive or intrusive, impulse-gratifying, acquisitive, or possessing other positive or negative characteristics. Mr. X's cognitive beliefs are that Jews are intrusive and acquisitive. Other illustrations of cognitive beliefs are that the Irish are heavy drinkers and fighters, African Americans are rhythmic and lazy, and the Poles are thick-headed and unintelligent. Generalizations shape both ethnocentric and prejudicial attitudes, but there is a difference. *Ethnocentrism* is a generalized rejection of all outgroups on the basis of an ingroup focus, whereas **prejudice** is a rejection of certain people solely on the basis of their membership in a particular group.

In many societies, members of the majority group may believe that a particular low-status minority group is dirty, immoral, violent, or law-breaking. In the United States, the Irish, Italians, African Americans, Mexicans, Chinese, Puerto Ricans, and others have at one time or another been labeled with most, if not all, of these adjectives. In most European countries and in the United States, the group lowest on the socioeconomic ladder has often been depicted in caricature as also lowest on the evolutionary ladder. The Irish and African Americans in the United States and the peasants and various ethnic groups in Europe have all been depicted in the past as apelike:

> The Victorian images of the Irish as "white Negro" and simian Celt, or a combination of the two, derived much of its force and inspiration from physiognomical beliefs ... [but] every country in Europe had its equivalent of "white Negroes" and simianized men, whether or not they happened to be stereotypes of criminals, assassins, political radicals, revolutionaries, Slavs, gypsies, Jews or peasants.[7]

The **emotional level of prejudice** refers to the feelings that a minority group arouses in an individual. Although these feelings may be based on stereotypes from the cognitive level, they represent a more intense stage of personal involvement. The emotional attitudes may be negative or positive, such as fear/envy, distrust/trust, disgust/admiration, or contempt/empathy. These feelings, based on beliefs about the group, may be triggered by social interaction or by the possibility of interaction. For example, Whites might react with fear or anger to the integration of their schools or neighborhoods, or Protestants might be jealous of the lifestyle of a highly successful Catholic business executive.

An **action-orientation level of prejudice** is the positive or negative predisposition to engage in discriminatory behavior. A person who harbors strong feelings about members of a certain racial or ethnic group may have a tendency to act for or against them—being aggressive or nonaggressive, offering assistance or withholding it. Such an individual would also be likely to want to exclude or include members of that group both in close, personal social relations and in peripheral social relations. For example, some people would want to exclude members of the disliked group from doing business with them or living in their neighborhood. Another manifestation of the action-orientation level of prejudice is the desire to change or maintain the status differential or inequality between the two groups, whether the area is economic, political, educational, social, or a combination. Note that an action orientation is a predisposition to act, not the action itself.

Self-Justification

The act of **self-justification** involves denigrating a person or group to justify maltreatment of them. In this situation, self-justification leads to prejudice and discrimination against members of another group.

Some philosophers argue that we are not so much rational creatures as we are rationalizing creatures. We require reassurance that the things we do and the lives we live are proper—that good reasons for our actions exist. If we can convince ourselves that another group is inferior, immoral, or dangerous, we may feel justified in discriminating against its members, enslaving them, or even killing them.

History is filled with examples of people who thought their maltreatment of others was just and necessary: As defenders of the "true faith," the Crusaders killed "Christ killers" (Jews) and "infidels" (Muslims). Participants in the Spanish Inquisition imprisoned, tortured, and executed "heretics," "the disciples of the Devil." Similarly, the Puritans burned witches, whose refusal to confess "proved they were evil"; pioneers exploited or killed Native Americans who were "heathen savages"; and Whites mistreated, enslaved, or killed African Americans, who were "an inferior species." According to U.S. Army officers, the civilians in the Vietnamese village of My Lai were "probably" aiding the Vietcong; so in 1968, U.S. soldiers fighting in the Vietnam War felt justified in slaughtering more than 300 unarmed people there, including women, children, and the elderly. The 2005 massacre of 24 Iraqi citizens in Haditha by U.S. Marines is a similar example.

Some sociologists believe that self-justification works the other way around. That is, instead of self-justification serving as a basis for subjugating others, the subjugation occurs first and the self-justification follows, result-ing in prejudice and continued discrimination.[8] The evolution of racism as a concept after the establishment of the African slave trade would seem to support this idea. Philip Mason offers an insight into this view:

> A specialized society is likely to defeat a simpler society and provide a lower tier still of enslaved and conquered peoples. The rulers and organizers sought security for themselves and their children; to perpetuate the power, the esteem, and the comfort they had achieved, it was necessary not only that the artisans and labourers should work contentedly but that the rulers should sleep without bad dreams. No one can say with certainty how the myths originated, but it is surely relevant that when one of the founders of Western thought set himself to frame an ideal state that would embody so-cial justice, he—like the earliest city dwellers—not only devised a society stratified in tiers but believed it would be necessary to persuade the traders and work-people that, by divine decree, they were made from brass and iron, while the warriors were made of silver and the rulers of gold.[9]

Another example of self-justification serving as a source of prejudice is the dominant group's assumption of an attitude of superiority over other groups. In this respect, establishing a prestige hierarchy—ranking the status of various ethnic groups—results in differential association. To enhance or maintain self-esteem, a person may avoid social contact with groups deemed inferior and associate only with those identified as being of high status. Through such behavior, self-justification may come to intensify the social distance between groups. As discussed in Chapter 1, *social distance* refers to the degree to which ingroup members do not engage in social or primary re-lationships with members of various outgroups.

Personality

In *The Authoritarian Personality*, T. W. Adorno and his colleagues reported a correlation between individuals' early childhood experiences of harsh parental discipline and their development of an **authoritarian personality** as adults.[10] If parents assume an excessively domineering posture in their rela-tions with a child, exercising stern measures and threatening to withdraw love if the child does not respond with weakness and submission, the child tends to be insecure and to nurture much latent hostility against the parents. When these children become adults, they may demonstrate **displaced ag-gression**, directing their hostility against a powerless group to compensate for their feelings of insecurity and fear. Highly prejudiced individuals tend to come from families that emphasize obedience.

The authors identified authoritarianism by the use of a measuring in-strument called an F scale (the *F* stands for potential fascism). Other tests in-cluded the A-S (anti-Semitism) and E (ethnocentrism) scales, the latter measuring attitudes toward various minorities. One of their major findings was that people who scored high on authoritarianism also consistently showed a high degree of prejudice against all minority groups. These highly prejudiced persons were characterized by rigidity of viewpoint, dislike of ambiguity, strict obedience to leaders, and intolerance of weakness in themselves and others.

No sooner did *The Authoritarian Personality* appear than controversy began. H. H. Hyman and P. B. Sheatsley challenged the methodology and analysis.[11] Solomon Asch questioned the assumptions that the F scale responses represented a belief system and that structural variables (e.g., ideologies, stratification, and mobility) do not play a role in shaping personality.[12] E. A. Shils argued that the authors were interested only in measuring authoritarianism of the political right while ignoring such tendencies in those at the other end of the political spectrum.[13] Other investigators sought alternative explanations for the authoritarian personality. D. Stewart and T. Hoult extended the framework beyond family childhood experiences to include other social factors.[14] H. C. Kelman and Janet Barclay pointed out that substantial evidence exists showing that lower intelligence and less education also correlate with high authoritarianism scores on the F scale.[15]

Despite the critical attacks, the underlying conceptions of *The Authoritarian Personality* were important, and research into personality as a factor in prejudice has continued. Subsequent investigators refined and modified the original study. Correcting scores for response bias, they conducted cross-cultural studies. Respondents in Germany and Near East countries, where more authoritarian social structures exist, scored higher on authoritarianism and social distance between groups. In Japan, Germany, and the United States, authoritarianism and social distance were moderately related. Other studies suggested that an inverse relationship exists between social class and F scale scores: the higher the social class, the lower the authoritarianism.[16]

Although studies of authoritarian personality have helped us understand some aspects of prejudice, they have not provided a causal explanation. Most of the findings in this area show a correlation, but the findings do not prove, for example, that harsh discipline of children causes them to become prejudiced adults. Perhaps the strict parents were themselves prejudiced, and the child learned those attitudes from them. Or, as George Simpson and J. Milton Yinger state:

> One must be careful not to assume too quickly that a certain tendency—rigidity of mind, for example—that is correlated with prejudice necessarily causes that prejudice. . . . The sequence may be the other way around. . . . It is more likely that both are related to more basic factors.[17]

For some people, prejudice may indeed be rooted in subconscious childhood tensions, but we do not know whether these tensions directly cause a high degree of prejudice in the adult or whether other powerful social forces are the determinants. Whatever the explanation, authoritarianism is a significant phenomenon worthy of continued investigation. Research, however, stresses social and situational factors, rather than personality, as primary causes of prejudice and discrimination.[18]

Yet another dimension of the personality component is that people with low self-esteem are more prejudiced than those who feel good about themselves. Some researchers have argued that individuals with low self-esteem deprecate others to improve their feelings about themselves.[19] One study asserts that "low self-esteem individuals seem to have a generally negative view of themselves, their ingroup, outgroups, and perhaps the world," and thus, their tendency to be more prejudiced is not due to rating the outgroup negatively in comparison to their ingroup.[20]

Frustration

Frustration is the result of relative deprivation in which expectations remain unsatisfied. **Relative deprivation** is a lack of resources, or rewards, in one's standard of living in comparison with those of others in the society. A number of investigators have suggested that frustrations tend to increase aggression toward others.[21] Frustrated people may easily strike out against the perceived cause of their frustration. However, this reaction may not be possible because the true source of the frustration is often too nebulous to be identified or too powerful to act against. In such instances, the result may be displaced aggression; in this situation, the frustrated individual or group usually redirects anger against a more visible, vulnerable, and socially sanctioned target that is unable to strike back. Minorities meet these criteria and are thus frequently the recipients of displaced aggression by the dominant group.

Blaming others for something that is not their fault is known as **scapegoating**. The term comes from the ancient Hebrew custom of using a goat during the Day of Atonement as a symbol of the sins of the people. In an annual ceremony, a priest placed his hands on the head of a goat and listed the people's sins in a symbolic transference of guilt; he then chased the goat out of the community, thereby freeing the people of sin.[22] Since those times, the powerful group has usually punished the scapegoat group rather than allowing it to escape.

There have been many instances throughout world history of minority groups serving as scapegoats, including the Christians in ancient Rome, the Huguenots in France, the Jews in Europe and Russia, and the Puritans and Quakers in England. Gordon Allport suggests that certain characteristics are necessary for a group to become a suitable scapegoat. The group must be (1) highly visible in physical appearance or observable customs and actions; (2) not strong enough to strike back; (3) situated within easy access of the dominant group and, ideally, concentrated in one area; (4) a past target of hostility for whom latent hostility still exists; and (5) the symbol of an un-popular concept.[23]

Some groups fit this typology better than others, but minority racial and ethnic groups have been a perennial choice. Irish, Italians, Catholics, Jews, Quakers, Mormons, Chinese, Japanese, Blacks, Puerto Ricans, Chicanos, and Koreans have all been treated, at one time or another, as the scapegoat in the United States. Especially in times of economic hardship, societies tend to blame some group for the general conditions, which often leads to aggressive action against the group as an expression of frustration. For example, a study by Carl Hovland and Robert Sears found that, between 1882 and 1930, a definite correlation existed between a decline in the price of cotton and an increase in the number of lynchings of Blacks.[24]

In several controlled experiments, social scientists have attempted to measure the validity of the scapegoat theory. Neal Miller and Richard Bugelski tested a group of young men aged 18 to 20 who were working in a government camp about their feelings toward various minority groups. The young men were reexamined about these feelings after experiencing frustration by being obliged to take a long, difficult test and being denied an opportunity to see a film at a local theater. This group showed some evidence of increased prejudicial feelings, whereas a control group, which did not experience any frustration, showed no change in prejudicial attitudes.[25]

Donald Weatherley conducted an experiment with a group of college students to measure the relationship between frustration and aggression against a specific disliked group.[26] After identifying students who were or were not highly anti-Semitic and subjecting them to a strongly frustrating experience, he asked the students to write stories about pictures shown to them. Some of the students were shown pictures of people who had been given Jewish names; other students were presented with pictures of unnamed people. When the pictures were unidentified, the stories of the anti-Semitic students did not differ from those of other students. When the pictures were identified, however, the anti-Semitic students wrote stories reflecting much more aggression against the Jews in the pictures than did the other students.

For more than 20 years, Leonard Berkowitz and his associates studied and experimented with aggressive behavior. They concluded that, confronted with equally frustrating situations, highly prejudiced individuals are more likely to seek scapegoats than are nonprejudiced individuals. Another intervening variable is that personal frustrations (marital failure, injury, or mental illness) make people more likely to seek scapegoats than do shared frustrations (dangers of flood or hurricane).[27]

Some experiments have shown that aggression does not increase if the frustration is understandable.[28] Other experiments have found that people become aggressive only if the aggression directly relieves their frustration.[29] Still other studies have shown that anger is a more likely result if the person responsible for the frustrating situation could have acted otherwise.[30]

Clearly, the results are mixed depending on the variables within a given social situation.

Frustration–aggression theory, although helpful, is not completely satisfactory. It ignores the role of culture and the reality of actual social conflict and fails to show any causal relationship. Most of the responses measured in these studies were of people already biased. Why did one group rather than another become the object of the aggression? Moreover, frustration does not necessarily precede aggression, and aggression does not necessarily flow from frustration.

The Sociology of Prejudice

Sociologist Talcott Parsons provided one bridge between psychology and sociology by introducing social forces as a variable in frustration–aggression theory. He suggested that both the family and the occupational structure may produce anxieties and insecurities that create frustration.[31] According to this view, the growing-up process (gaining parental affection and approval, identifying with and imitating sexual role models, and competing with others in adulthood) sometimes involves severe emotional strain. The result is an adult personality with a large reservoir of repressed aggression that becomes *free-floating*—susceptible to redirection against convenient scapegoats. Similarly, the occupational system is a source of frustration: Its emphasis on competitiveness and individual achievement, its function of conferring status, its requirement that people inhibit their natural impulses at work, and its ties to the state of the economy are among the factors that generate emotional anxieties. Parsons pessimistically concluded that minorities fulfill a functional "need" as targets for displaced aggression and therefore will remain targets.[32]

Perhaps most influential in staking out the sociological position on prejudice was Herbert Blumer, who suggested that prejudice always involves the "sense of group position" in society. Agreeing with Kramer's delineation of three levels of prejudice, Blumer argued that prejudice can include beliefs, feelings, and a predisposition to action, thus motivating behavior that derives from the social hierarchy.[33] By emphasizing historically established group positions and relationships, Blumer shifted his focus away from the attitudes and personality compositions of individuals. As a social phenomenon, prejudice rises or falls according to issues that alter one group's position vis-à-vis that of another group.

Socialization

In the **socialization process**, individuals acquire the values, attitudes, beliefs, and perceptions of their culture or subculture, including religion, nationality, and social class. Generally, the child conforms to the parents' expectations in acquiring an understanding of the world and its people. Being impressionable and knowing of no alternative conceptions of the world, the child usually accepts these concepts without questioning. We thus learn the prejudices of our parents and others, which then become part of our values and beliefs. Even when based on false stereotypes, prejudices shape our perceptions of various peoples and influence our attitudes and actions toward particular groups. For example, if we develop negative attitudes about Jews because we are taught that they are shrewd, acquisitive, and clannish—all-too-familiar stereotypes—as adults we may refrain from business or social relationships with them. We may not even realize the reason for such avoidance, so subtle has been the prejudice instilled within us.

People may learn certain prejudices because of their pervasiveness. The cultural screen that we develop and through which we view the surrounding world is not always accurate, but it does permit transmission of shared values and attitudes, which are reinforced by others. Prejudice, like cultural values, is taught and learned through the socialization process. The prevailing prejudicial attitudes and actions may be deeply embedded in custom or law (e.g., the **Jim Crow laws** of the 1890s and the early twentieth century establishing segregated public facilities throughout the South, which subsequent generations accepted as proper and maintained in their own adult lives).

Although socialization explains how prejudicial attitudes may be transmitted from one generation to the next, it does not explain their origin or why they intensify or diminish over the years. These aspects of prejudice must be explained in another way.

Economic Competition

People tend to be more hostile toward others when they feel that their security is threatened; thus, many social scientists conclude that economic competition and conflict breed prejudice. Certainly, considerable evidence shows that negative stereotyping, prejudice, and discrimination increase markedly whenever competition for available jobs increases.

An excellent illustration relates to the Chinese sojourners in the nineteenth-century United States. Prior to the 1870s, the transcontinental railroad was being built, and the Chinese filled many of the jobs made available by this project in the sparsely populated West. Although they were expelled from the region's gold mines and schools and could obtain no redress of grievances in the courts, they managed to convey to some Whites the image of being a clean, hardworking, law-abiding people. The completion of the railroad, the flood of former Civil War soldiers into the job market, and the economic depression of 1873 worsened their situation. The Chinese became more frequent victims of open discrimination and hostility. Their positive stereotype among some Whites was widely displaced by a negative one: They were now "conniving," "crafty," "criminal," "the Yellow menace." Only after they retreated into Chinatowns and entered specialty occupations that minimized their competition with Whites did the intense hostility abate.

One pioneer in the scientific study of prejudice, John Dollard, demonstrated how prejudice against the Germans, which had been virtually nonexistent, arose in a small U.S. industrial town when times got bad:

> Local Whites largely drawn from the surrounding farms manifested considerable direct aggression toward the newcomers. Scornful and derogatory opinions were expressed about the Germans, and the native Whites had a satisfying sense of superiority toward them. . . . The chief element in the permission to be aggressive against the Germans was rivalry for jobs and status in the local woodenware plants. The native Whites felt definitely crowded for their jobs by the entering German groups and in case of bad times had a chance to blame the Germans who by their presence provided more competitors for the scarcer jobs. There seemed to be no traditional pattern of prejudice against Germans unless the skeletal suspicion of all out-groupers (always present) be invoked in this place.[34]

Both experimental studies and historical analyses have added credence to the economic-competition theory. Muzafer Sherif directed several experiments showing how intergroup competition at a boys' camp led to conflict and escalating hostility.[35] Donald Young pointed out that, throughout U.S. history, in times of high unemployment and thus intense job competition, nativist movements against minorities have flourished.[36] This pattern has held true regionally—against Asians on the West Coast, Italians in Louisiana, and French Canadians in New England—and nationally, with the antiforeign movements always peaking during periods of depression. So it was with the Native American Party in the 1830s, the Know-Nothing Party in the 1850s, the American Protective Association in the 1890s, and the Ku Klux Klan after World War I. Since the passage of civil-rights laws on employment in the twentieth century, researchers have consistently detected the strongest anti-Black prejudice among working-class and middle-class Whites who feel threatened by Blacks entering their socioeconomic group in noticeable numbers.[37] It seems that any group applying the pressure of job competition most directly on another group becomes a target of its prejudice.

Once again, a theory that offers some excellent insights into prejudice—in particular, that adverse economic conditions correlate with increased hostility toward minorities—also has some serious shortcomings. Not all groups that have been objects of hostility (e.g., Quakers and Mormons) have been economic competitors. Moreover, why is hostility against some groups greater than against others? Why do the negative feelings in some communities run against groups whose numbers are so small that they cannot possibly pose an economic threat? Evidently, values besides economic ones cause people to be antagonistic to a group perceived as an actual or potential threat.

Social Norms

Some sociologists have suggested that a relationship exists between prejudice and a person's tendency to conform to societal expectations.[38] **Social norms**—the norms of one's culture—form the generally shared rules defining what is and is not proper behavior. By learning and automatically accepting the prevailing prejudices, an individual is simply conforming to those norms.

This theory holds that a direct relationship exists between degree of conformity and degree of prejudice. If so, people's prejudices should decrease or increase significantly when they move into areas where the prejudicial norm is lesser or greater. Evidence supports this view. Thomas Pettigrew found that Southerners in the 1950s became less prejudiced against Blacks when they interacted with them in the army, where the social norms were less prejudicial.[39] In another study, Jeanne Watson found that people moving into an anti-Semitic neighborhood in New York City became more anti-Semitic.[40]

John Dollard's study, *Caste and Class in a Southern Town*, provides an in-depth look at the emotional adjustment of Whites and Blacks to rigid social norms.[41] In his study of the processes, functions, and maintenance of accommodation, Dollard detailed the "carrot-and-stick" method social groups employed. Intimidation—sometimes even severe reprisals for going against social norms—ensured compliance. However, reprisals usually were unnecessary. The advantages Whites and Blacks gained in psychological, economic, or behavioral terms served to perpetuate the caste order. These gains in personal security and stability set in motion a vicious circle. They encouraged a way of life that reinforced the rationale of the social system in this community.

Two 1994 studies provided further evidence of the powerful influence of social norms. Joachim Krueger and Russell W. Clement found that consensus bias persisted despite the availability of statistical data and knowledge about such bias.[42] Michael R. Leippe and Donna Eisenstadt showed that induced compliance can change socially significant attitudes and that the change generalizes to broader beliefs.[43]

Although the social-norms theory explains prevailing attitudes, it does not explain either their origins or the reasons new prejudices develop when other groups move into an area. In addition, the theory does not explain why prejudicial attitudes against a particular group rise and fall cyclically over the years.

Although many social scientists have attempted to identify the causes of prejudice, no single factor provides an adequate explanation. Prejudice is a complex phenomenon, and it is most likely the product of more than one causal agent. Sociologists today tend either to emphasize multiple-cause explanations or to stress social forces encountered in specific and similar situations—forces such as economic conditions, stratification, and hostility toward an outgroup.

Stereotyping

One common reaction to strangers is to categorize them broadly. Prejudice at the cognitive level often arises from false perceptions that are enhanced by cultural or racial stereotypes. A **stereotype** is an oversimplified generalization by which we attribute certain traits or characteristics to a group without regard to individual differences. Sometimes stereotypes are positive—for example, that African Americans are good athletes and that Asians are good mathematicians. But even here, they can create pressures and problems—for example, for African Americans who are not athletic or for Asians who are weak in math. Stereotypes distort sociocultural truths but nevertheless are socially approved images held by one group about another.[44]

Stereotypes, which easily become ingrained within everyday thinking, serve to enhance a group's self-esteem and social identity—in accord with Blumer's concept of prejudice as a sense of group position. Even if an outgroup is economically successful, stereotyping it as clannish, mercenary, or unscrupulous enables other groups to affirm their own moral superiority.

Not only do stereotypes deny individuals the right to be judged and treated on the basis of their own personal merit, but also, by attributing a particular image to the entire group, they become a justification for discriminatory behavior. Negative stereotypes also serve as important reference points in people's evaluations of what they observe in everyday life. Following is an excellent illustration of how prejudice leads a person to attribute to other people's behavior motives and causes that are consistent with preexisting stereotypes:

> Prejudiced people see the world in ways that are consistent with their prejudice. If Mr. Bigot sees a well-dressed, white, Anglo-Saxon Protestant sitting on a park bench sunning himself at three o'clock on a Wednesday afternoon, he thinks nothing of it. If he sees a well-dressed black man doing the same thing, he is liable to leap to the conclusion that the person is unemployed— and he becomes infuriated, because he assumes that his hard-earned taxes are paying that shiftless good-for-nothing enough in welfare subsidies to keep him in good clothes. If Mr. Bigot passes Mr. Anglo's house and notices that a trash can is overturned and some garbage is strewn about, he is apt to conclude that a stray dog has been searching for food. If he passes Mr. Garcia's house and notices the same thing, he is inclined to become annoyed, and to assert that "those people live like pigs." Not only does prejudice

influence his conclusions, his erroneous conclusions justify and intensify his negative feelings.[45]

Once established, stereotypes are difficult to eradicate, even in succeeding generations. Evidence of the pervasiveness and persistence of stereotypes came from a study comparing responses of college students over three generations. Providing a list of eighty-four adjectives, the researchers asked the students to select five that they thought described the most characteristic traits of ten racial and ethnic groups.[46] Although each group showed increasing reluctance to make such generalizations, a high level of uniformity nonetheless marked the responses.

Notably, students either tended to agree on the same adjectives others had chosen in earlier studies or to pick a similar new adjective. Positive stereotypes regarding work achievement continued for "Americans," Germans, Japanese, and Jews. Emotional stereotypes for the Irish and for Ital-

"Mutual: Both Are Glad There Are Bars Between 'Em!"

This visual stereotype of an apelike Irishman reinforced prevailing beliefs that the Irish were emotionally unstable and morally primitive. This cartoon appeared in *Judge* on November 7, 1891, and is typical of a worldwide tendency to depict minorities as apelike.

ians, a carefree image for "Negroes" (the accepted word then), a negative stereotype for Turks, a positive and conservative image for the English, and commitment to family and tradition for Chinese—all remained constant generalizations over the 35-year span of the study. Other studies have reported similar findings.[47]

Both majority-group and minority-group members may hold stereotypes about each other. Such generalized labeling often begins with some small basis in fact as applied to a few particular individuals that is then erroneously applied to everyone in that group. Social barriers between the two groups, mass-media portrayals reinforcing the stereotypes (see the accompanying Ethnic Experience box), and societal pressures to conform to the stereotype combine to give such thinking a false aura of validity, encouraging people to ignore contrary evidence.

Ethnophaulisms

An **ethnophaulism** is a derogatory word or expression used to describe a racial or ethnic group. This is the language of prejudice, the verbal picture of a negative stereotype that reflects the prejudice and bigotry of a society's past and present. Howard J. Ehrlich divides ethnophaulisms into three types: (1) disparaging nicknames (e.g., chink, dago, polack, jungle bunny, or honky); (2) explicit group devaluations (e.g., "jew him down" for trying to get something for a lower price, "luck of the Irish" suggesting undeserved good fortune, or "to be in Dutch" meaning to be in trouble); (3) irrelevant ethnic names used as a mild disparagement (e.g., "jewbird" for black cuckoos having prominent beaks, "welsh" on a bet signifying failure to honor a debt, or "Irish confetti" for bricks thrown in a fight).[48]

Both majority and minority groups coin and use ethnophaulisms to denigrate outgroups. Such usage helps justify discrimination, inequality, and social privilege for the majority, and it helps the minority cope with social injustices caused by others. Them-versus-us name-calling is divisive, but it also indicates the state of intergroup relations. Erdman Palmore, for example, concluded that all racial and ethnic groups use ethnophaulisms. He found a correlation between the number of them used and the degree of group prejudice, and he observed that they express and support negative stereotypes about the most visible racial or cultural differences.[49]

Ethnophaulisms seem to appear most often during times of major social and economic change, such as migration or immigration waves, rapid urbanization or technological change, recessions and depressions, or war. Linguistic experts have identified about 1,200 ethnic-slur names or epithets used historically in U.S. speech.[50] Most of them are obsolete today, although a few remain, and new ones appear almost yearly.

Sometimes members of a racial or ethnic minority group use an ethnophaulism directed against themselves in their conversations with one another. On occasion, they may use the term as a reprimand to one of

The Ethnic Experience
The Impact of the Media

As a reflector of society's values, the media have a tremendous impact on the shaping of our personal and group identities. Radio, television, films, newspapers, magazines, and comics can convey the rich textures of a pluralistic society or they can, directly or indirectly (by omission and distortion), alter our perception of other ethnic groups and reinforce our defensiveness and ambivalence about our own cultural backgrounds. As an Italian-American, I've realized this myself when comparing the ethnic invisibility of 50s television with modern shows that concentrate on Mafia hit men and multiple biographies of Mussolini. Having squirmed as I watched some of these portrayals, I can empathize with Arabs who resent being characterized as villainous sheikhs, Jews seen as mendacious moguls or even the current vogue for matching a Russian accent with a kind of oafish villainy. Although such stereotypes may or may not serve political ends, they share the cartoonlike isolation of a few traits that ignore the humanity and variety of a group's members.

What is the impact of ethnic stereotypes on TV and in film on how people feel about themselves and how they perceive other ethnic groups?

Although research in this area is limited, what is available suggests that TV and film's portrayal of ethnics does have a deleterious effect on perceptions of self and others. In my own clinical work, I have found that minority children and adults will often internalize negative stereotypes about their own group. Other studies have shown that ethnic stereotypes on television and in the movies can contribute to prejudice against a particular group—especially when the person is not acquainted with any members of that group. . . .

In studies of youngsters who commit hate acts—desecration of religious institutions, racial and anti-Semitic incidents—many youngsters apprehended reported they got the idea of performing vandalism from news coverage of similar acts (the copy cat syndrome). They saw media coverage as conferring recognition and prestige, temporarily raising their low self-esteem.

Add to TV fiction and news the rash of "truly tasteless" joke books, radio call-in shows that invite bigoted calls from listeners, late-night TV hosts and comedians who denigrate ethnic groups, and the impact on people's perceptions is considerable. While the media cannot be blamed for creating the bigotry, their insensitive reporting and encouragement of inflammatory comments establishes a societal norm that gives license to such attitudes and behavior.

Source: Joseph Giordano, "Identity Crisis: Stereotypes Stifle Self-Development," accessed at www.sicilianculture.com/news/2002-idcrisis.htm on December 27, 2006.

their own kind for acting out the stereotype, but more often, they mean it as a humorous expression of friendship and endearment. However, when an outsider uses that same term, they resent it because of its prejudicial connotations.

The use of ethnophaulisms has behavioral consequences. For example, in an examination of archival research data spanning a 150-year period of U.S. history, Brian Mullen explored the effects of using ethnophaulisms in the representation of ethnic immigrant groups.[51] He found that the smaller, less familiar, and "more foreign" ethnic immigrant groups were typically portrayed in a simplistic and negative manner, with a corresponding tendency to exclude those groups from the host society. His study illustrates the "them" and "us" divisiveness, mentioned earlier, that results from the use of disparaging terms to refer to others.

The context of words is important, as in "Dutch treat" and "luck of the Irish," which are no longer recognized as derogatory.

Ethnic Humor

Why do some people find ethnic jokes funny, whereas others find them distasteful? Studies show the response often reflects the listener's attitude toward the group being ridiculed. If you hold favorable or positive attitudes toward the group that is the butt of the joke, then you are less likely to find it funny than if you hold unfavorable or negative views. If you dislike a group about which a joke implies something negative, you will tend to appreciate the joke.[52]

A common minority practice is to use ethnic humor as a strategy for defining one's ethnicity positively. Lois Leveen suggests that, in telling ethnic jokes about one's own group, the speaker challenges stereotypes within the dominant culture.[53] If an ethnic tells the joke to the ethnic ingroup, the act of laughing together through joke sharing is "an ethnicizing phenomenon" that develops a sense of "we-ness" in laughing with others. If an ethnic tells that joke to outsiders, it can serve as a means to undermine the stereotype by ridiculing it. Ethnic humor can thus serve as a powerful force to facilitate a positive, empowered position for the ethnic individual within the dominant culture. Of course, we must realize that there is also the potential risk that the joke will confirm the stereotype, not undermine it.

The Influence of Television

Virtually every U.S. household owns at least one television set, and families in the United States watch more than 7 hours of TV daily, on average. Does all this viewing make us think or act differently? Does it change our attitudes or shape our feelings and reactions about minority groups? Or is it only entertainment with no appreciable effect on perceptions and behavior? Abundant research evidence indicates television programming distorts reality, promotes stereotypical role models, and significantly shapes and reinforces our attitudes about men, women, and minority groups.

Perpetuation of Stereotypes

Twice in the late 1970s, the U.S. Commission on Civil Rights charged the television industry with perpetuating racial and sexual stereotypes in programming and news.[54] Besides criticizing the almost exclusively negative racial portrayals on police shows over the preceding 6 years, the report attacked the television industry for portraying

> a social structure in which males are very much in control of their lives, . . . older, more serious, more independent, and more likely to hold prestigious jobs. Women, on the other hand, were younger, often unemployed, more "family bound," and often found in comic roles. Those women who were employed were in stereotyped and sometimes subservient occupations.

In 1982, media expert George Gerbner continued the criticism, arguing that little had changed since the commission's reports.[55] A tiny percentage of Black characters, for example, were "unrealistically romanticized," but the overwhelming majority of them occupied subservient, supporting roles—such as the White hero's comic sidekick. Gerbner commented:

> When a black child looks at prime time, most of the people he sees doing interesting things are white. That imbalance tends to teach young blacks to accept minority status as naturally inevitable and even deserved.[56]

Despite some improvements since then, three recent studies revealed the continuance of stereotypes in commercials. One content analysis found that in the twenty-first century, prime-time commercials still perpetuate traditional stereotypes of women and men.[57] Another revealed that most major, active characters in commercials aired during children's cartoon programming were male, thus perpetuating stereotyped sex-typed behaviors, despite their decrease in the real world.[58] The third study found "distinct racial segregation" in prime-time ads, with Whites appearing in ads for upscale, beauty, or home products, while people of color, in contrast, appeared in ads for low-cost, low-nutrition products (e.g., fast food and soft drinks) and in athletic and sports equipment ads. Such depictions raise questions about the continuance of racial stereotypes, notably a somewhat one-dimensional view of people of color as key consumers of low-cost products.[59]

Influencing of Attitudes

Television influences attitudes toward racial or ethnic groups by the status of the parts it assigns to their members, the kind of behavior they display within these parts, and even the type of products they promote. Television greatly influences children's attitudes in this area. Children watch television during prime time more than any other time of day. Yet according to a 2002 Children Now's study, prime time remains overwhelmingly White, with

Critically acclaimed and honored, *The Sopranos* nonetheless drew complaints from many Italian American individuals and organizations for helping perpetuate the stereotype linking Italians with organized crime. Yet, in Italy, the show drew no such criticism as Italians said, "Everyone knows it's just a show." What explains these different reactions?

people of color appearing largely in secondary and guest roles. Whites account for 73 percent of the prime-time population, followed by African Americans (16 percent), Latinos (4 percent), Asian/Pacific Islanders (3 percent), and Native Americans (0.2 percent). However, prime-time diversity dramatically increases as the evening progresses, with the 8 P.M. hour the least racially diverse and the 10 P.M. hour the most racially diverse. Thus, children and youths are more likely to see a much more homogeneous prime time world than are adults who watch television later in the evening.[60]

Due to the near invisibility of characters of color (and the often negatively stereotyped portrayals when they do appear), children of color who watch television extensively may have low self-esteem, feel alienated, and be reluctant to participate in activities outside their own community.[61] This impact on identity development can be especially strong for Latino, Asian, and Native American children, who almost never see people who look like them on television. Children in these and other underrepresented groups can receive a strong, clear message that the majority culture does not value or respect them.[62]

All in the Family, a popular comedy series in the 1970s and still in syndicated reruns, received an NAACP award for its contribution to race relations but divided critics over the question of whether it reduced or reinforced racial bigotry.[63] Offering an explanation for both views, Neil Vidmar and Milton Rokeach reported findings that selective perception and prior attitudes determining reactions to the situations on screen governed viewers' affective responses.[64] Liberal viewers saw the program as satire, with son-in-law Mike effectively rebutting Archie's ignorance and bigotry or minority members besting Archie by the end of the program. In contrast, prejudiced viewers—particularly adolescents—were significantly more likely to admire Archie over Mike and to perceive Archie as winning in the end. Although most respondents indicated they thought Mike made better sense than Archie, highly prejudiced adolescents were significantly more likely to perceive Archie as making better sense. Thus, the program was probably doing more to reinforce prejudice and discrimination than to combat it.

Ingroup and Outgroup Perceptions

Two months before a 1986 racial attack in the Howard Beach area of Queens in New York City made national headlines, a study of 1,200 students at a public high school in the area revealed their attitudes toward race and ethnicity in real life and on television.[65] The school had been chosen because it contained a multiethnic population, with large numbers of Black, Hispanic, and Italian American students and smaller groups of students of Irish and Asian descent. Reasons for watching television varied by ethnic group.

One-fourth of these students said that TV accurately depicts what life and people are really like and that TV influences their racial and ethnic attitudes. Their responses to twenty then-popular TV ethnic characters as positive or negative were both realistic and revealing of broad patterns of consistent responses. Generally, group members saw their portrayed group members more favorably and as more typical than did nonmembers.

The Influence of Advertising and Music

Social scientists are paying increasing attention to the impact of corporate advertising, rap music lyrics, and music videos on attitudes about men and women. Beyond the obviousness of marketing products and entertainment lie their powers of seduction, imagery, and conditioning of attitudes.

Advertising

The average American is exposed to more than 3,000 advertisements a week and watches 3 years' worth of television ads over the course of a lifetime.

What effect do they have on our attitudes? In a content analysis of popular 1990s TV commercials designed for specific target audiences, researchers found the characters in them enjoyed more prominence and exercised more authority if they were White or male. Images of romantic and domestic fulfillment also differed by race and gender, with women and Whites disproportionately shown in family settings and in cross-sex interactions. In general, the researchers found that these commercials tended to portray White men as powerful, White women as sex objects, Black men as aggressive, and Black women as inconsequential. They suggest that these commercial images help perpetuate subtle prejudice against African Americans by exaggerating cultural differences and denying positive emotions.[66]

Another study of prime-time television ads in 2001 found Blacks generally portrayed in a more diverse, equitable manner compared to Whites, but Asians, Hispanics, and Native Americans underrepresented and sometimes negatively depicted. Latinos were often suggestively clad and shown engaging in alluring behaviors and sexual gazing, thus stressing physical appearance and sexuality over intelligence. Asians were most commonly young, passive adults at work in technology ads, thus promoting the stereotype of submissiveness and superior achievements as measures of their self-worth.[67]

Exploitation of women in ads is worse today than ever before, writes Jean Kilbourne, best known for her documentary film work (*Killing Us Softly; Pack of Lies*) and her college lecture tours. Kilbourne's research points out that women—and girls, in particular—need to be mindful of the influential power of advertising. Women's bodies, frequently portrayed as headless torsos, have long been used to sell everything from toothbrushes to chain saws. In addition, endless glossy spreads in women's magazines feature beauty products, fashion, and diets to keep women focused on exterior "problems." She doesn't blame ads alone for demonizing fat women or causing binge drinking, teenage pregnancy, and violence against women. The cumulative effect is what appalls her. Taken together, she says, advertising fosters an inescapable, poisonous environment in which sexist stereotypes, cynicism and self-hatred, and the search for quick fixes flourish. Consumers may think they are unaffected, but advertisers successfully create a false consciousness and teach young women that they are appetizing only when "plucked, polished and painted."[68]

Music

One of the major criticisms of rap music is that it may affect attitudes and behavior regarding the use of violence, especially violence against women. Although some rap artists—such as Arrested Development and Queen Latifah—reflect a concern for humanity and offer inspiration and hope, others—such as Eminem, 2 Live Crew, Apache, N.W.A., and Scarface—routinely endorse violence, homophobia, and portray women as punching bags, strippers, or simply sperm receptacles. Such portrayals prompted the National Black Women's Political Caucus to seek legislation to control the access to rap music. In 2005, *Essence,* one of the leading magazines for Black women, launched a one-year "Take Back the Music" campaign against anti-women lyrics in rap music.

Pop culture has enormous influence on how young men and women see themselves and each other in terms of sexuality and gender. Sut Jhally, best known for his documentary film *Dreamworlds* (which MTV tried to stop), says the powerful sexual imagery in hundreds of music videos, produced mostly by men, objectifies and dehumanizes women, frequently portraying them as existing solely for males' sexual satisfaction. In fact, one study found a strong link between increased exposure to rap music videos and problems with the law, drugs, and sexually transmitted diseases.[69]

Social scientists and activists fight against this onslaught to eliminate the prejudices that television shows and commercials, advertisements, music lyrics, and videos promulgate.

Can Prejudice Be Reduced?

A great many organizations and movements dedicated to reducing prejudice have existed over the years. Although they have varied in their orientation and focal point of activity, they have usually adopted two basic approaches: to promote greater interaction between dominant and minority groups in all aspects of living, by either voluntary or compulsory means; and to dispense information that destroys stereotypes and exposes rationalizations (self-justifications). Neither approach has been successful in all instances, probably because the inequalities that encourage prejudicial attitudes still exist.

Interaction

Contact between people of different racial and ethnic backgrounds does not necessarily lead to friendlier attitudes. In fact, the situation may worsen, as has happened frequently when schools and neighborhoods have experienced an influx of people from a different group. In many instances, however, interaction does reduce prejudice.[70] It would also appear that many other variables determine the effect of interaction, including the frequency and duration of contacts; the relative status of the two parties and their backgrounds; whether their meeting is voluntary or compulsory and competitive or cooperative; and whether they meet in a political, religious, occupational, residential, or recreational situation.[71]

A good example of the significance of the type of contact emerges from the experiments in **cooperative learning** of Elliot Aronson and Neal Osherow.[72] This research team observed that classroom competition for teacher recognition and approval often wreaked special hardship on minority children less fluent in English or less self-assured about participating in class. The researchers created interdependent learning groups of five or six children, each member charged with learning one portion of the day's lesson in a particular subject. The children learned the complete lesson from one another and then took a test on all the material. Because it creates interdependent groups, this technique is not the same as the cooperative learning approach so common in U.S. schools. In fact, Australian researchers compared use of the two approaches among children in grades 4 to 6 and found that the cooperative learning method produced significant improvements on measures of academic performance, liking of peers, and racial prejudice, in contrast to the effect of the cooperative approach that exacerbated preexisting intergroup tensions[73] (see the accompanying Ethnic Experience box).

Information

Many people have long cherished the hope that education would reduce prejudice. Some studies have found a definite correlation between level of education and degree of tolerance.[74] Charles Stember's research, however, led him to conclude that more highly educated persons were not more tolerant; they were simply more sophisticated in recognizing measures of bias and more subtle in expressing their prejudices.[75] In sum, it appears that formal education is far from a perfect means of reducing prejudice.

One reason for this failure is that people tend to use **selective perception**; that is, they absorb information that accords with their own beliefs and rationalize away information that does not. Another reason is the almost quantum leap from the classroom to real-life situations. Dealing with prejudice from a detached perspective is one thing; dealing with it in actuality is quite another because emotions, social pressures, and many other factors are involved.

Despite these criticisms, courses in race and ethnic relations certainly have value because they raise the students' level of consciousness about intergroup dynamics. However, a significant reduction or elimination of prejudice is more likely to occur by changing the structural conditions of inequality that promote and maintain prejudicial attitudes. As Herbert Blumer suggests, the sense of group position dissolves and racial prejudice declines when major shifts in the social order overtake the current definition of a group's characteristics.[76] As long as the dominant group does not react with fear and institute a countermovement, the improvement of a minority's social position changes power relations and reduces negative stereotypes. Therefore, continued efforts at public enlightenment and extension of constitutional rights and equal opportunities to all Americans, regardless of race, religion, or national origin, appear to be the most promising means of attaining an unprejudiced society.

The Ethnic Experience
Reducing Prejudice through Cooperative Learning

The experience of a Mexican-American child in one of our groups serves as a useful illustration. We will call him Carlos. Carlos was not very articulate in English, his second language. Because he was often ridiculed when he had spoken up in the past, over the years he learned to keep quiet in class. He was one of those students . . . who had entered into an implicit contract of silence with his teacher, he opting for anonymity and she calling on him only rarely.

While Carlos hated school and was learning very little in the traditional classroom, at least he was left alone. Accordingly, he was quite uncomfortable with the jigsaw system, which required him to talk to his groupmates. He had a great deal of trouble communicating his paragraph, stammering and hesitating. The other children reacted out of old habits, resorting to insults and teasing. "Aw, you don't know it," Susan accused. "You're dumb, you're stupid. You don't know what you are doing."

One of the researchers, assigned to observe the group process, intervened with a bit of advice when she overheard such comments: "Okay, you can tease him if you want to. It might be fun for you, but it's not going to help you learn about Eleanor Roosevelt's young adulthood. And let me remind you, the exam will take place in less than an hour." Note how this statement brings home the fact that the reinforcement contingencies have shifted considerably. Now Susan does not gain much from putting Carlos down. And she stands to lose a great deal, not just from the teacher singling her out for criticism but because she needs to know Carlos's information.

Gradually, but inexorably, it began to dawn on the students that the only chance they had to learn about Carlos's segment was by paying attention to what he had to say. If they ignored Carlos or continued to ridicule him, his segment would be unavailable to them and the most they could hope for would be an 80 percent score on the exam—an unattractive prospect to most of the children. And with that realization, the kids began to develop into pretty good interviewers, learning to pay attention to Carlos, to draw him out, and to ask probing questions. Carlos, in turn, began to relax more and found it easier to explain out loud what was in his head. What the children came to learn about Carlos is even more important than the information about the lesson that they got from him. After a couple of days, they began to appreciate that Carlos was not nearly as dumb as they had thought he was. After a few weeks they noticed talents in him they had not seen before. They began to like Carlos, and he began to enjoy school more and to think of his Anglo classmates as helpful friends and interested colleagues rather than as tormentors.

Source: Elliot Aronson and Neal Osherow. "Cooperation, Prosocial Behavior, and Academic Performance: Experiments in the Desegregated Classroom," *Applied Social Psychology Annual* 1 (1980): 174–75. Reprinted by permission.

Cooperative learning, where each child tells the others about parts of the lesson, is now a common teaching technique in U.S. elementary schools. Experiments by social scientists show this approach is also an effective means of reducing the walls of prejudice and social distance and building self-esteem and motivation in minority youngsters, particularly in interdependent learning groups.

One measure of shifting group positions is the expanding inclusiveness of the mainstream U.S. ingroup; previously excluded minority groups, once victims of prejudice, are gaining the social acceptance of structural assimilation. In its over-200-year history, the United States has experienced a changing definition of *mainstream "American"*—from only those whose ancestry was English, to the British (English, Welsh, Scots, and Scots Irish), to peoples from Northern and Western Europe, and now to all Europeans. People of color, however, have yet to gain entry into this national cultural identity group, and that entry is the challenge before us.[77]

Diversity Training

A workplace environment that promotes positive intergroup interaction is more efficient, has higher morale, and retains experienced personnel. Conversely, a hostile work environment has lower productivity, disgruntled personnel, and a higher attrition rate. Moreover, if an organization develops a reputation for insensitivity to diversity, it will attract fewer qualified job applicants among women and people of color, and businesses will lose market share by attracting fewer clients from our increasingly diverse society for their goods and services.

With women and non-White males now constituting 75 percent of the people entering the U.S. labor force, and with nearly 36 percent of the nation's enlisted military personnel identifying themselves as a minority, it has become critical for all organizations to take steps to prevent prejudice from creating dysfunctions within their daily operations.[78]

As someone who has conducted numerous diversity training workshops for military leaders and corporate management (including health care), let me give you some insight into these programs. The best ones heighten awareness by providing informational insights into the diversity of cultural value orientations, as well as into the current and future demographics of employees and clients. Most valuable in broadening perceptions is the inclusion of interactive learning sessions such as role-playing demonstrations of wrong–right handlings of situations and the creation of small groups to discuss and offer solutions to hypothetical but realistic problems.

Although programs vary greatly in their length, structure, and content, the most effective ones are comprehensive, actively supported by management as part of the organization's general mission statement, and fully integrated into all aspects of the organization. The latter includes a diversity orientation session for new employees, occasional reinforcement sessions for continuing employees, and all levels of management working together to promote an inclusive, hospitable work climate. Such efforts can make a significant contribution to reducing prejudice in the workplace.

Retrospect

The psychology of prejudice focuses on individuals' subjective states of mind, emphasizing the levels of prejudice held and the factors of self-justification, personality, frustration, and scapegoating. The sociology of prejudice examines objective conditions of society as social forces behind prejudicial attitudes; socialization, economic competition, and social norms constitute major considerations.

Stereotyping often reflects prejudice as a sense of group position. Once established, stereotypes are difficult to eradicate and often are manifest in ethnophaulisms and ethnic humor. Television has a profound impact in shaping and reinforcing attitudes; unfortunately, it tends to perpetuate racial and sexual stereotypes instead of combating them.

Increased contact between groups and improved information do not necessarily reduce prejudice. The nature of the contact, particularly whether it is competitive or cooperative, is a key determinant. Information can develop heightened awareness as a means of improving relations, but external factors (economic conditions and social pressures) may override rational considerations.

The imagery in advertising, rap music lyrics, and music videos can have a cumulative effect in shaping values about men and women. These images and words help perpetuate subtle prejudice and a false consciousness.

Diversity in the workplace, whether corporate or military, has prompted many organizations to create a more positive, inclusive environment through diversity training workshops. The most effective ones are comprehensive, actively supported by management, and fully integrated into all aspects of the organization.

KEY TERMS

Action-orientation level of prejudice
Authoritarian personality
Cognitive level of prejudice
Cooperative learning
Displaced aggression
Emotional level of prejudice
Ethnophaulism
Jim Crow laws

Prejudice
Relative deprivation
Scapegoating
Selective perception
Self-justification
Social norms
Socialization process
Stereotype

REVIEW QUESTIONS

1. What is prejudice? What are some of its manifestations?

2. What are some of the possible causes of prejudice?

3. What role does television play in combating or reinforcing stereotypes?

4. In what ways can advertising be harmful to minorities?

5. What are the criticisms against some rap music and music videos?

6. How can we reduce prejudice?

SUGGESTED READINGS

Delgado, Richard, and Jean Stefancic. *Understanding Words That Wound.* Boulder, Colo.: West-view Press, 2004.
    Addresses the issue of hate speech as a serious social problem and the pros and cons of regulating or suppressing it.

Kilbourne, Jean, and Mary Pipher. *Can't Buy My Love: How Advertising Changes the Way We Think and Feel*. New York: Free Press, 2000.

A gripping portrait on how the onslaught of advertising affects young people, especially girls, and feeds an addictive mentality that often continues throughout adulthood.

Lester, Paul M. (ed.). *Images That Injure: Pictorial Stereotypes in the Media*, 2d ed. New York: Praeger, 2003.

A collection of essays that discuss media stereotypes, their impact on individuals and society, and the motivations of those who made the images.

Perlmutter, Philip. *Legacy of Hate: A Short History of Ethnic, Religious, and Racial Prejudice in America*. New York: M. E. Sharpe, 1999.

A comprehensive study of bigotry in the United States against various groups, from colonial beginnings to the present.

Pickering, Michael. *Stereotyping: The Politics of Representation*. New York: Palgrave Macmillan, 2001.

An interdisciplinary treatment of stereotyping, the roots of prejudice and bigotry in modern society, and the figure of the stranger in the modern city.

Sowell, Thomas. *Migrations and Cultures: A World View*. New York: HarperCollins, 1997.

A provocative book that draws from case histories of the Germans, Italians, Japanese, Chinese, Jews, and Asian Indians and argues that immigrants' habits and beliefs are more important to their fate than a country's economy, culture, or politics.

INTERNET RESOURCES

At http://stop-the-hate.org, you'll find intriguing and inspiring quotations and poetry that also offer insights into how prejudice and hatred undermine the beauty of life.

At the Institute for Research on Poverty (www.irp.wisc.edu), you'll be able to access answers to frequently asked questions about poverty and recent articles.

CHAPTER

5 Discrimination

"In the end antiblack, antifemale, and all forms of discrimination are equivalent to the same thing—antihumanism."
—Shirley Chisholm

Whereas prejudice is an attitudinal system, **discrimination** is actual behavior, the practice of differential and unequal treatment of other groups of people, usually along racial, religious, or ethnic lines. The Latin word *discriminatus*, from which the English word is derived, means "to divide or distinguish," and its subsequent negative connotation has remained relatively unchanged through the centuries.

Levels of Discrimination

Actions, like attitudes, have different levels of intensity. As a result, discrimination may be analyzed at five levels.[1] The first level is *verbal expression*, a statement of dislike or the use of a derogatory term. The next level is *avoidance*, in which the prejudiced person takes steps to avoid social interaction with a group. Actions of this type may include choice of residence, organizational membership, activities located in urban centers, and primary relationships in any social setting.

At the third level, *exclusion* from certain jobs, housing, education, or social organizations occurs. In the United States, the practice of **de jure segregation** was once widespread throughout the South. Not only were children specifically assigned to certain schools to maintain racial separation, but segregationist laws kept all public places (theaters, restaurants, restrooms, transportation, etc.) racially separated as well. This exclusion can also take the form of **de facto segregation** as residential patterns become embedded

105

in social customs and institutions. Thus, the standard practice of building and maintaining neighborhood schools in racially segregated communities creates and preserves segregated schools.

Another form of exclusion is **redlining**—designating certain neighborhoods as "bad risk" areas for mortgages and home improvement loans. Although this is an illegal practice, it still occurs, creating a self-fulfilling prophecy. Unable to secure loans to fix up their property and buyers unable to obtain mortgages for properties in such areas, market values drop, and the neighborhood declines, intensifying the racial segregation in that area. Such mortgage disinvestment is most common in African American neighborhoods.[2]

The fourth level of discrimination is *physical abuse*—violent attacks on members of the disliked group. Unfortunately, this behavior still occurs often in the United States. The Prejudice Institute defines **ethnoviolence** as encompassing a range of action—harassment, group insults, vandalism, graffiti, swastika painting, arson, cross burning, physical assault, and murder—committed against people targeted solely because of their race, religion, ethnic background, or sexual orientation.[3] Thousands of incidents of ethnoviolence against members of various minority groups occur each year throughout the United States on college campuses and in both suburban and urban areas.

The most extreme level of discrimination is *extermination*: massacres, genocide, or pogroms conducted against a people. Such barbarous actions continue to occur sporadically, as in the 9/11 attacks in New York City and Washington, D.C., in 2001, and more recently, the killings in Darfur and the terrorist bombing in Asia, Europe, and the Middle East.

Relationships between Prejudice and Discrimination

Prejudice can lead to discrimination, and discrimination can lead to prejudice, although no certainty exists that one will follow the other. Our attitudes and our overt behavior are closely related, but they are not identical. We may harbor hostile feelings toward certain groups without ever making them known through word or deed. Conversely, our overt behavior may effectively conceal our real attitudes.

Prejudiced people are more likely than others to practice discrimination; thus, discrimination quite often represents the overt expression of prejudice. It is wrong, however, to assume that discrimination is always the simple acting out of prejudice. It may instead be the result of a policy decision protecting the interests of the majority group, as happens when legal immigration is curtailed for economic reasons. It may be due to social conformity, as when people submit to outside pressures despite their personal views.[4] Discriminators may explain their actions with reasons other than prejudice toward a particular group, and those reasons may be valid to the discriminators. Sometimes discriminatory behavior may precede prejudicial attitudes as, for example, when organizations insist that all job applicants take aptitude or IQ tests based on middle-class experiences and then form negative judgments of lower-income people who do not score well.

Robert Merton formulated a model showing the possible relationships between prejudice and discrimination (Figure 5.1). Merton demonstrated that, quite conceivably, a nonprejudiced person may discriminate and a prejudiced person may not. In his paradigm, Merton classified four types of people according to how they accept or reject the American Creed: "the right of equitable access to justice, freedom and opportunity, irrespective of race or religion, or ethnic origin."[5]

The Nonprejudiced Nondiscriminator.   Nonprejudiced nondiscriminators are neither prejudiced nor practicers of discrimination. Of course, as Merton observes, these are virtues of omission, not commission. He criticizes members of this class who show no inclination to illuminate others and to fight actively against all forms of discrimination. They talk chiefly to others sharing their viewpoint, and so they deceive themselves into thinking that they represent the consensus of the community. Furthermore, because their "own spiritual house is in order," they feel no pangs of conscience pressing them to work collectively on the problem. On the other hand, some nonprejudiced nondiscriminators obviously are activists and do engage in dialogue with others who hold different viewpoints, thereby transforming belief into action.

Prejudiced	Discriminates	
	No	Yes
No	All-weather liberal	Fair-weather liberal
Yes	Timid bigot	Active bigot

FIGURE 5.1   **Relationships between Prejudice and Discrimination**

The Nonprejudiced Discriminator.   Expedience is the byword for those in the category of the nonprejudiced discriminator, for their actions often conflict with their personal beliefs. They may, for example, be free of racial prejudice, but they will join clubs that exclude people who belong to outgroups, they will vote for regressive measures if they would benefit materially from these, and they will support efforts to keep African Americans out of their neighborhood for fear of its deterioration. These people frequently feel guilt and shame because they are acting against their beliefs.

The Prejudiced Nondiscriminator.   Merton's term *timid bigots* best describes prejudiced nondiscriminators. They believe in many stereotypes about other groups and definitely feel hostility toward these groups. However, they keep silent in the presence of those who are more tolerant; they conform because they must. If there were no law or pressure to avoid bias in certain actions, they would discriminate.

The Prejudiced Discriminator.   Prejudiced discriminators are active bigots. They demonstrate no conflict between attitudes and behavior. Not only do they openly express their beliefs, practice discrimination, and defy the law if necessary, but they consider such conduct virtuous.

The second and third categories—the nonprejudiced discriminator and the prejudiced nondiscriminator—are the most sociologically interesting classifications because they demonstrate that social-situational variables often determine whether discriminatory behavior occurs. The pressure of group norms may force individuals to act in a manner inconsistent with their beliefs.

Social and Institutional Discrimination

Discriminatory practices are encountered frequently in the areas of employment and residence, although such actions often are taken covertly and are denied by those who take them. Another dimension of discrimination, often unrealized, is **social discrimination**—the creation of a "social distance" between groups. Simply stated, in their intimate primary relationships, people tend to associate with others of similar ethnic background and socioeconomic level; dominant-group members thus usually exclude minority-group members from close relations with them.

Discrimination is more than the biased actions of individuals, though. In their influential book, *Black Power*, Stokely Carmichael and Charles Hamilton called attention to the fact that far greater harm occurs from **institutional discrimination**—unequal treatment of subordinate groups inherent in the ongoing operations of society's institutions.[6] Entrenched in customs, laws, and practices, these discriminatory patterns can exist in banking, criminal justice, employment, education, health care, housing, and many other areas in the private and public sectors. Critical to understanding this concept is the fact the practices are so widespread that individuals helping to perpetuate them may be completely unaware of their existence. Examples would be banks rejecting home mortgage applications of minorities at a higher rate, the sentencing inequities in our justice system, the concentration of minorities in low-paying jobs, the former "separate but equal" educational structure in the South, and segregated housing.

Hubert Blalock, offering conflict-perspective reasoning, suggested that, when the dominant group feels that its self-interests—such as primacy and the preservation of cherished values—are threatened, extreme discrimination usually results.[7] Blalock believed that the dominant group will not hesitate to act discriminatorily if it thinks that this approach will effectively undercut the minority group as a social competitor (see the accompanying International Scene box). Further, the dominant group will aggressively discriminate if it interprets minority variation from cultural norms as a form of social deviance that threatens society's sacred traditions (e.g., the large influx of Catholic immigrants in the nineteenth-century Protestant-dominated United States or the appearance of "dishonest" Gypsies among "decent, hardworking" people). Discrimination, in this view, is "a technique designed to neutralize minority group efforts."[8]

The Affirmative-Action Controversy

At what point do efforts to secure justice and equal opportunities in life for one group infringe on the rights of other groups? Is justice a utilitarian concept—the greatest happiness for the greatest number? Or is it a moral concept—a sense of good that all people share? Is the proper role of government to foster a climate in which people have equal opportunity to participate in a competitive system of occupations and rewards, or should government ensure equal results in any competition? These issues have engaged moral and political philosophers for centuries, and they go to the core of the affirmative-action controversy.

The Concepts of Justice, Liberty, and Equality

Over 2,300 years ago, Plato wrote in the *Republic* that justice must be relative to the needs of the people who are served, not to the desires of those who serve them. For example, physicians must make patients' health their primary concern if they are to be just. In *A Theory of Justice*, John Rawls interprets justice as fairness, which maximizes equal liberty for all.[9] To provide the greatest benefit to the least advantaged, society must eliminate social and economic inequalities, placing minority persons in offices and positions that are open to all under conditions of fair equality of

The International Scene
Discrimination in Northern Ireland

Northern Ireland contains about 1 million Protestants with loyalties to the over-whelmingly Protestant United Kingdom and about 600,000 Catholics with a preference for unification with the Catholic-dominated Republic of Ireland. Despite some progress toward reconciliation since the 1998 peace agreement, it remains today a polarized society, its sporadic violence fed by centuries of deep-seated hostility.

Sociologically, Catholics are the minority group, with limited political power. They are more likely than Protestants to be poor, to suffer prolonged unemployment, and to live in substandard housing in segregated communities. Catholics tend to be in low-status, low-skill jobs and Protestants in high-status, high-skill positions. It is difficult, however, to determine whether these employment patterns result from overt job discrimination, from structural factors of community segregation, education, and class, or from both.

Although the degree of actual discrimination employed to maintain their dominance is unclear, Protestants rationalize about the situation through a set of negative beliefs about Catholics. Many Protestants stereotype Catholics as lazy welfare cheats who are dirty, superstitious, and ignorant. They also view them as oversexed (as "proved" by the typically larger size of Catholic families) and brainwashed by priests, whose primary allegiance, they say, is to a foreign entity—the Pope. Moreover, many Protestants suspect that Catholics are intent on undermining the Ulster government to force reunification with the Republic of Ireland. Most Protestants see no discrimination on the basis of religion in jobs, housing, and other social areas. Catholics "get what they deserve" because of their values, attitudes, and disloyalty.

For their part, most Catholics in Northern Ireland strongly believe that they suffer from discrimination as a direct consequence of their religion. They view Protestants as narrow-minded bigots who stubbornly hold onto political power and have no desire to relinquish any part of it. A vicious circle of prejudice and discrimination, despite the peace accord, intensifies Protestant resistance to sharing power and Catholic reluctance to support the government.

Not yet fully implemented, the hard-fought pragmatism and promise of the 1998 peace accord could still fall victim to political opportunism, fickle public opinion, or the evil intent of the radicals on both sides, who have never agreed to forswear the use of bombs and murder to pursue their political ends.

In contrast, Protestants in the Republic of Ireland, who constitute only 3 percent of the population, live in harmony with their Catholic neighbors. They are fully integrated socioeconomically and do not, for the most part, experience prejudice.

Critical thinking question: What must be done to reduce the prejudice and discrimination that sows the seeds of violence in Northern Ireland?

opportunity. However, when a government takes action to ensure equality (such as passing a law against housing discrimination), it is also restricting the liberty of property owners to rent or sell as they choose. While the goal of an antidiscriminatory law is laudable, the result is nonetheless the government telling people what they can or cannot do with their own property (or business, if we consider job discrimination). The quest for equality thus curtails the liberty of others, and has led to some to denounce "big brother" interference with calls to "get the government off our backs." Critics counter that "the greater good" sometimes outweighs individual choice, as it also does in wartime restrictions or the public confiscation of private property for redevelopment ("eminent domain").

Anticipating the emergence of the equal-protection-under-the-law clause of the Fourteenth Amendment as a major force for social change, Joseph Tussman and Jacobus tenBroek examined the problems of the doctrine of equality five years before the 1954 Supreme Court school desegregation

In 2003, as the U.S. Supreme Court justices heard arguments for and against the use of affirmative action in admissions decisions at the University of Michigan, demonstrators outside made their views known. The court's subsequent 5–4 ruling was a broad one, endorsing continuance of this practice, but under broad guidelines not intended for an indefinite period.

ruling. Americans, they argued, have always been more concerned with liberty than with equality, identifying liberty with the absence of government interference:

> What happens, then, when government becomes more ubiquitous? Whenever an area of activity is brought within the control or regulation of government, to that extent equality supplants liberty as the dominant ideal and constitutional demand.[10]

Tussman and tenBroek noted that those who insist on constitutional rights for all are not so much demanding the removal of government restraints as they are asking for positive government action to provide equal treatment for "minority groups, parties, or organizations whose rights are too easily sacrificed or ignored in periods of popular hysteria."[11] Responsibility for promoting individual rights has increasingly been placed on the federal government and its efforts through affirmative action have sparked a conservative countermovement.

Affirmative Action Begins

We can trace the origin of government affirmative-action policy to July 1941, when President Franklin D. Roosevelt issued Executive Order 8802, obligating defense contractors "not to discriminate against any worker because of race, creed, color, or national origin." Subsequent executive orders by virtually all presidents continued or expanded the government's efforts to curb discrimination in employment. President Kennedy's Executive Order 10925 in 1961 was the first to use the term **affirmative action**; it stipulated that government contractors would "take affirmative action that applicants are employed, and that employees are treated during employment, without regard to their race, creed, color, or national origin."

The legal basis for affirmative action appears to rest on two points. Stanford M. Lyman argued that passage of the Thirteenth Amendment, which abolished slavery, set the precedent for action against any vestiges of slavery manifest through racial discrimination.[12] Both supporters and opponents, however, point to Title VII, Section 703(j), of the 1964 Civil Rights Act as the keystone of their positions on affirmative action.

Title VII seems to address the need for fairness, openness, and color-blind equal opportunity. It specifically bans preference by race, ethnicity, gender, and religion in business and government. Opponents claim that this clear language outlawing preferences makes affirmative action unnecessary and illegal.[13] Supporters contend that President Lyndon Johnson's Executive Order 11246 is linked to Title VII by mandating employer affirmative-action plans to correct existing deficiencies through specific goals and deadlines. This was, supporters say, a logical step from concern about equal rights to concern about actual equal opportunity.[14]

Addressing an expanded list of protected categories (Asians, Blacks, Hispanics, Native Americans, women, the aged, people with disabilities, and homosexuals), an array of state and federal policy guidelines began to regulate many aspects of business, education, and government practices. Legislation in 1972 amended the 1964 Civil Rights Act, giving the courts the power to enforce affirmative-action standards. Preference programs became the rule, through reserved minority quotas in college and graduate school admissions and in job hirings and promotions, as well as through government set-aside work contracts for minority firms.[15]

Court Challenges and Rulings

The resentment of Whites over "reverse discrimination" crystallized in the 1978 *Regents of the University of California v. Bakke* case, when the U.S. Supreme Court ruled that quotas were not permitted but race could be a factor in university admissions. In a separate opinion, Justice Harry A. Blackmun stated:

> In order to get beyond racism, we must first take account of race. There is no other way. And in order to treat some persons equally, we must treat them differently. We cannot—we dare not—let the Equal Protection Clause perpetuate racial superiority.

For the next 11 years, the court upheld the principle of affirmative action in a series of rulings (see Affirmative Action box). Since 1989, however, a more conservative court has shown a growing reluctance to use "race-conscious remedies"—the practice of trying to overcome the effects of past discrimination by helping minorities. This has been true not only in affirmative-action cases involving jobs and contracts but in school desegregation and voting rights as well. The 1995 *Adarand Constructors v. Pena* decision scaled back the federal government's own affirmative-action program, mandating "strict scrutiny and evidence" of alleged past discrimination, not just a "general history of racial discrimination in the nation." In another 1995 decision, the Supreme Court declared that race could no longer be the "predominant factor" in drawing congressional districts—or by implication, any jurisdiction for any government body, from school boards to state legislatures.

In 1995, the California Board of Regents banned affirmative action for graduate and undergraduate admissions. The following year, California voters overwhelmingly passed the California Civil Rights Initiative, which prohibited the use of race, ethnicity, or gender "as a criterion for either discriminating against, or granting preferential treatment to, any individual or group," thereby dismantling state affirmative-action programs. Also in 1996, a sweeping ruling by the U.S. Circuit Court of Appeals in *Hopwood v. Texas* led the Texas attorney general to interpret the opinion as banning affirmative action in admissions, scholarships, and outreach programs.

Affirmative Action: Forty Years
of Actions and Decisions

1964   The Civil Rights Act of 1964 established legal recourse against discrimination based on race, color, religion, sex, or national origin in public accommodations, transportation, public education, and federally assisted programs.

1972   Legislation gives the courts power to enforce affirmative-action standards.

1978   The Court ruled that racial quotas are illegal but colleges and universities could consider race as one factor in admitting students.

1980   The Court ruled that a federal public works program that set aside 10 percent of its spending for minority contractors was constitutional.

1981   The Court ruled that the city of Hartford, Connecticut, could require that 15 percent of all workers on city-financed projects be women or minorities.

1987   For the first time, the Court upheld an affirmative-action plan for women, ruling that companies can give special preferences to hire and promote female employees to create a more balanced work force.

1989   The Court threw out a set-aside program in Richmond, Virginia, in which contractors on city building contracts were required to give at least 30 percent of the value of the project to firms at least one-half minority owned.

1990   The Court upheld federal policies favoring women and minorities in granting broadcasting licenses.

1995   The Court set a stricter standard on state programs or laws designed to help minorities. Only race-based preferences narrowly tailored to address identifiable past discrimination would be deemed constitutional.

1996   The Court declined to hear an appeal of a Fifth U.S. Circuit Court of Appeals ruling that "race itself cannot be taken into account" by the University of Texas in admitting students to its law school, which knocked down its affirmative-action admissions plan.

1996   The Court ordered the Virginia Military Institute to admit women or give up state funding. The decision also affected The Citadel, South Carolina's state-run military school.

1996   Californians voted to forbid any consideration of race, gender, or national origin in hiring or school admissions.

1997   The Court declined to hear a challenge to California's Proposition 209, the measure that banned race or gender from being a factor in state hiring or school admission.

1998   Washington state voters eliminated all preferential treatment based on race or gender in government hiring and school admissions.

2000   Florida ended the consideration of race in university admissions and state contracts, instead calling for more aid based on financial need.

2003   The Court upheld an affirmative-action program at the University of Michigan law school but struck down the university's system that awarded extra points to minorities in its points-based admissions policy.

Without affirmative action, California and Texas universities initially suffered minority enrollment drops in their undergraduate and graduate programs. However, both states then implemented percentage plans as a viable alternative to achieve a race/ethnic balance in higher education without the stigma of set-asides and lowered admission standards. California guaranteed university admission to the top 4 percent of high school graduates, and Texas guaranteed the top 10 percent. When Florida ended its affirmative-action program, it guaranteed college admission to the top 20 percent if students completed a minimum of 2 years of foreign language and other academic credits.

A major Supreme Court decision in 2003 preserved affirmative action in university admissions at the University of Michigan law school by a 5 to 4 vote, while at the same time striking down that university's undergraduate admissions program that used a point system based in part on race. In making a forceful endorsement of the role of racial diversity on campus in achieving a more equal society, the court's ruling was a broad one that applies to all admissions programs. Moreover, this ruling strengthened the solitary view of Justice Lewis Powell at the time of the *Bakke* decision that there was a "compelling state interest" in racial diversity. At the same time, the court suggested a time limit on such programs, with Justice Sandra Day O'Connor writing in the majority opinion, "We expect that 25 years from now the use of racial preferences will no longer be necessary to further the interest approved today."[16]

Adding significance to this ruling is the fact that it also sends a strong signal to the nation's employers that they should continue their own affirmative-action plans to hire more women and minorities. Perhaps demonstrating the commitment of business to affirmative action were the series of friend-of-the-court briefs filed by sixty-five corporations (including General Motors and Microsoft) in support of the university.[17]

This ruling, however, is not the final word on affirmative action, as numerous groups still oppose it. With several Supreme Court justices about to end their careers on the bench, new challenges to a differently constituted court may result in different rulings.

Has Affirmative Action Worked?

Evidence about the success of affirmative-action programs is as mixed as public debate on the subject. John Gpuhl and Susan Welch revealed in 1990 that the *Bakke* decision had little impact on the enrollment of African Americans and Hispanics in medical and law schools; their enrollment had already leveled off 2 or 3 years before this 1978 ruling. However, in a 1995 study, Alfred Blumrosen found that 5 million minority workers and 6 million women had better jobs than they would have had without preferences and antidiscrimination laws.[18]

Although some of the motivations behind the challenges to affirmative action may well be racist or sexist, the preservation of white privilege and conservative political ideology appear to be more significant underpinnings.[19] Addressing this point as one of the more articulate defenders of affirmative action, Tim J. Wise argues that reverse discrimination is a myth fueled by White hysteria, and he insists "affirmative action remains important and necessary because racism remains prevalent and damaging to the life prospects of people of color in the United States."[20]

Still, some minority group spokespersons, conservatives themselves, have also spoken against affirmative action, arguing that it has had a destructive influence on their own communities. Thomas Sowell and Linda Chavez maintain that universities recruit talented minority students away from local colleges where they might do very well and into learning environments where the competition for grades is intense. Opponents also argue that affirmative action is "misplaced condescension" that has poisoned race relations—a view that seems to posit a golden age of race relations in the United States at some point prior to the advent of affirmative action. According to this line of reasoning, the achievements of minorities become tainted by the possibility that they resulted from special favorable treatment rather than being earned on merit.[21]

Public Opinion

Negative public opinion about affirmative action gathered strength in the 1990s as the United States experienced a slow-growth economy, stagnant middle-class incomes, and corporate downsizing, all of which made the question of who gets fired—or hired—unusually volatile. James Q. Wilson and Seymour Martin Lipset cynically suggested that the long-term resentment of affirmative action by Whites influenced policy only when the remedy's effects finally touched the people who set the national agenda. The middle and upper classes, they argue, paid scant attention to mandated minority hirings among trade unionists or to busing orders in working-class neighborhoods. Now, however, women and minorities are competing for managerial positions that the elite once dominated and for admission to universities that the elites' sons and daughters also wish to attend.[22]

When asked in a 2006 CBS News poll what should happen to affirmative action, 12 percent thought it should be ended right away while 37 percent thought it should be phased out. Another 36 percent thought it should be continued, while 19 percent were unsure.[23] But while divided about preferences based on race and gender (Blacks less in opposition than Whites), most Americans seemed eager to support affirmative action based on economic class.[24] Under such a provision, for example, the White son of a poor coal miner in West Virginia could be eligible for special help, but the daughter of an affluent African American stockbroker would not.

Another poll, conducted by the Associated Press in 2003, just a few weeks before the Supreme Court ruling on the Michigan case, found that four in five Americans said it was important that colleges have racially diverse student bodies. However, only 51 percent thought affirmative-action programs were still needed to help Blacks, Hispanics, and other minorities, while 43 percent did not and 35 percent wanted them abolished. Among Blacks, 89 percent thought the programs were necessary. About six in ten young adults in the poll, from 18 to 34 years old, said affirmative action was still needed.[25] An obvious split along racial and generational lines exists on this subject.

Even as affirmative action withers in some states, it continues in others. Proposed federal legislation in the Congress would end it everywhere. Supporters of affirmative action argue "mend it, don't end it," whereas opponents urge that it be dismantled completely. The next few years undoubtedly will see a continuing battle and significant changes in affirmative action as we know it.

Racial Profiling

Although racial profiling has a long history, only in recent years have the government and public given it much attention. **Racial profiling** refers to action taken by law enforcement officials on the presumption that individuals of one race or ethnicity are more likely to engage in illegal activity than individuals of other races or ethnicities. Such thinking led authorities routinely to stop vehicles driven by Blacks and Latinos in the expectation of finding drugs in their possession.

Some argued that overall discrepancies in crime rates among racial groups justified such profiling in traffic enforcement activities to produce a greater number of arrests for nontraffic offenses (e.g., narcotics trafficking). Critics contended that an emphasis on minority-group drug use would naturally result in more minority arrests, but the evidence shows that about 75 percent of all illicit drug users are White.[26]

In the 1990s, racial profiling received a great deal of attention through media exposés, special reports, commissions, and legislative initiatives. In 2001, the Bush administration became the first to take action to ban it in federal law enforcement. However, the terrorist attacks later that year changed the government view of racial profiling from an undesirable police activity to one of necessity for national security. As a result, airline security, customs officials, and police place Arab and Muslim Americans under special scrutiny, and immigration officials prosecute them for minor violations often ignored for resident aliens of other ethnic backgrounds.

In 2003, the U.S. Department of Justice issued guidelines rejecting racial profiling. It argued that such activity is immoral and perpetuates negative racial stereotypes that are "harmful to our diverse democracy, and ma-

Although Whites are as likely to commit moving traffic violations as non-Whites, the tendency of police officers to stop a disproportionate number of minority drivers led to charges of biased actions through racial profiling. After 9/11, national security concerns extended racial profiling specifically to Arabs and Muslims, an action some see as necessary and others decry as biased.

terially impair our efforts to maintain a fair and just society." However, in that same statement, it included a broad and largely undefined exception when "national security" concerns come into play.[27] At the present time, then, a dichotomy exists between racial profiling attitudes and actions.

Retrospect

Discriminatory behavior operates at five levels of intensity: verbal expression, avoidance, exclusion, physical abuse, and extermination. Discrimination is not necessarily an acting-out of prejudice. Social pressures may oblige nonprejudiced individuals to discriminate or may prevent prejudiced people from discriminating.

The debate over affirmative action involves these questions: Is it a democratic government's responsibility to provide a climate for equal opportunity or to ensure equal results? If the latter, at what point do efforts to secure equality for one group infringe on the rights of other groups? After several decades of implementation, affirmative-action programs face a mixture of support and dismantling through court decisions, public initiatives, and state action.

Racial profiling remains a serious concern, given its mixed interpretation since the 2001 terrorist attacks.

KEY TERMS

Affirmative action
De facto segregation
De jure segregation
Discrimination
Ethnoviolence

Institutional discrimination
Racial profiling
Redlining
Social discrimination

REVIEW QUESTIONS

1. What is discrimination? What are some of its manifestations?

2. What is the relationship between prejudice and discrimination?

3. Why would institutional discrimination be difficult to eliminate?

4. What is the intent of affirmative action?

5. Discuss the pros and cons of affirmative action.

6. Is racial profiling an important tool in law enforcement?

SUGGESTED READINGS

Cohen, Carl, and James P. Sterba. *Affirmative Action and Racial Preference: A Debate*. New York: Oxford University Press, 2003.

An enlightening presentation of the pros and cons of affirmative action framed both by past and contemporary events and court decisions.

Harris, David A. *Profiles in Injustice: Why Racial Profiling Cannot Work*. Nevada City, Cal.: New Press, 2003.

A thoughtful and scrupulous analysis of racial profiling's history, its failure in crime prevention, and recent steps at improvement.

Irons, Peter H. *Jim Crow's Children: The Broken Promise of the Brown Decision*. New York: Viking Press, 2002.

Clearly exposes the gaping divide among our ideals, laws, and social realities as well as the interconnection of poverty, race, and education.

Lott, Bernice E., and Dianne Maluso (eds.). *The Social Psychology of Interpersonal Discrimination*. Guilford, Conn.: Guilford Press, 1995.

Provides an overview of current research focusing on behavior rather than attitudes and beliefs, exploring how and why people discriminate against others in everyday life.

Wang, Lu-In. *Discrimination by Default: How Racism Becomes Routine*. New York: New York University Press, 2006.

An intriguing explanation of how and why discrimination still plays a strong role in our society, with suggestions on how to overcome the default processes.

Wise, Tim J. *Affirmative Action: Racial Preference in Black and White*. New York: Routledge, 2005.

A well-written, compelling, and provocative book about race, privilege, and education that offers an insightful defense of affirmative action.

INTERNET RESOURCES

At http://results.about.com/affirmative_action/, you will find pro and con arguments on affirmative action, as well as a wealth of other material on this subject.

The U.S. Department of Justice released a Resource Guide on Racial Profiling (www.ncjrs.gov/pdffiles1/bja/184768.pdf), in which you will gain insights into its nature and extent, as well as a profile of several states' experiences in this area.

CHAPTER

6 Dominant–Minority Relations

"We've learned to fly the air like birds, we've learned to swim the seas like fish, and yet we haven't learned to walk the earth as brothers and sisters."

—Martin Luther King, Jr.

So far, we have looked at people's behavioral patterns in relating to strangers, the role of culture and social structure in shaping perceptions and interactions, and the complexity of prejudice and discrimination. In this chapter, we examine response patterns that dominant and minority groups follow in their dealings with each other.

The following pages suggest that these patterns occur in varying degrees for most groups, regardless of race, ethnicity, or time period. They are not mutually exclusive categories, and groups do not necessarily follow all these patterns at one time. To some degree, though, each minority or dominant group in any society shares these pattern commonalities. Before we examine the patterns, we must consider two notes of caution. First, all groups are not alike, for each has its own unique beliefs, habits, and history. And second, variations *within* a group prevent any group from being a homogeneous entity.

Minority-Group Responses

Although personality characteristics play a large role in determining how individuals respond to unfavorable situations, behavioral patterns for the group in general are similar to those of other groups in comparable circumstances. External factors play an important role, but social interpretation is also a critical determinant, as explained in the next section on ethnic- and racial-group identity. Also, the minority group's perception of its power resource—its power to change established relationships with the dominant group in a significant way—to a large extent determines the response it makes.[1] The responses include avoidance, deviance, defiance, acceptance, and negative self-image.

Ethnic- and Racial-Group Identity

Any group unable to participate fully in the societal mainstream typically develops its own group identity. This is a normal pattern in ingroup–outgroup relationships. In the field of race and ethnic relations, group identity can serve as a basis for positive encounters, a source of comfort and strength, or entry into the mainstream. It can also be a foundation for prejudice and discrimination, negative self-image, a detriment to social acceptance, or a source of conflict.

Ethnic-group identity exists when individuals choose to emphasize cultural or national ties as the basis for their primary social interactions and sense of self. Leaving the taken-for-granted world of their homeland, immigrants—as strangers in a strange land—become more self-conscious of their group identity. Even as the acculturation process and ethnogenesis unfold, these group members retain some of the "cultural baggage" they brought with them and see themselves—as does the mainstream society—as possessing distinctiveness because of their ethnicity.

Many factors determine the duration of an ethnic-group identity. A cohesive ethnic community, continually revitalized by the steady influx of newcomers, will maintain a strong resilience. Ethnic-minority media can play a significant role in strengthening that sense of identity. Indeed, minority media can even affect the assimilation process, either by promoting it (as did the New York *Daily Forward* newspaper among Jewish immigrants in the late nineteenth and early twentieth centuries) or by delaying that process by stressing the retention of language, customs, and values.

Socialization into one's own ethnic group also engenders this identity. Often, part of the growing-up process for minorities involves the existence of a dual identity: one in the larger society and another within one's own group. This multiple reality affects one's roles and behavior, and sense of self, depending on the social setting and other participants.

Ethnic-group identity can be especially protracted on the basis of religion. Some good examples are persistent subcultures such as the Amish, Hutterites, and Hasidic Jews mentioned in Chapter 2. Although a group identity usually remains among the adherents of any faith, its existence along other ethnic lines depends on racial and assimilation considerations. For example, Catholic immigrants in the nineteenth century and other Catholic and Jewish immigrants in the early twentieth century once stood apart not only for their religion but for their other subcultural traits as well. Although traces of anti-Catholicism and anti-Semitism remain today in the United States, most members of these religious groups hold a mainstream-group identity alongside their religious-group identity, which was not the case a few generations ago. More recent arrivals—such as Buddhists, Hindus, Muslims, and Sikhs—are not only religiously distinct from the previously three main U.S. religions but are culturally distinct in other ways along with their usual racial differences. Currently, their ethnic-group identities embody all these aspects (religion, race, culture), and only time will tell what evolution in group identity will occur among them.

For most but not all European groups, everyday ethnicity eventually yields to assimilation over the generations, and ethnic-group identity declines. That change is possible because gradually the group identifies more and more with mainstream society and its subcultural "marks" (clothing, language, customs, behavior, residential clustering) disappear, making the group less noticeable to the rest of society as they become absorbed into the dominant White culture.

Ethnic festivals, such as the Cinco de Mayo Festival in Los Angeles where Hispanics line up to buy food at booths, provide an opportunity to celebrate one's cultural heritage and reaffirm ethnic identity. At the same time such events enable non-group members to enrich their intercultural experiences by enjoying the foods, music, and crafts that are part of America's diversity.

Because of the social definition of race, this metamorphosis is difficult for non-Europeans in a color-conscious society. Physical identification through skin color, facial features, and/or hair texture thus maintains differences between the mainstream racial group and others. With their race an inescapable feature affecting their social acceptance and interaction patterns, non-Europeans typically develop a *racial-group identity*. This ingroup bonding satisfies the human need for a sense of belonging while simultaneously serving as a basis for racial and cultural pride. Such an arrangement can foster a healthier, more positive self-identity than would otherwise develop among racial minorities relegated to secondary social status.

People of color—whether black, brown, yellow, or red—typically affirm their identity and heritage in a variety of ways. These include combating their stereotypes, teaching the younger generation about their racial history and achievements, adopting slogans (e.g., "Black is beautiful" and "La Raza" [the race]), and using a dual identity (e.g., African American, Mexican American, Korean American, Native American) as a positive designator of their dual reality. The more militant racial group members often use ethnophaulisms against their own whom they criticize for "thinking or acting White" and call them, depending on the racial group, an "oreo," "coconut," "banana," or "apple"—that is, one color on the outside, but White on the inside.

Ethnic- or racial-group identity, then, can have positive and negative consequences. Examining it in both a social and historical context will lead to a more complete understanding of this social phenomenon.

Avoidance

One way of dealing with discriminatory practices is through **avoidance**, if this avenue is available. Throughout history, minority groups—from the ancient Hebrews to the Pilgrims to today's new arrivals—have attempted to solve their problems by leaving them behind. One motive for migrating, then, is to avoid discrimination. If leaving is not possible, minorities may turn inward to their own group for all or most of their social and economic activities. This approach insulates the minority group from antagonistic actions by the dominant group, but it also promotes charges of "clannishness" and "nonassimilation." Lacking adequate economic, legal, or political power, however, the minority group may find avoidance the only choice open to it.

By clustering together in small subcommunities, minority peoples not only create a miniature version of their familiar world but also establish a safe place in which they can live, relax, and interact with others like themselves, who understand their needs and interests. For some minority groups, seeking shelter from prejudice is probably a secondary motivation, following a primary desire to live among their own kind.

Asian immigrants, for example, have followed this pattern. When the Chinese first came to this country, they worked in many occupations in which workers were needed, frequently clustering together in neighborhoods close to their jobs. In the United States, prejudicial attitudes had commonly existed against the Chinese, but in the post–Civil War period, they became even more the targets of bitter hatred and discrimination for economic and other reasons. Evicted from their jobs as a result of race-baiting union strikes and limited in their choice of residence by restrictive housing covenants, many had no choice but to live in insular Chinatowns within the larger cities. They entered businesses that did not compete with those of Whites (curio shops, laundries, restaurants, etc.) and followed their old-country tradition of settling disputes among themselves rather than appealing to government authorities for adjudication.

Deviance

When a group continually experiences rejection and discrimination, some of its members can't identify with the dominant society or accept its norms. People at the bottom of the socioeconomic ladder, particularly members of victimized racial and ethnic groups, may respond to the pressures of everyday life in ways they consider reasonable but that others view as **deviance**. This situation occurs in particular when laws serve to impose the moral standards of the dominant group on the behavior of other groups.

Many minority groups in the United States—Irish, Germans, Chinese, Italians, African Americans, Native Americans, and Hispanics—have at one time or another been arrested and punished in disproportionate numbers for so-called crimes of personal disorganization. Among the offenses to the dominant group's morality have been public drunkenness, drug abuse, gambling, and sexual "misconduct." It is unclear whether this disproportion reflects the frequency of misconduct or a pattern of selective arrests. Moreover, some types of conduct are deviant only from the perspective of the majority group, such as cockfighting or female genital mutilation, whereas other types, such as wife beating, may also be deviant within the minority community.

Part of the problem with law enforcement is its subjective nature and the discretionary handling of violations. Many people have criticized the U.S. criminal justice system for its failure to accord fair and equal treatment to the poor and to minority-group members as compared with people from the middle and upper classes.[2] Criticisms have included (1) the tendency of police to arrest suspects from minority groups at substantially higher rates than those from the majority group in situations where discretionary judgment is possible; (2) the overrepresentation of certain dominant social, ethnic, and racial groups on juries; (3) the difficulty the poor encounter in affording bail; (4) the poor quality of free legal defense; and (5) the disparities in sentencing for members of dominant and minority groups. Because social background constitutes one of the factors that the police and courts consider, individuals who belong to a racial or ethnic group with a negative stereotype find themselves at a severe disadvantage.

When a particular racial or ethnic group commits a noticeable number of deviant offenses, such as delinquency, crime, drunkenness, or some public-nuisance problem, the public often extends a negative image to all members of that group even if it applies to only a few. Some common associations, for example, are Italians and gangsters, Irish and heavy drinking and fighting, Chinese and opium, African Americans and street crimes such as mugging and purse snatching, Puerto Ricans and knife fighting. Even though a very small percentage of a group actually engages in such behavior, the entire group may become negatively stereotyped. A number of factors—including values, behavior patterns, and structural conditions in both the native and adopted lands—help explain the various kinds of so-called deviance among different minority groups. The appropriate means of stopping the deviance is itself subject to debate between proponents of corrective versus preventive measures.

Deviant behavior among minority groups occurs not because of race or ethnicity, as prejudiced people think, but usually because of poverty and lack of opportunity. Clifford Shaw and Henry McKay, in a classic study of juvenile delinquency in Chicago, suggested that structural conditions, not membership in a particular minority group, determine crime and delinquency rates.[3] They found that the highest rates of juvenile delinquency occurred in areas with poor housing, few job opportunities, and widespread prostitution, gambling, and drug use. The delinquency rate was consistently high over a 30-year period, even though five different ethnic groups moved in and out of those areas during that period. Nationality was unimportant; the unchanged conditions brought unchanged results. Other studies have demonstrated a correlation between higher rates of juvenile or adult crime and income level and place of residence.[4]

Because many minority groups are heavily represented among low-income populations, studies emphasizing social-class variables provide insight into the minority experience. The most common finding is that a lack of opportunities encourages delinquency among lower-class males.[5] Social aspirations may be similar in all levels of society, but opportunities are not. Belonging to a gang may give a youth a sense of power and help overcome feelings of inadequacy; hoodlumism becomes a conduit for expressing resentment against a society whose approved norms seem impossible to follow.[6] Notwithstanding the economic and environmental difficulties they face, the large majority of racial-group and ethnic-group members do not join gangs or engage in criminally deviant behavior. But because some minority groups are represented disproportionately in such activities, the public image of the group as a whole suffers.

Some social factors, particularly parental attitudes about education and social ascent, appear to be related to delinquency rates. Generally, parental emphasis on academic achievement and extensive involvement in their children's schooling leads to more educationally committed adolescents. The greater their commitment, the lower the rates of delinquency, and vice versa.[7]

Defiance

If a minority group is sufficiently cohesive and conscious of its growing economic or political power, its members may act openly to challenge and eliminate discriminatory practices—**defiance**. In defying discrimination, the minority group takes a strong stance regarding its position in the society. Prior to this time, certain individuals of that group may have pioneered the movement (e.g., by challenging laws in court).

Sometimes the defiance is violent and seems spontaneous, although it usually grows out of long-standing conditions. One example is the Irish draft riot in New York in 1863 during the Civil War. When its volunteer armies proved insufficient, the Union used a military draft to secure needed troops. In those days, well-to-do males of draft age could legally avoid conscription by buying the military services of a substitute. Meanwhile, because the Irish were mostly poor and concentrated in urban areas, many of them had no recourse when drafted. Their defiance at what they considered an unfair practice blossomed into a riot in which Blacks became the scapegoats, with lives lost and property destroyed or damaged. Similarly, the 1991 Washington, D.C., Hispanic riot after a Black female police officer shot a Salvadoran immigrant and the 1992 Los Angeles riot following the acquittal of police officers videotaped beating Rodney King may both have been spontaneous reactions, but only within the larger context of smoldering, deep-seated, long-standing resentments.

A militant action, such as the takeover of a symbolic site, is a moderately aggressive act of defiance. The late 1960s witnessed many building takeovers by African Americans and other disaffected, angry, alienated students on college campuses. In many instances, the purpose of the action was to call public attention to what the group considered society's indifference toward or discrimination against their people. Similar actions occurred in this period to protest the war in Vietnam. A small group of Native Americans took this approach in the 1970s to protest their living conditions; at different times, they seized Alcatraz Island in California, the Bureau of Indian Affairs in Washington, D.C., and the village of Wounded Knee in South Dakota. Media attention helped validate and spread the idea of using militant actions to promote a group's agenda.

Any peaceful action that challenges the status quo, though less aggressive, is defiant nonetheless; parades, marches, picket lines, mass meetings,

Gang membership has existed among minority youths at least since the time of massive Irish immigration. Some actions may be new, such as using hand signals to identify their gang, but motives for joining remain similar. Peer pressure, a sense of identity and importance, and rebelliousness offset society's rebuke of their deviant behavior.

boycotts, and demonstrations are examples. Another form of peaceful protest consists of civil disobedience: deliberately breaking discriminatory laws and then challenging their constitutionality, or breaking a discriminatory tradition. The civil-rights actions of the 1960s—sit-ins, lie-ins, and freedom rides—challenged decades-old Jim Crow laws that restricted access by Blacks to public establishments in the South. Shop-ins at stores that catered to an exclusively White clientele represented deliberate efforts to break traditional store practices.

Acceptance

Many minority people, to the frequent consternation of their leaders and sympathizers, accept the situation in which they find themselves. Some do so stoically, justifying their decision by subtle rationalizations. Others are resentful but accept the situation for reasons of personal security or economic necessity. Still others accept it through false consciousness, a consequence of the dominant group's control over sources of information. Although **acceptance** maintains the superior position in society of the dominant group and the subordinate position of the minority group, it does diminish the open tensions and conflicts between the two groups.

In some instances, conforming to prevailing patterns of interaction between dominant and minority groups occurs subconsciously, as the end result of social conditioning. Just as socialization can inculcate prejudice, so too it can cause minority-group members to disregard or be unaware of alternative status possibilities. How much acceptance of lower status takes this form and how much is characterized by resentful submission and mental rejection have not been completely settled.

African Americans, Mexican Americans, and Native Americans have experienced a subordinate position in the United States for multiple generations. Until the 1960s, a combination of structural discrimination, racial stratification, powerlessness, and a sense of the futility of trying to change things caused many to acquiesce in the situation imposed on them. Similarly, Japanese Americans had little choice when, following the bombing of Pearl Harbor and the subsequent rise in anti-Japanese sentiment, the U.S. government in 1942 dispossessed and imprisoned 110,000 of them in "temporary relocation centers."[8]

Acceptance as a minority response is less common in the United States than it once was. More aware of the alternative ways of living presented in the media, today's minorities are more hopeful about sharing in them. No longer do they passively accept the status quo, which denies them the comfortable life and leisure pursuits others enjoy. Simultaneously, through court decisions, legislation, new social services, and other efforts, society has created a more favorable climate for improving the status of minority groups. Televised news features and behavioral-science courses may have heightened the public's social awareness as well.

Consequences of Minority-Group Status

Minority groups that experience sustained inequality face four possible outcomes: negative self-image, a vicious circle of continued discrimination, marginality, and status as middleman minorities.

Negative Self-Image

The apathy that militant leaders find among their own people may result from a **negative self-image**, a common consequence of prejudice and discrimination. Continual treatment as an inferior encourages a loss of self-confidence. If everything about a person's position and experiences—jobs with low pay, substandard housing, the hostility of others, and the need for assistance from government agencies—works to destroy pride and hope, the person may become apathetic. To remain optimistic and determined in the face of constant negative experiences from all directions is extremely difficult.

Kurt Lewin once observed that minority-group members had a fairly general tendency to develop a negative self-image.[9] The pervasiveness of dominant-group values and attitudes, which include negative stereotypes of the minority group, may cause the minority-group member to absorb them. A person's self-image includes race, religion, and nationality; thus, individuals may feel embarrassed and inferior if they see that one or more of the attributes they possess are despised within the society. In effect, minority-group members begin to perceive themselves as negatively as the dominant group originally did.

Negative self-image, or self-hatred, manifests itself in many ways. People may try to "pass" as members of the dominant group and deny membership in a disparaged group. They may adopt the dominant group's prejudices and accept their devalued status. They may engage in ego defense by blaming others within the group for the low esteem in which society holds them:

> Some Jews refer to other Jews as "kikes"—blaming them exclusively for the anti-Semitism from which all alike suffer. Class distinctions within groups are often a result of trying to free oneself from responsibility for the handicap from which the group as a whole suffers. "Lace curtain" Irish look down on "shanty" Irish. Wealthy Spanish and Portuguese Jews have long regarded themselves as the top of the pyramid of Hebraic peoples. But Jews of German origin, having a rich culture, view themselves as the aristocrats, often looking down on Austrian, Hungarian, and Balkan Jews, and regarding Polish and Russian Jews at the very bottom.[10]

Negative self-image, then, can cause people to accept their fate passively. It also can encourage personal shame for possessing undesired qualities or antipathy toward other members of the group for possessing them. Minority-group members may attempt to overcome their negative self-image by changing their name or religion, having cosmetic surgery, or moving to a locale where the stereotype is less prevalent.

But Lewin's view that negative self-image is a fairly general tendency among minority-group members may be too broad. For example, members of tightly cohesive religious groups may draw emotional support from their faith and from one another. The insulation of living in an ethnic community, strong ingroup loyalty, or a determination to maintain a cultural heritage may prevent minority-group members from developing a negative self-image.

Recent experiments have shown that people who are stigmatized can protect their self-esteem by attributing the negative feedback they receive to prejudice. In a study analyzing minority children's attitudes toward their own group, Frances E. Aboud suggested group visibility as a possible link to positive self-image. In another analysis, Margaret Beale Spencer argued that, since parents are the first source of a child's "sense of self," their instilling racial pride contributes to resilience and may lead to coping strategies against prejudice that have positive consequences.[11]

The Vicious Circle

Sometimes the relationship between prejudice and discrimination is circular. Gunnar Myrdal refers to this pattern as **cumulative causation**—a **vicious circle** in which prejudice and discrimination perpetuate each other.[12] The dynamics of the relations between dominant and minority groups set in motion a cyclical sequence of reciprocal stimuli and responses. For example, a discriminatory action in filling jobs leads to a minority reaction, poverty, which in turn reinforces the dominant-group attitude that the minority group is inferior, leading to more discrimination and so on.

Myrdal points out that the pattern of expectation and reaction may produce desirable or undesirable results. The expectations held about the newcomers determine the pattern that develops.[13] If the dominant group makes the newcomers welcome, they in turn are likely to react in a positive manner, which reinforces their friendly reception. If the new group is ignored or made to feel unwelcome, the members may react negatively, which again reaffirms original attitudes and actions. As Allport says, "If we foresee evil in our fellow man, we tend to provoke it; if good, we elicit it."[14] In other words, negative expectations engender negative reactions, broadening the social distance between the groups and causing the vicious circle to continue.

When Jews were denied access to many U.S. vacation resorts during the nineteenth century, their reactions served to reinforce their negative stereotype in the minds of some, reinforcing their discriminatory behavior. Some Jews demanded equal access, which the resort operators took as proof that Jews were "pushy." When Jews responded to this discriminatory policy by establishing and patronizing their own resorts in the Catskill Mountains of New York, the majority group labeled them "clannish." Similarly, the Irish encountered severe job discrimination in the mid-nineteenth century; the resulting poverty forced many of them to live in urban slums, where they often had trouble with the law. Given this evidence of their "inferiority" and "undesirability," majority-group employers curtailed their job opportunities further. In the same way, discrimination by Whites against Blacks, based partly on the low standard of living endured by many of the latter, exacerbates the problems of poverty, fueling even more the antipathy of some Whites toward Blacks.

Marginality

Minority-group members sometimes find themselves caught in a conflict between their own identity and values and the necessity to behave in a certain way to gain acceptance by the dominant group. This situation—**marginality**—usually arises when a member of a minority group is passing through a transitional period. In attempting to enter the mainstream of society, the marginal person internalizes the dominant group's cultural patterns without having gained full acceptance. Such individuals occupy an ill-defined position, no longer at ease within their own group but not yet fully a part of the *reference group*, the one by whose standards they evaluate themselves and their behavior.

Over the years, sociologists have differed in their interpretation of the effects of marginality. Robert E. Park, who gave this social phenomenon its name, believed that it caused the individual a great deal of strain and difficulty. A marginal person, he observed, is one "whom fate has condemned to live in two societies and in two not merely different but antagonistic cultures."[15]

According to Park, this situation can cause the marginal person, whether an adult or a child, to suffer anxiety over a conflict of values and loyalties. Adults leave the security of their cultural group and thereby risk being labeled renegades by their own people. They seek sustained social contacts with members of the dominant group, which may view them as outsiders. No longer comfortable with the old ways but nonetheless influenced by them and identified with them, marginal adults often experience feelings of frustration, hypersensitivity, and self-consciousness.

Children of immigrants likewise find themselves caught between two worlds. At home, their parents attempt to raise them in their social heritage, according to the established ways of the old country. Meanwhile, through school and other outside experiences, the children are exposed to the U.S. culture and want to be like other children in the society. Moreover, they quickly learn that the dominant group views their parents' ways as inferior and that they too are socially rejected because of their background. Consequently, many young people in transition develop emotional problems and are embarrassed to bring classmates home.

According to this view, marginality is an example of cultural conflict caused primarily by the clash of values within the individual. Many sociologists now believe, however, that the reaction to marginal status depends largely on whether the individual receives reassurances of self-worth from the surrounding community. Thus, successfully defining the situation and adjusting to it are contingent on the individual's sense of security within the community.[16] Supportive ethnic subcommunities and institutions and a sense of solidarity among members of the ethnic group contribute to that sense of well-being. These observations have led some sociologists to emphasize that the transitional phase involves stable individuals in a marginal culture rather than marginal persons in a dominant culture. Individuals in a marginal culture share their cultural duality with many others in primary-group relationships, in institutional activities, and in interacting with members of the dominant society without encountering any dichotomy between their desires and actuality.[17]

Whether this phase of the assimilation process represents an emotionally stressful experience or a comfortably protected one, minority-group members nonetheless pass through a transitional period during which they are not fully a part of either world. An immigrant group may move into the mainstream of U.S. society within the lifetimes of the first-generation members, it may choose not to do so, or it may not be permitted to. Usually, marginality is a one- or two-generation phenomenon. After that, members of the minority group either have assimilated or have formed a distinctive subculture. Whichever route they take, they are no longer caught between two cultural worlds.

Middleman Minorities

Building on theories of marginality, Hubert Blalock suggested the model of **middleman minorities**.[18] This model, based on a dominant–subordinate stratification system, places middleman minorities in an intermediate rather than a low-status position.[19] Feudal and colonial societies, with their ruling elite and large peasant masses, often rely on middleman minorities to forge mediating commerce links between the two. Consequently, such minorities commonly are trading peoples whose history of persecution (Jews, Greeks, and Armenians) or sojourner orientation (Chinese, Japanese, and Koreans)

Once German, Irish, Italian, and Jewish merchants and small businesses served as middleman minorities to other ethnic groups. Today some Africans, Asians, and Hispanics repeat the pattern, such as in this Black neighborhood pizzeria where a Hispanic cook sells slices and whole pies, along with other foods and drinks.

have obliged them to perform risky or marginal tasks that permitted easy liquidation of their assets when necessary.[20]

Middleman groups often serve as buffers and hence experience hostility and conflict from above and below. Jews in Nazi Germany and Asians in Uganda in the early 1970s, for instance, became scapegoats for the economic turmoil in those societies. Their susceptibility to such antagonism and their nonassimilation into the host society promote high ingroup solidarity.

Systematic discrimination can prolong the duration of a group's middleman-minority status, as in the case of European Jews throughout the medieval period. Sometimes the entrepreneurial skills developed in trade and commerce provide middleman minorities with adaptive capabilities and competitive advantages, enabling them to achieve upward mobility and to assimilate more easily; this occurred for Jewish immigrants to the United States and may similarly occur for Korean Americans. In other cases, a group may emerge as a middleman minority because of changing residential patterns. One example is Jewish store owners in city neighborhoods where they once served their own people; when their original neighbors moved away and they found themselves unable to follow them, these urban merchants served new urban minority groups who were situated lower on the socioeconomic ladder.

Dominant-Group Responses

Members of a dominant group may react to minority peoples with hostility, indifference, welcoming tolerance, or condescension. The more favorable responses usually occur when the minority is numerically small, not perceived as a threat, or both. As the minority group's population increases, threatening the natives' monopoly on jobs and other claims to privileged cultural resources, the dominant group's attitude is likely to become suspicious or fearful. If the fear becomes great enough, the dominant group may take action against the minority group.

Dominant groups often use religion in varying aggressive ways against minority groups. Besides religious persecution (a push factor in many migrations throughout world history), they often use missionaries to convert minorities. Dominant groups do not necessarily conduct these sometimes forced conversions with the intent of assimilating a minority group. For example, teaching Christianity to slaves enabled Southern Whites to create a false consciousness among the Africans in accepting their fate but working hard to please their masters. In the case of Native Americans, the federal government gave reservation land to several Protestant religions in an effort to convert the "heathens" and remake them in the White man's image, while maintaining their isolated, segregated confinement.

Legislative Controls

If the influx of racial and ethnic groups appears to the dominant group to be too great for a country to absorb, or if prejudicial fears prevail, the nation may enact measures to regulate and restrict their entry. Australia, Canada, and the United States—the three greatest receiving countries in international migration—once had discriminatory immigration laws that either excluded or curtailed the number of immigrants from countries other than those of northern and western Europe. Through similar patterns of policy change, Canada (in 1962), the United States (in 1965), and Australia (in 1973) began to permit entry from all parts of the world.

To maintain a paternalistic social system, the dominant group frequently restricts the subordinate group's educational and voting opportunities. This denial assures the dominant group of maintaining its system of control, whether over internal minorities, such as Blacks in the Old South and various ethnic minorities in the former Soviet Union, or over colonized peoples, such as those ruled by the Belgians, British, Dutch, French, Japanese, and Portuguese. Most colonial powers have committed themselves to stability, trade, and tapping the natural resources of a country rather than to developing its infrastructure and preparing it for self-governance. As a result, the usual experience of native populations under colonial rule has been largely ceremonial leadership from figureheads, who lack real power in important matters, installed and approved by the colonial authority; limited educational opportunities; and restricted political participation. Other means of denying political power have included disenfranchising voters through high property qualifications (British West Indies), high income qualifications (Trinidad), and poll taxes (United States), although none of these practices exist today in these areas. The most conspicuous recent example of rigid social control was in South Africa, where a legislated apartheid society denied Blacks not only equal education and the ballot but also almost every other privilege.

Segregation

Through a policy of containment—avoiding social interaction with members of a minority group as much as possible and keeping them "in their place"—the dominant group can effectively create both spatial and social segregation.

Spatial segregation is the physical separation of a minority people from the rest of society. This most commonly occurs in residential patterns, but it also takes place in education, in the use of public facilities, and in occupations. The majority group may institutionalize this form of segregation by law (de jure segregation) or establish it informally through pervasive practice (de facto segregation).

Spatial segregation of minorities has a long history. Since the days of the preindustrial city, with its heterogeneous populations, the dominant group has relegated racial and ethnic minorities to special sections of the city, often the least desirable areas.[21] In Europe, this medieval ecological pattern resulted in minority groups being situated on the city outskirts nearest the encircling wall. Because this pattern remains in much of Europe today, Europeans, unlike people in the United States, consider it a sign of high prestige to live near the center of the city.[22]

The dominant group may use covert or overt means to achieve spatial segregation of a minority group. Examples of covert actions include restrictive covenants, "gentlemen's agreements," and collusion between the community and real estate agents to steer "undesirable" minorities into certain neighborhoods.[23] Overt actions include restrictive zoning, segregation laws, and intimidation. Both covert and overt methods of segregation have been found unlawful by U.S. courts since the mid-1970s.

An important dimension of spatial segregation is that the dominant group can achieve it through avoidance or residential mobility. Usually referred to as the invasion-succession ecological pattern, this common process has involved different religions and nationalities as well as different races. The most widely recognized example in the United States is previously all-White neighborhoods becoming Black, but any study of old urban neighborhoods would reveal the same pattern as successive waves of immigrants came here over the years. Residents of a neighborhood may resist the influx of a minority group but eventually abandon the area when their efforts are not successful. This pattern results in neighborhoods with a concentration of a new racial or ethnic group—a new segregated area.

Social segregation involves confining participation in social, service, political, and other types of activities to members of the ingroup. The dominant group excludes the outgroup from any involvement in meaningful primary-group activities and in secondary-group activities. Organizations use screening procedures to keep out unwanted types, and informal groups act to preserve their composition.

Segregation, whether spatial or social, may be voluntary or involuntary. Minority-group members may choose to live by themselves rather than among the dominant group; this is an avoidance response, discussed previously. On the other hand, minority-group members may have no choice about where they live because of economic or residential discrimination.

Whether by choice or against their will, minority groups form ethnic subcommunities, whose existence in turn promotes and maintains the social distance between them and the rest of society. Not only do minority-group members physically congregate in one area and thus find themselves spatially segregated, but they do not engage in much social interaction with others outside their own group.

Under the right conditions, frequent interaction reduces prejudice, but when interaction is severely limited, the acculturation process slows considerably. Meanwhile, values regarding what is normal or different are reinforced, paving the way for stereotyping, social comparisons, and prestige ranking.

Expulsion

When other methods of dealing with a minority group fail—and sometimes not even as a last resort—an intolerant dominant group may persecute the minority group or eject it from the territory where it resides—**expulsion**. Henry VIII banished the Gypsies from England in the sixteenth century, Spanish rulers drove out the Moors in the early seventeenth century, and the British expelled the French Acadians from Nova Scotia in the mid-eighteenth century. More recent examples include Idi Amin, who decreed in 1972 that all Asians must leave Uganda, Muammar Ghadafi, who expelled Libya's ethnic Italian community in 1970, and Serbs, who forced ethnic Albanians out of Kosovo in 1999.

The United States also has its examples of mass expulsion. In colonial times, the Puritans forced Roger Williams and his followers out of Massachusetts for their nonconformity; the group then settled in what became Rhode Island. The forcible removal of the Cherokee from fertile Georgia land and the subsequent "Trail of Tears," during which 4,000 perished along the 1,000-mile forced march to Oklahoma Territory, is another illustration.

Mass expulsion is an effort to drive out a group that is seen as a social problem rather than attempting to resolve the problem cooperatively. This policy often arises after other methods, such as assimilation or extermination, have failed. Whether a dominant group chooses to remove a minority group by extermination or by expulsion depends in part on how sensitive the country is to world opinion, which in turn may be related to the country's economic dependence on other nations.

Xenophobia

If the dominant group's suspicions and fears of the minority group become serious enough, they may produce volatile, irrational feelings and actions. This overreaction is known as **xenophobia**—the undue fear of or contempt for strangers or foreigners. This almost hysterical response—reflected in print, speeches, sermons, legislation, and violent actions—begins with ethnocentric views. Ethnocentrism encourages the creation of negative stereotypes, which in turn invites prejudice and discrimination and can escalate through some catalyst into a highly emotional reaction (see the accompanying International Scene box).

Many examples of xenophobia exist in U.S. history. In 1798, the Federalists, fearful of "wild Irishmen" and "French radicals" and anxious to eliminate what they saw as a foreign threat to the country's stability, passed the Alien and Sedition Acts. When a bomb exploded at an anarchist gathering at

The International Scene
Segregation and Defiance in France

In late 2005, several months of riots and violent clashes broke out in Paris and spread to other French cities, eventually engulfing all fifteen of the country's largest urban areas. By the time the riots ended, the counts were one dead, about 2,900 arrested, and thousands of vehicles and numerous public buildings burned, including a Roman Catholic Church.

The spiraling events began with the accidental electrocution of two teenagers—one the son of West African immigrants and the other the son of Tunisian immigrants—who ran from police (conducting one of their frequent ID checks of minorities) and hid in a power substation. A third teenager, the son of Turkish Kurdish immigrants, was injured and hospitalized. The three victims thus represented the primary minority groups in France—Arab, Black, and Muslim—and became the catalyst to ignite the pre-existing tensions.

For decades, French government policy had concentrated immigrants and their families in well-defined districts of poorly maintained public housing projects on the edges of cities. Isolated from the city center, these de facto ethnic ghettos have little activity at night or on Sunday, and there is limited public transportation to the center. In addition, much higher unemployment for the foreign-born compared to the native-born—even worse among college graduates—contributed extensively to the mounting frustration and desperation.

Amid charges of job discrimination and police harassment, the common use by the media and general population of the expression "second generation of immigrants," even for those born in France, suggested a cultural mindset that differentiated who was "really" French. (At age 18, immigrant children born in France may go through a bureaucratic application process to be citizens; their birth there does not automatically bestow citizenship on them as in the United States.)

Experts cite the racial and social discrimination against persons with dark skin or Arabic- and/or African-sounding names as a major cause of unhappiness in the riot-torn areas. Although such discrimination is illegal, children of immigrants claim that they frequently encounter economic segregation, problems getting a job or renting a flat, or even getting into a nightclub, just because of their name or the color of their skin.

Critical thinking questions: How similar or dissimilar are the experiences of U.S. minorities today? Does the difference in French and U.S. citizenship laws have any impact on the acceptance and integration of minorities into society? How so?

Chicago's Haymarket Square in 1886, many Americans thereafter linked foreigners with radicals. The Bolshevik Revolution in 1917 led to the Palmer raids, in which foreign-born U.S. residents were illegally rounded up and incarcerated for their alleged Communist Party affiliation; some were even deported. In 1942, 110,000 Japanese Americans, many of them second- and third-generation U.S. citizens, were interned in concentration camps as a result of irrational suspicions that they would prove less loyal during the ongoing World War II than German Americans and Italian Americans. The U.S. English movement's current efforts to pass English-only laws reflect a xenophobic fear that foreigners won't learn English.

Annihilation

The Nazi extermination of more than 6 million Jews brought the term *genocide* into the English language, but the practice of **annihilation**—killing all the men, women, and children of a particular group—goes back to ancient times. In warfare among the ancient Assyrians, Babylonians, Egyptians, Hebrews, and others, the usual practice was for the victor to slay all the enemy, partly to prevent their children from seeking revenge. For example, preserved in Deuteronomy are these words of Moses:

> . . . when Sehon offered battle at Jasa, coming out to meet us with all his forces. . . . We made an end of him and of his sons and of all his people, took all his cities there and then, putting all that dwelt there, men, women, and children, to the sword, and spared nothing except the beasts we drove off for our use, and such plunder as captured cities yield.
>
> . . . Og, that was king of Basan, came out to meet us with all his forces, and offered battle at Edrai. . . . So the Lord our God gave us a fresh victory over Og, king of Basan, and all his people, and we exterminated them, there and then laying waste all his cities. . . . We made an end of them as we had made an end of Sehon, that reigned in Hesebon, destroying all the inhabitants of their cities, men, women, and children, plundering their cattle and all the plunder their cities yielded.[24]

In modern times, various countries have used extermination as a means of solving a so-called race problem. Arnold Toynbee once said that the "English method of settlement" followed this pattern.[25] The British, through extermination and close confinement of survivors, annihilated the entire aboriginal population of Tasmania between 1803 and 1876.[26] The Dutch considered South African San (Bushmen) to be less than human and attempted to obliterate them.[27] When native peoples of Brazil resisted Portuguese settlement of their lands, the Whites solved the problem by systematically killing them. One favored means of doing so was to place the clothing of recent smallpox victims in their villages and allow the contagion to destroy the native population.[28] In the 1890s and again in 1915, the Turkish government systematically massacred hundreds of thousands of Armenians, events still solemnly remembered each year by Armenian Americans. One of the largest genocides in U.S. history occurred at Wounded Knee in 1890, when the U.S. Seventh Cavalry killed about 200 Native American men, women, and children. In the past 50 years, campaigns of genocide have occurred around the globe in such countries as Sudan, Burundi, Rwanda, Nigeria, Cambodia, Indonesia, Iraq, Bangladesh, Bosnia, and Kosovo.

Lynchings are not a form of annihilation because the intent is not to exterminate an entire group but to set an example through selective, drastic punishment. Nonetheless, the victims usually are minority-group members. Although lynchings have occurred in the United States throughout its history, only since 1882 have reasonably reliable statistics on their frequency been kept (Figure 6.1). Sources such as the *Chicago Tribune* and the Tuskegee Institute, which have kept data on this subject, reveal that at least 5,000 lynchings have occurred since 1882. They have taken place in every state except the New England states, with the Deep South (including Texas) claiming the most victims. In fact, 90 percent of all lynchings during this period have occurred in the southern states; Blacks have accounted for 80 percent of the victims. The statistics do not, however, cover lynchings during the nation's first 100 years, including those in the western frontier, when many Native Americans and Hispanics also met this fate.[29]

Annihilation sometimes occurs unintentionally, as when Whites inadvertently spread Old World sicknesses to Native Americans in the United States and Canada, to Inuit (Eskimos), and to Polynesians. Having no prior exposure to such ailments as measles, mumps, chicken pox, and smallpox, the native populations had little physiological resistance to them, and thus

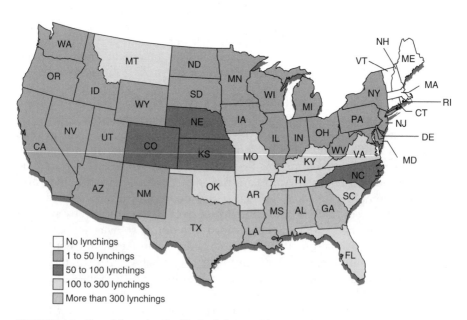

FIGURE 6.1   **Lynchings in the United States Since 1882**

succumbed to these contagious diseases in unusually high numbers. Other forms of annihilation, usually intentional, occur during times of mob violence, overzealous police actions, and the calculated actions of small private groups.[30]

Hate Groups

Like most nations, the United States has had its share of hate groups and hate crimes. Most prominent among hate groups of the past were the Know-Nothings of the mid-nineteenth century and the Ku Klux Klan in the late nineteenth and early twentieth centuries. In fact, bias crimes against Europeans, Native Americans, Asians, and numerous religious groups occurred frequently in the nineteenth and twentieth centuries. Deplorably, this ugly pattern remains a brutal force in U.S. society in the twenty-first century.

The Intelligence Project of the Southern Poverty Law Center—the nation's pre-eminent monitor and analyst of American extremism—reported that the number of hate groups operating in the United States increased by 33 percent between 2000 and 2005 to reach a total of 803 active groups (Figure 6.2).[31] The Center reported that a number of factors spurred this growth. These include an increased Internet presence—524 hate sites in 2005, up 12 percent from 468 in 2004—and the racist music scene, largely dominated by

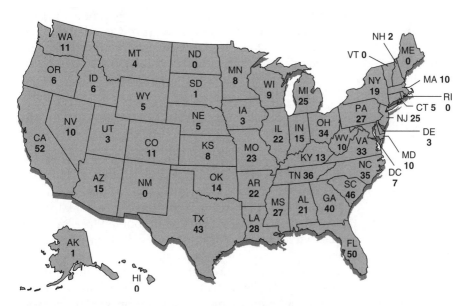

FIGURE 6.2   Hate Groups in the United States: 2005

Source: Southern Poverty Law Center Intelligence Project.

Skinhead groups. Racist music and concerts continue to attract new young people into the movement, no doubt aided by such campaigns as "Operation Schoolyard" in 2004–2005, during which 100,000 free racist music CDs were distributed to schoolchildren.

Also aiding hate group recruitment has been their aggressive tactics resulting in extensive media coverage, such as repeated attempts to march through Black, inner-city neighborhoods and their picketing the funerals of soldiers, saying God was punishing America for tolerating homosexuality. Hispanic immigration, however, was the primary reason for the continuing rise, giving these groups an issue that connects with many of those opposed to the changing demographics. Still another factor is the war in Iraq, erroneously seen by many hate groups as a struggle the United States was forced into by Jews.

Ku Klux Klan groups comprise 179 of the 803 hate groups in 2005, with neo-Nazi groups accounting for another 157, followed by 106 Black separatist groups, most of whom are anti-White and anti-Semitic. Totaling 99, some neo-Confederate groups—most particularly the League of the South—have a racist agenda, saying that minorities are destroying the "Anglo-Celtic" (White) culture of the South. Christian Identity groups—which depict Jews as satanic—total 35. A hodge-podge of other groups—notably the Council of Conservative Citizens, a reincarnation of the White Citizens Councils that sprung up in the 1950s and 1960s to oppose school desegregation—complete the list with 171 groups.

California contained the largest number of active hate groups (52), followed by Florida (50), South Carolina (46), Texas (43), Georgia (40), Tennessee (36), North Carolina (35), Ohio (34), Louisiana (28), Pennsylvania (27), and New Jersey (25). One or more hate groups existed in 44 states; the exceptions were Hawaii, Maine, New Mexico, North Dakota, Rhode Island, and Vermont.

Hate Crimes

Reported hate crimes—only some of which are committed by members of organized hate groups—numbered 8,376 in 2005 and claimed 8,804 victims. Racial bias motivated 55 percent of the incidents, religious bias another 17 percent, sexual-orientation bias 14 percent, and ethnicity/national origin bias 13 percent (Table 6.1). Crimes against persons accounted for 62 percent of hate crime offenses, while damage/destruction/vandalism of property constituted 37 percent.[32]

To combat hate crimes—commonly defined as any criminal offense against a person or property that is motivated in whole or part by the offender's bias against a race, religion, ethnic/national origin, group, or sexual orientation—many states have passed laws mandating severe punishments for persons convicted of such crimes. Federal law (18 U.S.C. 245) also permits federal prosecution of a hate crime as a civil-rights violation if the as-

TABLE 6.1   Bias Motivation of Hate Crime Incidents in 2005

	Percentage of Category	Percentage of Total
Race		54.7
Anti-Black	68.2	
Anti-White	19.9	
Anti-Asian/Pacific Islander	4.9	
Anti-multiracial group	4.9	
Anti-Native American	2.0	
Religion		17.1
Anti-Jewish	68.5	
Anti-Islamic	11.1	
Anti-Protestant	4.4	
Anti-Catholic	4.6	
Anti-multireligious group	3.2	
Other	7.8	
Ethnicity/National Origin		13.2
Anti-Hispanic	57.7	
Other	42.3	
Sexual Orientation		14.2
Anti-male homosexual	60.9	
Anti-female homosexual	15.4	
Anti-homosexual	19.5	
Anti-heterosexual	2.0	
Anti-bisexual	2.3	

Source: Federal Bureau of Investigation, "Hate Crimes," *Crime in the United States 2005*, adapted from Table 1. Accessed online at www.gov/ucr/hc2005/incidentsoffenses.htm.

sailant intended to prevent the victim from exercising a "federally protected right" such as voting or attending school.

Exploitation

Countless writings have documented instances of the **exploitation** of minority groups in various countries. Sometimes the perpetrators of this abuse are members of the same group—the operators of Asian sweatshops in U.S. cities, for instance, and the *padroni* of old Italian immigrant communities, both of whom often benefited at the expense of their own people. Most often, however, members of dominant groups exploit minority groups.

Middle-range conflict theories are often helpful in understanding specific forms of exploitation, such as the internal-colonialism theory discussed in Chapter 3. Another analytical explanation comes to us from

Edna Bonacich, who suggests a **split-labor-market theory** as a means of understanding the ethnic antagonism arising from economic exploitation.

To understand how a split labor market works, we must first understand its structural context. Racial or ethnic differences do not in themselves create labor price differentials, as these arise out of the resource conditions of both groups. As Bonacich says:

> With the possible exception of sojourners, cheaper labor does not intentionally undermine more expensive labor; it is paradoxically its weakness that makes it so threatening, for business can more thoroughly control it.[33]

Bonacich theorizes that ethnic antagonism results from a combination of economic exploitation by employers and economic competition between two or more groups of laborers that produce a wage differential for labor. She contends that much ethnic antagonism is based not on ethnicity and race but on the conflict between higher-paid and lower-paid labor—the split-labor-market theory:

> Ethnic antagonism is specifically produced by the competition that arises from a price differential. An oversupply of equal-priced labor does not produce such antagonism, though it too threatens people with the loss of their job. However, hiring practices will not necessarily fall along ethnic lines. ...All workingmen are on the same footing, competing for scarce jobs. When one ethnic group is decidedly cheaper than another (i.e., when the labor market is split), the higher paid worker faces more than the loss of his job; he faces the possibility that the wage standard in all jobs will be undermined by cheaper labor.[34]

The lower-paid group—its wages nonetheless higher than its members can find elsewhere—threatens the higher-paid labor group with possible displacement with such wage undercutting. In turn, higher-paid labor may respond, says Bonacich, in one of three ways.

First, if the higher-paid labor group is strong enough, it may be able to block the cheaper competition through exclusion. To some degree, the United States's restriction of Chinese and Japanese immigrant labor and Australia's restriction of Asian and Polynesian immigrants represented victories for organized labor against lower-paid competition.

Second, it may create a caste system of occupational segregation. In a caste system, higher-paid labor controls certain high-paying jobs exclusively and limits the minority group to other lower-paying jobs (often lacking health benefits and pension plans). This creates an aristocracy of labor and submerges the labor-market split by stratifying the differentially priced workers. This phenomenon can be seen in the job differentials between Blacks and Whites—and between men and women in certain trade unions.

A third response is radicalism, where the workers form a multi-ethnic coalition against the employers. Here the action may include mass demonstrations and protests, sometimes provoked into violent outbreaks by counter-demonstrations, employer race-baiting, or police activity.

Among the factors that lower the price of one group's labor are exploitation by management, unfamiliarity with wage standards, limiting language skills and customs, and lack of economic resources. All of these factors force them into low-paying jobs, into making contractual commitments before emigrating, or into seeking political support from a labor organization or government:

> Governments vary in the degree to which they protect their emigrants. Japan kept close watch over the fate of her nationals who migrated to Hawaii and the Pacific coast. . . . In contrast Mexican migrant workers to the United States have received little protection from their government, and African states were unable to intervene on behalf of slaves brought to America.[35]

When a labor market splits along ethnic lines, racial and ethnic stereotyping becomes a key factor in the labor conflict, and prejudice, ethnic antagonism, and racism become overt. The conflict may not be due to religious differences or even depend on which group was first to move into the

Today, sweatshops remain a form of economic exploitation just as they did three generations ago. The labor union movement of the early twentieth century ended this practice for European immigrants, but now Asian and Hispanic newcomers—many undocumented aliens—work long hours for low pay without any advocates for them.

area because examples of ethnic antagonism can be found in which these variables were controlled. Bonacich argues that the one characteristic shared by all societies where ethnic antagonism is acute is an indigenous working class that earns higher wages than do immigrant workers.

This common characteristic fuels anti-immigration sentiments, intensified even more these days by the concern over the millions of undocumented immigrants in the country. The generations-old complaint that "they're taking jobs away from Americans" has at its core the fear of higher-priced American labor displaced by cheaper immigrant labor.

Employers are seldom passive observers of this clash between higher-priced and cheaper labor along racial and ethnic lines. As suggested earlier, it is they who control the lower wages offered to the minority workers. Moreover, employers will often actively manipulate the situation to keep the groups divided. For example, they could practice *majority paternalism* (promoting a racial hierarchy to cultivate majority group loyalty) or *minority paternalism* (cultivating minority group loyalty through jobs, home loans, or funds for community projects to encourage company unionism). A more militant approach would be a divide-and-rule strategy either by hiring minorities as strikebreakers or by encouraging state intervention to demobilize a possible coalition of workers.[36]

Also, employers can more easily persuade a group to work for a lower price if its initial standard of living—either in the United States or in the homeland left behind—is low, than it could tempt another group coming from a more favorable economic resource position. In addition, a group's political resources may affect the price of labor, by using the law to criminalize labor protests and thus prevent a threat to its control over wages.[37]

Retrospect

Ethnic- and racial-group identity is a normal pattern in ingroup–outgroup relationships. It can have positive and negative results depending on the social context in which it exists. A group identity based on immigrant status is normally of shorter duration than one based on religion or race. Minorities typically experience a dual identity, one in the larger society and another within their own group.

Minority-group responses to prejudice and discrimination include avoidance, deviance, defiance, and acceptance depending in large measure on the group's perception of its power to change the status quo. After prolonged treatment as an inferior, a person may develop a negative self-image. Continued inequality intensifies through a vicious circle or cumulative causation.

Marginality is a social phenomenon that occurs during the transitional period of assimilation; it may be either a stressful or a sheltered experience depending on the support system of the ethnic community. Some groups become middleman minorities because of their historical background or sojourner orientation; they may remain indefinitely in that intermediate place in the social hierarchy, a potential scapegoat for those above and below them, or they may achieve upward mobility and assimilation.

Dominant-group actions toward the minority group may take various forms, including favorable, indifferent, or hostile responses. When the reaction is negative, the group in power may place restraints on the minority group (e.g., legislative controls and segregation). If the reaction becomes more emotional or even xenophobic, expulsion or annihilation may occur. Sensitivity to world opinion and economic dependence on other nations may restrain such actions. Another dominant response is exploitation as illustrated by the internal-colonialism theory, discussed in Chapter 3, or by the split-labor-market theory, in which differential wage levels can spark ethnic antagonism.

KEY TERMS

Acceptance
Annihilation
Avoidance
Cumulative causation
Defiance
Deviance
Exploitation
Expulsion

Marginality
Middleman minorities
Negative self-image
Social segregation
Spatial segregation
Split-labor-market theory
Vicious circle
Xenophobia

REVIEW QUESTIONS

1. What are some common minority-group responses to prejudice and discrimination?

2. What are some common majority-group responses to minorities?

3. What is marginality? Why may it be a stressful experience in some cases but not in others?

4. What are middleman minorities? How do they affect acceptance?

5. Discuss the split-labor-market theory in regard to the exploitation of minorities.

SUGGESTED READINGS

Bender, Daniel E., and Richard A. Greenwald (eds.). *Sweatshop U.S.A.: The American Sweatshop in Historical and Global Perspective*. New York: Routledge, 2003.

An examination of the exploitation of minorities in U.S. sweatshops, their role in global migration and economics, and efforts to control and eradicate them.

Gourevitch, Philip. *We Wish to Inform You That Tomorrow We Will Be Killed with Our Families.* New York: Farrar Straus Giroux, 1999.

A journalist's dramatic narrative of the 1994 Hutu massacre of 800,000 Tutsi within 100 days in Rwanda—its history, aftermath, and the temptation for revenge in the refugee camps.

Knobel, Dale T. *"America for the Americans": The Nativist Movement in the United States.* Boston: Twayne, 1996.

A detailed account of the xenophobic spirit in the United States and the nativist fear that the newcomers threaten U.S. culture.

Levin, Jack, and Jack McDevitt. *Hate Crimes Revisited: America's War on Those Who Are Different.* Boulder, Colo: Westview Press, 2002.

Analysis of how seemingly random hate crimes share certain characteristics and are encouraged by stereotypes, a "culture of Hate," and economic hard times.

Mahler, Sarah J. *American Dreaming: Immigrant Life on the Margins.* Princeton, N.J.: Princeton University Press, 1995.

The struggles of immigrants who fled troubled homelands in search of a better life, only to be marginalized by the U.S. society they had hoped would embrace them.

Massey, Douglas S., and Nancy A. Denton. *American Apartheid: Segregation and the Making of the Underclass,* reprint ed. Cambridge, Mass.: Harvard University Press, 1998.

A richly documented account of how segregation and dissociation from other cultures and ways of life lie at the root of many problems facing African Americans today.

Wachtel, Paul L. *Race in the Mind of America: Breaking the Vicious Circle between Blacks and Whites.* New Haven, Conn.: Yale University Press, 2000.

Examines how Blacks and Whites unknowingly perpetuate and maintain racial problems that inhibit progress toward resolution and offers guidance on how to break the cycle.

INTERNET RESOURCES

Want to do something about bias? Go to www.tolerance.org/campus/index.jsp to learn ten ways to fight hate on campus.

CHAPTER

7 Contemporary Patterns and Issues

"Ultimately, America's answer to the intolerant man is diversity, the very diversity which our heritage of religious freedom has inspired."

—Robert F. Kennedy

As a nation of immigrants, the United States has seen many different groups of strangers arrive and interact with its people. The strangers perceived a different world that the native population took for granted, and their reactions ranged from wonder to bewilderment to dismay, from fulfilled expectations to culture shock. Because their language, appearance, and cultural background often made them conspicuous, the newcomers were categorically identified and judged as a group rather than as individuals. Native-born U.S. residents' responses ranged from receptive to impatient and intolerant, while their actions ranged from indifferent to helpful to exploitative.

Throughout the nation's history, then, varied patterns of majority–minority relations existed. Ethnocentric values prompted the natural development of ingroup loyalty and outgroup hostility among both indigenous and migrant groups. Competition for scarce resources, colonialism, and political dominance by the Anglo-Saxon core groups also provided a basis for conflict. However, the resulting prejudicial attitudes and discriminatory actions varied greatly in intensity. In addition, attitudes and social and economic conditions in this country changed over the years, affecting the newcomers' experiences.

Not all groups came for the same reasons or from the same backgrounds. Because of variations in social class, education, and occupational skills, not all immigrants began at the bottom of the socioeconomic ladder. Some came as sojourners, intending to stay only as long as necessary to earn enough money for a better life back in their homeland. Some came with the desire to become U.S. citizens in every sense of the word; others insisted on retaining their own culture.

Dominant attitudes, as well as sociological analyses, tend to focus on either assimilation or pluralism as the preferred minority adaptation. Which process the public considers more acceptable greatly influences dominant–minority relations. For example, if assimilation is held to be the "proper" goal, then evidence of pluralism will probably draw negative reactions, even though pluralism is a normal manifestation among first- and second-generation Americans. In recent years, the growing presence in U.S. cities and suburbs of Spanish-speaking peoples and of people of color from non-Western cultures has led many other U.S. residents to question the country's immigration policies. Although race and economics are undoubtedly influencing factors, so too are genuine concerns about widespread pluralism overwhelming the "melting-pot" capabilities of the United States.

Stir in words such as *affirmative action, illegal aliens,* and *multiculturalism,* and the debate reaches "white heat" temperatures. These aspects of intergroup relations suggest to many that the majority group and the dominant culture are seriously threatened. In many quarters, the level of intolerance for any manifestation of pluralism has risen to alarming proportions.

How important is ethnicity today? Are immigration and assimilation concerns justified? What is the future of race and ethnicity in the United States? In this chapter, we attempt to answer these questions as we examine concepts of ethnic consciousness; evolutionary changes in ethnicity; and issues of legal and illegal immigration, bilingual education, and the future of our in a multicultural society.

Ethnic Consciousness

Sociologists have long been interested in the attitudinal and behavioral patterns that emerge when people migrate into a society with a different culture. For example, what factors encourage or discourage ethnic self-awareness or culture preservation? If succeeding generations supposedly identify less with their country of origin, how do we explain the resurgence of ethnicity among White ethnics in recent years? Are there ethnic differences in social mobility, social change, and behavior patterns even among third-generation U.S. citizens? Sociologists frequently raise these questions and offer a number of sociological explanations in an effort to describe scientifically the diversity of ethnic experience.

Country of Origin as a Factor

Focusing on the relationship between the migrant and the country of origin will produce a better understanding of the degree of assimilation.[1] Assuming that a migrant group today is affected primarily by factors in the receiving country is incorrect, although this may have been truer of groups that came to the United States before World War I, when transportation and communication were limited. Furthermore, immigration restrictions in the 1920s sharply curtailed the number of new immigrants, thereby aiding the assimilation process since fewer newcomers arrived to reinforce the language and customs of the old country.

In today's world, however, an immigrant group can maintain contact with the country of origin not only through airmail letters but also (and more importantly) through telecommunications, rapid transportation, and the continued arrival of newcomers. Mexican and West Indian immigrant communities benefit from geographical proximity, and the homeland can exert more influence over its emigrants than in years past. Where greater social contact occurs, cultural transmission is greater too.

That contact with one's country of origin also affects politics. In an analysis of the political activities of Asian Americans, I identified three general and overlapping phases of acculturation in their political activities. These were: (1) the *alien phase*, when the political locus remains with the country of origin; (2) the *reactionary phase*, when immigrants form political organizations to protect their interests and fight discrimination; and (3) the *acceptance phase*, when they display a greater degree of cultural and structural discrimination.[2]

In examining the political activities of immigrants from the Dominican Republic, Haiti, and El Salvador, Jose Itzigsohn found manifestations of that first phase. Immigrants' transnational politics rested heavily on the government structure and political parties in the country of origin. The rise of a pattern of transnational politics, he states, is contingent on the home country's need for a steady flow of remittances, migrant organizations in the country of reception, and consolidation of competitive politics in democratic regimes.[3]

Sheila E. Henry finds a connection between country of origin and recent levels of ethnic and racial inequality in the United States. Focusing on Chinese, Japanese, and African Americans, she suggests that the U.S. stratification system closely reflects global economic stratification systems. Because Japan ranks among the leading capitalist nations, its immigrants enjoy a status of "honorary Whites," something she suggests Chinese immigrants may soon enjoy, given their country's current economic boom. However, since no African country is likely to achieve economic global success in the near future, she thinks it is unlikely that the ethnic-group status of African Americans will change.[4]

The degree of stability or social change in the homeland, suggests Mary Sengstock, has a profound effect on the migrant community's sociocultural patterns and lifestyle:

> Where the country of origin has experienced a relatively stable or gradually changing culture, the effect on the immigrant community will most likely be

to encourage retention of the ethnic culture. This is much the same case as has occurred with Puerto Ricans and Mexican Americans.

Some societies, however, have experienced drastic changes in recent years. When groups of immigrants from such areas experience constant immigration and other types of contact with the mother country, one might expect such contact to produce profound effects on the immigrant community as well.[5]

To illustrate her position, Sengstock used a study of Chaldean immigrants from Iraq who settled in Detroit both before and after World War II. Iraq, presently occupied by U.S. troops, is nonetheless an independent nation-state, not a colonial land of different tribes all under the control of another nation. It replaced centuries-old tribal rivalries with the unity of nationalism, and these changes reached the Detroit community through visitors and immigrants. Recent immigrants, who have more education and more experience with urban settings and bureaucracies, are more likely to interact with others. Thus, willingness to extend one's social contacts to members of other groups could, suggests Sengstock, produce a more assimilable group. The social structure of an immigrant group's country of origin, then, may help explain both nationalistic sentiment and social interaction with others in the adopted country.[6]

The Three-Generation Hypothesis

Pulitzer Prize–winner and historian Marcus Hansen conceptualized a normal pattern of ethnic revival in what he called the "Law of the Return of the Third Generation."[7] The third generation, more secure in its socioeconomic status and U.S. identity, becomes interested in the ethnic heritage that the second generation neglected in its efforts to overcome discrimination and marginality. Simply stated, "What the child wishes to forget, the grandchild wishes to remember." Hansen, who based his conclusions mainly on midwestern Swedish Americans, reaffirmed his position several years later:

> Whenever any immigrant group reaches the third-generation stage in its development a spontaneous and almost irresistible impulse arises which forces the thoughts of many people of different professions, different positions in life and different points of view to interest themselves in that one factor which they have in common: heritage—the heritage of blood.[8]

Hansen suggested a pattern in the fall and rise of ethnic identity in succeeding generations of Americans. His hypothesis generated extensive discussion in the academic community, resulting in studies and commentaries that both supported and criticized his views.

Hansen's law assumes that the second generation perceives its ethnicity as a disadvantage in being accepted in U.S. society. However, Peter

Skerry sees a different pattern in the reawakening of one's ethnic identity on college campuses as well as group competition and conflict. In relating the complexities of the assimilation process to Hansen's hypothesis, Skerry states, "However flawed as a precise predictor of generational differences within specific ethnic groups, Hansen's basic insight remains valid: the process of assimilation is a dialectical one."[9] By this, he means that assimilation is not simply a linear progression but instead is a process that moves back and forth across the generations. Assimilation is not irreversible. Subsequent generations, even those who are the product of intermarriages, may emphasize their ethnic identity and learn the language of their cultural heritage.

In contrast, a study by Neil Sandburg found that Polish Americans in the Los Angeles area tended to become less ethnic over several generations.[10] In a similar study of Italian Americans in two suburbs of Providence, Rhode Island, John P. Roche also found increased assimilation over several generations and lower levels of attitudinal ethnicity.[11]

Studies of more recently arrived groups also find a similar decline in ethnicity among second-generation Asian and Hispanic Americans as they seek to assimilate. In fact, Valentine found a negative relationship between cultural assimilation and Hispanic identity; the acculturation process functioned as a trade-off between traditional Latino tendencies and mainstream Anglo-American practices.[12] Similarly, Portes and MacLeod, in a survey of immigrant children from south Florida and southern California, reported that children who adopt the "Hispanic" label are the least well assimilated; these children had poorer English skills, lower self-esteem, and higher rates of poverty than those who identified themselves as Americans or as hyphenated Americans.[13]

Among Asian Americans, Kibria found that second-generation East Asian Americans (those whose ancestry was from China, Japan, or Korea) developed a sense of a shared Asian American culture in their socialization into the Asian values of education, family, hard work, and respect for elders. In this instance, the "backlash" in the construction of a common cultural background was an attempt to distinguish it from the homogeneously conceived White mainstream culture.[14]

Although most Asian and Hispanic Americans are too recently part of U.S. society to apply the three-generation hypothesis, the experience of Japanese Americans, among whom many are third-, fourth-, and even fifth-generation Americans, may offer an insight. With above average educational, occupational, and income levels, as well as high intermarriage rates, they are arguably the most assimilated of all Asian Americans. Still, they retain symbolic vestiges of their heritage and cling to the aforementioned values as part of their sense of self and group identity.[15] Perhaps a similar future awaits our newest groups, although undoubtedly their racial experiences will mediate their identity formation.

Harold Abramson dismissed the three-generation hypothesis, arguing that the many dimensions of ethnic diversity preclude any macrosocial theory about ethnic consciousness.[16] Besides differences in time period—which may have influenced the experience, adjustment, and intergenerational conflict or consensus of ethnic groups—diversity exists within the groups themselves. Possibly, only the better educated among each ethnic group, being in wider contact with the outside world and more ambivalent about their identity, experience an ethnic resurgence, while the majority quietly progress in some steady fashion. In addition, the enormous variability in the U.S. social structure affects what happens to the grandchildren of all ethnic groups:

> Here I am talking about the diversity of region, of social stratification, of urban and rural settlement. In other words, the immigrants of Old and New and continuing migrations, the blacks of the North and of the South, the native American Indians, all experience their encounters with America under vastly different conditions. The French-Canadians in depressed mill towns of New England, the Hungarians and Czechs in company coal towns of Pennsylvania, and the Chicanos in migrant labor fields of California, do not experience the social mobility or social change of the Irish in Boston politics, the Jews in the garment industry of New York, or the Japanese in the professions of Hawaii. Not only are there traditional cultural factors to explain these phenomena, but there are structural reasons of settlement, region, and the local composition of the ethnic mosaic as well.[17]

Furthermore, the responses of different cultural groups to the host society vary. Conservative social scientists such as Thomas Sowell argue that cultural characteristics that either mesh or clash with the dominant cultural values determine a group's upward mobility.[18] Liberal social scientists such as Stephen Steinberg downplay cultural characteristics and emphasize social-structural variables instead. Steinberg maintains that pluralism appeals only to groups that benefit from maintaining ethnic boundaries, while disadvantaged groups willingly compromise their ethnicity to gain economic security and social acceptance.[19] More likely, the interplay of culture and social structure enables groups to achieve economic success or prevents them from doing so.

The Changing Face of Ethnicity

We can gain helpful insights into the complex, varied experiences and adjustments of different racial and ethnic groups by considering three important concepts: transnationalism, social capital, and segmented assimilation.

Transnationalism

We have long recognized the fact that immigrants, even when intent on blending into the societal mainstream of the host country, nevertheless retain much of their "cultural baggage" that affects not only their adjustment to their new land but also serves as a stabilizing link to their homeland and sense of self.[20] Despite that "old world" influence, the traditional view of social scientists was that the political and social behavior of the newcomers occurred within the cultural/structural framework of the host society. However, an expanding global economy, together with rapid communications and travel, has led scholars in recent years to revise traditional migration theory in recognition of a changed interaction pattern between immigrants and the host society.[21]

This new orientation recognizes that recent global transformations have led to the creation of social ties and support networks no longer restricted by national boundaries. **Transnationalism** thus refers to sustained ties of persons, networks, and organizations across national borders that result from the current international migration patterns and refugee flows.[22] The easy flow of people and their ideas back and forth between two countries has given many people the ability to maintain dual identities, with strong cultural ties and the capacity to make contributions to both places.[23] Instant transactions and communications have compressed time and space, allowing populations to be culturally and socially anchored at multiple sites. Instead of a permanent move from one country to another, today's immigrant retains more intense, interconnected, even legitimized links (cultural, economic, familial, political) than ever before. Some scholars therefore argue that transnationalism makes the traditional terms of assimilation, integration, or segregation, in which states have dealt with immigration, obsolete.[24]

Social Capital

The term **social capital** refers to actual or virtual resources available to an individual or group through a "durable network" of "institutionalized relationships of mutual acquaintance and recognition." Social capital thus refers to the potential value of information, social support, and personal connections inherent in social network relationships that are indispensable for achieving social, economic, and political goals.[25]

When we examine ethnic communities in terms of social capital, we can determine how community-based support systems and cultural orientations do or do not assist first- and second-generation Americans in their quest to share in the American Dream. Social capital is not a fixed object but rather a constantly changing means that facilitates access to benefits and resources that best suit the goals of specific immigrant groups.[26]

Essentially, social capital offers resources to racial or ethnic minorities that are beyond their individual reach by creating connections and support. The presence of these networks cultivate hope, trust, communication, mutual assistance, and problem solving through cooperative, collective action. Although the presence of strong social capital does not guarantee a minority group's successful integration into the economic and political mainstream, it certainly makes life easier than in a community lacking it.

Ethnic communities with strong social capital can offer help to new arrivals in securing informal sources of credit, insurance, child support, English language training, and job referrals. Less successful communities display a short-term commitment to their host country and are less able to provide their members with important services. Thus, Koreans in Los Angeles and Chinese in San Francisco can better assist new immigrants than can Dominicans in New York or Mexicans in San Diego.[27]

Segmented Assimilation

Building on the concept that immigrant groups possess different levels of social capital, Alejandro Portés and Min Zhou advanced their theory of **segmented assimilation**. As its name implies, this hypothesis suggests a variety of outcomes among, and even within, contemporary immigrant streams. Instead of a uniform adaptation process that becomes more successful with longer residence in the United States, new immigrant groups may follow different assimilation paths than did previous immigrants. Besides the variants in available social capital, such factors as country of origin, settlement area, social class, race, and education also play an important role.[28]

In a positive scenario, those groups that are received favorably and possess high levels of human capital may quickly move up the socioeconomic ladder and integrate into the societal mainstream. In contrast, a second scenario depicts groups with limited resources as unable to find stable employment to earn enough income to support their children's education. Moreover, longer residence in an inner-city environment may result in their children's acculturation to other minority peers, leading to lower educational aspirations and downward mobility, somewhat of a "new rainbow underclass."[29] Yet a third scenario is limited assimilation where immigrant parents support their children's educational success but reinforce traditional cultural values and thus limit their acculturation into the American youth subculture.[30]

The segmented-assimilation hypothesis provides a lens for understanding the discrepancy in research findings on the educational enrollment of recent immigrants and the children of immigrants in the United States. Reynolds Farley and Richard Alba, for example, saw significant intergenerational progress in educational attainment for many second-generation groups. Indeed, some surpassed those of third-generation or higher whites and African Americans. However, those of Mexican and Puerto Rican heritage languished behind the other groups.[31] Charles Herschman found that a downward mobility pattern for Hispanic Caribbean youths was consistent with the second possible outcome of the segmented-assimilation hypothesis, whereas Afro-Caribbean youths appeared to illustrate the third type of outcome.[32] Similarly, in their study of the Vietnamese community in New Orleans, Min Zhou and Carl Bankston reported that those more successful in school were those who were able to retain their mother tongue and traditional values.[33] In another study, Mary Waters found that Caribbean immigrants often pass along to their children an immigrant or ethnic identity that retards acculturation into the African American community.[34]

If, therefore, we are to understand more completely the acculturation patterns among today's immigrants, the segmented-assimilation hypothesis informs us that one model does not fit all groups or even all members of any group. Groups differ in their incorporation into the U.S. stratification system, and this theory attempts to explain how and why they do.

Naturalization

After five years of continuous legal residence in the United States, immigrants are eligible to become naturalized citizens, provided they are of good moral character and demonstrate a command of English as well a knowledge of U.S. history and government. It is a reasonable assumption that those who become U.S. citizens are demonstrating a desire to join fully in U.S. society through this formal process.

As Figure 7.1 shows, the longer the residence in the United States, the higher the percentage of naturalized citizens. Those who arrived in the

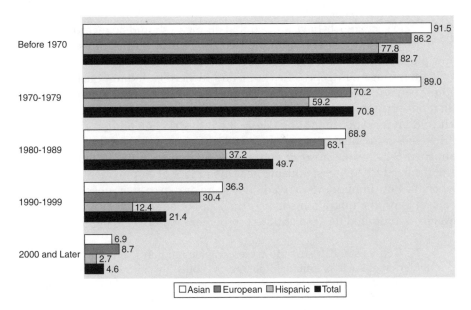

FIGURE 7.1   **Percentage of Naturalized Citizens in 2004 by Period of Entry by Percent**

Source: U.S. Office of Immigration Statistics.

1970s, for example, have a greater proportion of naturalized citizens than those who arrived in the 1980s, who in turn exceed those who arrived in the 1990s. Moreover, Asian immigrants lead all other groups in all time periods in the percentage of those who became U.S. citizens. How much of a role transnationalism or segmented assimilation plays in the level of naturalization among groups is a matter of great interest to social scientists.

We must be careful in analyzing the citizenship data. At first glance, the smaller proportion of newer arrivals compared to earlier immigrants in becoming naturalized citizens would seem to support the argument that newcomers are less likely to "become Americans." However, the correlation between length of U.S. residence and the proportion of those becoming citizens has been fairly constant for a great many decades. For example, although seven in ten of all immigrants who arrived in the 1970s are now citizens, less than half of them were citizens in the early 1990s.

Ethnicity as a Social Process

Ethnicity is a creation of a pluralistic U.S. society. Usually, culture shock and an emerging self-consciousness lead immigrant groups to think of themselves in terms of an ethnic identity and to become part of an ethnic community to gain the social and emotional support they need to begin a new life in their adopted country. That community is revitalized with a continual influx of new arrivals.

Some sociologists have argued that ethnicity should be regarded not as an ascribed attribute, with only the two discrete categories of assimilation and pluralism, but as a continuous variable. In a review of the literature, William L. Yancey, Eugene P. Ericksen, and Richard N. Juliani concluded that ethnic behavior is conditioned by occupation, residence, and institutional affiliation—the structural situations in which groups have found themselves.[35] The old immigrants, migrating before the Industrial Revolution, had a more dispersed residential pattern than did the new immigrants, who were bunched together because of concentrated large-scale urban employment and the need for low-cost housing near their place of employment. Similarly, when the new immigrants arrived, they were drawn to areas of economic expansion, and the migration chains—the subsequent arrival of relatives and friends—continued the concentrated settlement pattern (see Figure 7.2).

> The Germans and Irish, who were earlier immigrants, concentrated in the older cities such as Philadelphia and St. Louis. By contrast, the new immigrants from Poland, Italy and Russia concentrated in Buffalo, Cleveland, Detroit and Milwaukee, as well as in some of the older cities with expanding opportunities. Different migration patterns occurred for immigrants with and without skills. . . . Rewards for skilled occupations were greater, and the skilled immigrant went to the cities where there were opportunities to practice his trade. Less highly skilled workers went to the cities with expanding oppor-

tunities. Thus, the Italian concentration in construction and the Polish in steel were related to the expansion of these industries as these groups arrived. The Jewish concentration in the garment industry may have been a function of their previous experience as tailors, but it is also dependent upon the emergence of the mass production of clothing in the late nineteenth century.[36]

The authors conclude that group consciousness arises and crystallizes within the work relationships, common residential areas, interests, and lifestyles of working-class conditions. Moreover, normal communication and participation in ethnic organizations on a cosmopolitan level can reinforce ethnic identity even among residentially dispersed groups.[37]

Migration Patterns

Stanley Lieberson and Mary C. Waters examined the location of ethnic and racial groups in the United States on the basis and patterns of internal migration. They found that the longer a group had been in the United States, the less geographically concentrated it was. This was hardly a surprising finding, but their analysis of internal migration patterns revealed that ethnicity still affected the changing spatial patterns:

> We have concluded that although current patterns of internal migration are tending to reduce some of the distinctive geographic concentrations in the nation, this will still not fully eliminate distinctive ethnic concentrations. This is because groups differ in their propensity to leave and in their propensity to enter each area in a way that reflects the existing ethnic compositions of the areas. Thus, even with the massive level of internal migration in the United States, there is no evidence that the ethnic linkage to region is disappearing.[38]

Lieberson and Waters observed that a numerically small group, if highly concentrated in a small number of localities, possesses greater political and social influence than one dispersed more uniformly. Thus, the linkage between demographic size and location will influence visibility, occupational patterns, interaction patterns, intermarriage, and assimilation.

In 2005, 62 percent of the 1.1 million immigrants who came to the United States entered through just six states.[39] At the same time, three of these gateway states—California, New York, and Texas—had considerable net outmigration of their foreign-born populations to other states. As the leading destination for migrants from abroad, California and New York were also the leaders in this internal migration, sending 237,000 and 205,000, respectively, to other states over a five-year period.[40]

Just as chain migration is an important factor in migration from abroad, so too does it appear to play an important role in this population

FIGURE 7.2 Where We Settled

Go west, go east

At first they came to New England, the Carolinas and what are now the mid-Atlantic states. Then they crossed the Appalachians and headed west. Now, the destination for many immigrants is California, and most are reaching it by going east or north—from Asia or Latin America. In 2005, 21 percent of new immigrants settled in California, compared to 12 percent settling in New York, which until 1976 was the first choice of new arrivals.

These maps show the biggest concentration of ethnic groups—500,000 or more in a state—as identified in the 2000 census. California is the top choice for immigrants from China, El Salvador, Guatemala, Hong Kong, India, Iran, Korea, Mexico, the Philippines, and Vietnam. New York has the most from Bangladesh, Colombia, the Dominican Republic, Ecuador, Guyana, Jamaica, Pakistan, and the former Soviet Union.

Captions below the maps show where specific ethnic groups make up the biggest shares of the state's population, such as South Dakota with its large percentage of people of German descent.

German

Highest densities: North Dakota 46%, South Dakota 46%, Nebraska 43%, Wisconsin 43%, Minnesota 38%, Iowa 37%, Kansas 33%, Ohio 30%, Indiana 27%.

English

States with the highest densities of English: Utah 30%, Maine 25%, Idaho 22%, New Hampshire 21%, Wyoming 19%, Vermont 18%, Oregon 15%, Delaware 14%.

Irish

Highest densities: Massachusetts 23%, New Hampshire 21%, Rhode Island 20%, Delaware 19%, Connecticut 18%, New Jersey 17%, Missouri 14%, New York 14%, West Virginia 14%.

Italian

Highest densities: Rhode Island 20%, Connecticut 20%, New Jersey 18%, New York 15%, Massachusetts 14%, Alabama 11%, New Mexico 8%.

☐ States in color are those with at least 500,000 persons of the indicated ethnic groups in the latest census.

French or French Canadian

Highest densities: Vermont 27%, New Hampshire 27%, Maine 25%, Rhode Island 20%, Louisiana 18%, Massachusetts 14%, Connecticut 11%.

Asian

Highest densities: Hawaii 42%, California 11%, New Jersey 6%, New York 6%, Washington 6%, Nevada 5%, Maryland 4%, Massachusetts 4%, Virginia 4%.

African American

Highest densities: Mississippi 36%, Louisiana 33%, South Carolina 30%, Georgia 29%, Alabama 26%, Maryland 25%, North Carolina 22%.

Mexican

Highest densities: California 25%, Texas 24%, Arizona 21%, New Mexico 18%, Nevada 14%, Colorado 11%, Illinois 9%.

Hispanic

Highest densities: New Mexico 42%, California 32%, Texas 32%, Arizona 25%, Colorado 17%, Florida 17%, New York 15%, New Jersey 13%, Illinois 12%.

Polish

Highest densities: Wisconsin 9%, Michigan 9%, Connecticut 8%, Illinois 7%, New Jersey 7%, Pennsylvania 7%, New York 5%.

Source: Basic data from U.S. Bureau of the Census.

redistribution of the foreign-born to other states. As a result, the ethnic dimension in internal migration patterns that Lieberson and Waters found 20 years earlier is still significant. By far, the greatest numbers of interstate movers were Asians (667,000), followed by Mexicans (472,000) and other Latin Americans (438,000). States where this internal migration had the most dramatic impact on population composition were Nevada, North Carolina, Georgia, Arkansas, Minnesota, Nebraska, and Indiana.[41]

Focusing on ethnic and racial settlement patterns is helpful in understanding part of the assimilation process. In his ecological model of Chicago's growth and development, Robert Park noted the linkage between social and spatial mobility. Where one lives is as valid an indicator of upward mobility as income, education, and occupation.[42] Housing markets are segmented along class and racial lines, and since the most desirable neighborhoods tend to be inhabited by non-Hispanic Whites, the relocation by minority members typically involves a process of integration.[43] Because such spatial mobility implies greater access to cultural, economic, physical, and social resources and is indicative of social and economic assimilation, the term **spatial assimilation** is often used to identify this process.

Symbolic Ethnicity

Among first-generation U.S. immigrants, ethnicity is an everyday reality that everyone takes for granted. For most immigrants living within an ethnic community or network, shared communal interactions make ethnic identity a major factor in daily life. Not yet structurally assimilated, these immigrants find that their ethnicity provides the link to virtually everything they say or do, what they join, and whom they befriend or marry.

What happens to the ethnicity of subsequent generations depends on the immediate environment. As Richard D. Alba reaffirmed in a 1990 study in Albany, New York, the presence of ethnic neighborhoods or organizations in the vicinity helps sustain a strong sense of ethnic identity.[44] For most Whites of European origin, living away from visible ethnic links and becoming part of the societal mainstream reduces the importance of their ethnic identity in comparison to their occupational and social identity. At this point, ethnicity rests on acknowledging ancestry through attachment to a few ethnic symbols not pertinent to everyday life.[45]

Alba speaks of a twilight stage of ethnicity among White ethnics. High intermarriage rates not only have reduced the intergenerational transmission of distinctive cultural traits but also have diversified the ethnic ancestry of third- and fourth-generation European Americans. A coalesced new ethnic group, European Americans, has emerged. Its ethnicity is muted and symbolic, a personal and voluntary identity that finds expression in such activities as "church and synagogue attendance, marching in a St. Patrick's or Columbus Day parade, voting for a political candidate of a similar ethnicity, or supporting a political cause associated with the country of origin, such as the emigration of Russian Jews to Israel or the reunification of Ireland."[46]

Although socially assimilated and integrated into middle-class society, third- and fourth-generation European Americans maintain this quiet link to their origins. As Gans suggests, it can find form in small details, such as objects in the home with an ethnic meaning, occasional participation in an old-country ritual, or a fondness for ethnic cuisine.[47] Individuals may remain interested in the immigrant experience, participate in ethnic political and social activities, or even visit the ancestral homeland. All these private, leisure-time activities help preserve ethnicity in symbolic ways, giving people a special sense of self in the homogenized world of White U.S. culture.

African Americans express symbolic ethnicity through such elements as musical styles, fashion and dress styles (Afros, braids, dreadlocks, tribal symbols cut into the hair, bandanna headbands, Kufi hats, harem pants, African beads), cuisine (soul food), and festivals (such as Kwanzaa, a holiday based on traditional African harvest celebrations). Sometimes called *manifestations of cultural nationalism*—a movement toward African American solidarity based on encouraging African culture and values—these activities resemble those of the descendants of other ethnic groups proudly recalling their heritage.

Current Issues

Two highly controversial issues punctuate race and ethnic relations in the United States: immigration and bilingual education. Although the latter is a fairly new issue, arguments against both repeat objections hotly asserted in the late nineteenth and early twentieth centuries. Nativist fears of being overrun by too many "non-American types" and losing societal cohesion as a result of their cultural pluralism are quite similar to concerns raised by dominant-group members of past generations. Closely related to these two issues is a third one: multiculturalism. This subject causes ongoing debates between its advocates and those insisting on assimilation.

Immigration Fears

The ebb and flow of immigrant waves have an impact on the host nation in many ways. Their cultural impact can enrich the society—in architecture, art, foods, and music, to name just a few—but some fear language retention and non-assimilation will undermine societal cohesion. Immigrant labor can be a boon to the economy, but critics express concern about the lowering of wages and loss of jobs for native workers. Because most immigrants are now people of color and have a higher birth rate than native-born Americans, some worry about the changing racial demographics.

Symbolic ethnicity is an occasional means for native-born U.S. residents to reaffirm their cultural heritage. Sometimes these activities are carryovers from the old country, but other times they are of U.S. origin, as with Kwanzaa, a fairly recently developed observance based on traditional African harvest celebrations. This three-generation group of African Americans, whose native-born roots predate the Civil War, enjoy this special event together.

Moreover, with developing countries now the primary sending areas, the interests of the newly naturalized citizens—and, in turn, U.S. foreign policy—become increasingly involved in the developments in those parts of the world (see Table 7.1).

Many immigrants still come from European countries, but they now account for less than 16 percent annually of the total number, due to the large increase in Asian and Hispanic immigrants. Given the ongoing processes of chain migration and family reunification—and contrasting birth rates in Europe as compared to Asia and Latin America—we can safely assume the continued dominance of developing countries in sending additional immigrants.

Almost 9.1 million legal immigrants (including undocumented immigrants who were subsequently granted amnesty) came to the United States in the 1990s, exceeding the previous record set in 1901–1910, when 8.8 million arrived. Current trends suggest this decade will set an even higher record number of immigrants. Add in the millions of undocumented immi-

TABLE 7.1   Major Sources of Newcomers to the United States: 2005

1. Mexico	161,445	9. Colombia	25,571
2. India	84,681	10. Ukraine	22,761
3. China	69,967	11. Canada	21,878
4. Philippines	60,748	12. El Salvador	21,539
5. Cuba	36,261	13. United Kingdom	19,800
6. Vietnam	32,784	14. Jamaica	18,346
7. Dominican Republic	27,504	15. Russia	18,083
8. Korea	26,562	16. Guatemala	16,825

Source: U.S. Office of Immigration Statistics.

grants, now thought to exceed 12 million, and the issue of immigration becomes a fiercely debated one.

Some opposition to current immigration results from concern about the ability of the United States to absorb so many immigrants. Echoing xenophobic fears of earlier generations, immigration opponents worry that U.S. citizens will lose control of the country to foreigners. This time, instead of fears about the religiously different Catholics and Jews or the physically different Mediterranean Whites who were dark-complexioned, the new anti-immigration groups fear the significantly growing presence of religiously and physically different immigrants of color. Visible differences, together with the prevalence of languages other than English, constantly remind multiple-generation U.S. residents about the strangers in their midst, whom some perceive as a threat to U.S. society as they know it. This is especially true for Arab and Muslim Americans, whom anti-immigration advocates point to as illustrating a too-liberal immigration policy that allowed terrorists in our midst. The reality that virtually all Arab and Muslim Americans denounce terrorism does little to assuage public fears.

It is not just the increasing visibility of so many "strangers" in neighborhoods, schools, and workplaces that encourages this backlash. The nation's stable birthrate means that immigrants account for a larger share of population growth than in previous years. According to the Population Reference Bureau, that share is currently 44 percent.[48] Accordingly, the Census Bureau projects that the racial composition of the United States will change dramatically in the next two generations, a prospect that displeases some people.

Another concern about immigration is economic. The public worries that immigrants take away jobs, drive down wages, and use too many government services at taxpayers' expense. How real are these fears?

Jobs.   A common belief is that immigrants take jobs away from Americans, a fear that has been expressed for more than 100 years. On the one hand, immigrants create many new jobs by starting new businesses (about 18 percent of the total) and by increasing the demand for goods and services that others fill through those new jobs. At the same time, between 2000 and 2004, the decline in native-born employment was most pronounced in states where immigrants increased their share of workers the most. Immigration has its biggest impact on the lower part of the labor market—particularly building maintenance, construction, and food services—where native-born unemployment numbers closely match the increase in immigrant employment increases. In other labor sectors, there appears to be far less impact.[49]

Wages.   Most economists agree that immigration has lowered the wages of native-born Americans with limited education and few skills. For example, George Borjas and Leonard Katz, in a study of Mexican immigration throughout the twentieth century, concluded that high school dropouts would earn as much as 8 percent more if it weren't for Mexican immigration.[50] However, for all other U.S. workers, the impact has not been significant.[51]

Costs and Contributions.   Here, too, the findings are mixed. At the local and state levels, immigrants use more in services than they pay in local taxes (which is also true for the majority of native-born citizens as well). Those with very low levels of education and job skills cost the most, particularly in health care and use of schools. A National Academy of Sciences study found that the average immigrant imposes a net lifetime fiscal cost on state and local governments of $25,000 for these services.[52]

Research shows a consensus that the picture is quite different on the national level. The taxes that immigrants pay, including Social Security payments, are well in excess of federal benefits received. Furthermore, when all levels of government are combined, immigrants pay substantially more than the benefits they receive.[53] Another important fact is the value of immigration to the future financial strength of the Social Security and Medicare systems. In the absence of immigration, the U.S. workforce is projected to grow very slowly—much more slowly than the size of the retired population as the Baby Boom generation reaches its golden years. Because immigrants add to the supply of younger workers who contribute payroll taxes that finance the Social Security and Medicare system, they are an important reason why forecasts show that the programs will be able to pay benefits in full until 2042 for Social Security and 2019 for Medicare's hospital insurance program. The projections of Social Security's trustees show that higher levels of immigration in the future will improve the long-term financial condition of Social Security, while lower levels will have the opposite effect. The higher fertility levels of immigrants also slow the rate at which the average age of the overall population will rise, keeping more people on the contribution side of the equation.[54]

To summarize, immigrant labor allows many goods and services to be produced more cheaply and provides the work force for some businesses that otherwise could not exist. These include U.S. textile and agricultural industries, as well as restaurants and domestic household services. They compete primarily with each other and with U.S. citizens who lack a high school diploma; wages of the latter have dropped by about 5 percent in the past 15 years. In some areas with large concentrations of low-skilled, low-paid immigrants, such as California, taxpayers at both state and local levels pay more on average to support the publicly funded services needed by these immigrants. Still, economists say, immigrants and their children bring long-term benefits for most U.S. taxpayers because—like most U.S. residents—they and their descendants will add more to government coffers than they receive over their lifetimes.

Public Opinion Polls.   Statistics notwithstanding, Americans have mixed opinions about immigration. A 2004 poll conducted jointly by National Public Radio, the Kaiser Family Foundation, and Harvard's Kennedy School of Government found that 52 percent of respondents thought that there were too many immigrants in the United States, but only 31 percent thought that the country was too open to immigrants. Yet in a 2005 Gallup poll, 61 percent of respondents said they thought that, on the whole, immigration was a good thing for the country.[55]

Undocumented Migrants

What fuels public debate about immigration is the rising number of unauthorized foreign-born people in the United States, now estimated to be around 12 million. Jeffrey Passel estimates that 1.8 million undocumented migrants arrived in the 1980s, 5 million in the 1990s, and 4.4 million between 2000 and 2003. About two-thirds have been in the United States for less than ten years.[56]

Mexicans comprise the largest segment of undocumented migrants, estimated to be 57 percent of the total, a proportion that has remained steady for a decade. Another 24 percent are from elsewhere in Latin America. About 9 percent come from Asia, 6 percent from Europe and Canada, and 4 percent from other parts of the world (see Figure 7.3).[57]

Entering the country easily and then disappearing within it, these undocumented aliens usually escape detection by Immigration and Customs Enforcement agents who patrol the border of the United States. In the Southwest, where the problem draws the greatest amount of public attention, the most apprehension about undocumented aliens occurs (about one million annually).

In the aftermath of the 9/11 attacks, amid concerns about insufficient screening of aliens coming to the United States and the growing presence of undocumented aliens, the government reorganized in March 2003. Services once provided by the much-criticized Immigration and Naturalization Service now occur within the Department of Homeland Security under

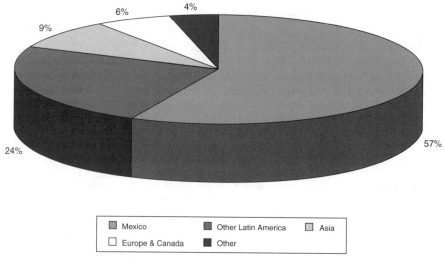

FIGURE 7.3   Undocumented Migrants: 2005

Source: Pew Hispanic Center.

the U.S. Citizenship and Immigration Services (USCIS). Immediate priorities "are to promote national security, continue to eliminate immigration adjudication backlogs, and improve the delivery of immigration and citizenship services."[58] With ongoing public and government concern about further acts of terrorism, the national security priority may lead to stronger enforcement against all undocumented aliens, not just those from Muslim countries.

Certainly public pressure mounted in 2006 to do something about securing our borders and dealing with those undocumented migrants already here. Political debates, opposing legislative proposals, calls for a 700-mile wall along the border, congressional hearings, and mass demonstrations in many U.S. cities all illustrated the fundamental disagreements about how to deal with the situation.

Calls for reform come at a time when parts of the U.S. economy are dependent on the labor of undocumented migrants. Mostly Latinos, these unskilled workers have spread to a wide range of industries (see Figure 7.4). Moreover, about 10 percent of the labor force of Mexico—as well as several other Central American and Caribbean countries—are now working in the United States, and sending money to their families back home as a major source of financial support there.[59]

Hostility against undocumented aliens is strong and often carries over to negative reactions toward legal immigrants. Until some solution is found, this indiscriminate reaction to legal immigrants will continue.

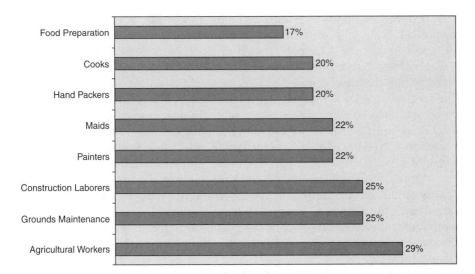

FIGURE 7.4   Percent of Undocumented Migrants in U.S. Labor Force: 2005

Source: Jeffrey Passel, "The Size and Characteristics of the Unauthorized Migrant Population in the United States," *Pew Hispanic Center Research Report* 61 (2006).

Language Retention

One of the most divisive issues in majority–minority relations is language retention. For many native-born Americans, the presence of groups not speaking English goes to the heart of their assumptions that the newcomers aren't even trying to assimilate. The large-scale presence of an immigrant group—whether on a national level such as the Hispanics or in a local area such as the Vietnamese in California—intensifies this perception. On a personal level, witnessing foreign-born parents speaking in public to their children in the language of their homeland, or seeing signs or television programs in languages other than English, also deepens an individual's concern about societal cohesion.

However, if we examine language retention concerns about past immigrants, we find similar patterns. For example, when colonial Pennsylvania was one-third German, Benjamin Franklin asked,

> Why [should] the Pennsylvanians . . . allow the Palatine Germans to swarm into our settlements, and by herding together to establish their language and Manners to the exclusion of ours? Why should Pennsylvania, founded by the English, become a colony of Aliens, who will shortly be so numerous as to Germanize us instead of our Anglifying them?[60]

Concerned about their meager command of English and need for interpreters, Franklin also remarked, "I suppose in a few years they will also be necessary in the Assembly, to tell one-half of our legislators what the other half say."[61] A century later, so many hundreds of thousands of Germans lived within the area bounded by Cincinnati, Milwaukee, and St. Louis, that the area became known as the "German triangle." Here, everyday speaking in German was so commonplace that several states in the region passed legislation permitting the use of German in public schools for all classroom instruction.[62] Needless to say, many Americans were aghast at what they thought was the encouragement of German non-assimilation.

Similarly, as millions of Italian immigrants in the first two decades of the twentieth century settled in what became the Little Italys of many U.S. cities, the prevalence of Italian language usage, signs, newspapers, and radio programs led many Americans to denounce these "inassimilable" Italians and to seek restrictive legislation to stop any more from coming here. Sound familiar?

Although Spanish is now the secondmost language spoken at home (about 31 million do so), other languages have also been increasing significantly. Foremost among these are Arabic, Russian, Tagalog (Philippines), and Vietnamese. In 1990, French was the thirdmost language spoken; today it is Chinese (see Figure 7.5).

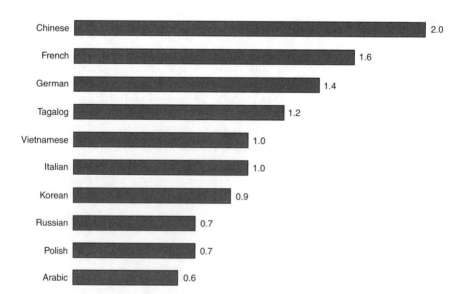

FIGURE 7.5   Ten Languages Most Frequently Spoken at Home Other Than English and Spanish, Age 5 Years and Older, in Millions: 2000

Source: U.S. Bureau of the Census.

With about a million or more immigrants entering the United States each year, the extensive use of other languages alarms many nativists. Of course, many Asian and other non-English-speaking immigrants add to nativists' concerns. The Census Bureau estimates revealed that nearly one in five Americans does not speak English at home. In fact, more than 10.5 million said they speak little or no English, up from 6.5 million in 1990. According to experts, some of the rise is due to the fast growth of the new-immigrant population, which included millions of people who came here illegally. The share of people who speak little English is highest among those in their working years, ages 18 to 64.[63]

Bilingual Education

Offering **bilingual education**—teaching subjects in both English and the student's native language—can take the form of a transitional program (gradually phasing in English completely over several years) or a maintenance program (continued native-language teaching to sustain the students' heritage with a simultaneous but relatively limited emphasis on English proficiency).

For the many U.S. residents who assume that English-speaking schools provided the heat for the melting pot, the popularity of bilingual education—particularly maintenance programs—is a sore point. Some see these efforts as counterproductive because they tend to reduce assimilation in and the cohesiveness of U.S. society, while simultaneously isolating ethnic groups from one another. Advocates of bilingual programs emphasize that they are developing **bilingualism**—fluency in both English and the students' native tongue—and that many youngsters are illiterate in both when they begin school.

Public funding for bilingual education began in 1968, when Congress passed the Bilingual Education Act, designed for low-income families only. Two years later, the Department of Health, Education, and Welfare specified that school districts in which any national-origin group constitutes more than 5 percent of the student population had a legal obligation to provide bilingual programs for low-income families.

In 1974, two laws significantly expanded bilingual programs. The Bilingual Act eliminated the low-income requirement and urged that children receive various courses that provided appreciation of their cultural heritage. The Equal Opportunity Act identified failure to take "appropriate action" to overcome language barriers impeding equal participation in school as a form of illegal denial of equal educational opportunity. **English as a Second Language (ESL) programs** have since expanded to function in about 125 languages, including 20 Native American languages. With 10 million immigrant children now enrolled in the public schools—both urban and suburban—schools must overcome cultural, language, and literacy barriers to provide for their education.

Schools thus face an enormous challenge in overcoming the language barrier so many students face. Between 1979 and 2004, the number of school-age children (ages 5–17) who spoke a language other than English at home increased from 9 to 19 percent, from 3.8 to 9.9 million. If current trends continue, by 2010, children of immigrants will constitute 25 percent of the total K–12 student population.[64]

Because 95 percent of all immigrant children attend urban schools, this challenge falls primarily to these urban areas, most especially those in the six states where immigrants are most concentrated: California, New York, Florida, Texas, New Jersey, and Illinois. For example, almost half of all school-age children in California are children of immigrants. However, new immigrant patterns are doubling, even tripling the enrollment of immigrant children in such states as Nevada, North Carolina, Georgia, and Nebraska.[65]

Three-fourths of all limited-English-proficient (LEP) students receive English as a Second Language instruction, and only one-fourth have this in-

On May 1, 2006, demonstrators nationwide marched in many U.S. city downtowns, as here in Chicago, to show support for immigration reform and opposition to legislation that would criminalize the actions of an estimated 12 million illegal immigrants. When President Bush signed the U.S.-Mexico border fence bill in October 2006, which called for construction of a 700-mile fence, the issue became even more polarized.

struction paired with native-language academic instruction, more commonly known as bilingual programs.

The practical value of ESL programs over native-language instruction is readily apparent since it is practically impossible to offer native-tongue classes in so many languages. As it is, urban and suburban schools struggle for funds, space, and qualified teachers for their various bilingual programs.

Older naturalized U.S. citizens often cite difficulty with the English language while they were students as one of the most difficult aspects of adjusting to the United States and gaining acceptance. Bilingual proponents argue that their programs ease that adjustment and accelerate the learning process. Since the 1970s, the National Education Association has supported an **English-plus program** to promote the integration of language minority students into the U.S. mainstream and to develop foreign language competence in native-born U.S. students to function in a global economy.[66]

How effective is bilingual education in helping children learn English? Christine H. Rossell and Keith Baker examined three hundred studies pursuing this question and found that in only 22 percent of methodologically acceptable studies was transitional bilingual education better than regular classroom instruction when the outcome is reading; for math, it was only 9 percent.[67] Most recent studies are inconclusive, showing neither bilingual education nor English immersion to be superior to the other. Some concluded that it's not the model of instruction that matters, but the quality. Other researchers completed a synthesis of all available research on literacy, including that of the U.S. Department of Education, and found that children did somewhat better if they received some instruction in their home language, in addition to that in English, but it was unclear how much or what kind of home language instruction was best.[68]

Since bilingual programs vary so widely in approach and quality, it is difficult to assess their overall effectiveness. However, studies show that students who are given enough time in well-taught bilingual programs to gain English proficiency test better in the eleventh grade than do those with no prior preparation in any bilingual program.[69]

The English-Only Movement

Opponents of bilingual education argue that the program encourages "ethnic tribalism," fostering separation instead of a cohesive society. Their objections come in response to Hispanic leaders in such groups as the National Council of La Raza and the League of United Latin American Citizens (LULAC), who claim that "language rights" entitle Hispanic people to have their language and culture maintained at public expense, both in the schools and in the workplace. The oldest Hispanic civil-rights group still in existence, LULAC was founded in 1929. Ironically, it began as an assimilationist organization, accepting only U.S. citizens as members, conducting its official proceedings in English, and declaring as one of its goals "to foster the acquisition and facile use of the official language of our country."[70]

In reaction, the nativists have pressed to make English the official language for all public business. The largest national lobbying group, U.S. English, was cofounded by Japanese immigrant S. I. Hayakawa, a former U.S. senator from California and former president of and linguistics professor at San Francisco State University. By 2006, the group claimed 1.8 million members, and its success prompted critics to attack it as being anti-immigrant, racist, divisive, and dangerous.[71] The group's goals are to reduce or eliminate bilingual education, to abolish multilingual ballots, and to prevent state and local expenditures on translating road signs and government documents and translating to assist non–English-speaking patients at public hospitals.

By 2007, twenty-eight states had passed English-only legislation; thirteen other states had rejected similar proposals. New Mexico's legislature went beyond rejecting the proposal; in 1989, it approved "English Plus," stating, "Proficiency in more than one language is to the economic and cultural benefit of our State and Nation." Then, in 1998, the Arizona Supreme Court struck down the state's official English law as unconstitutional. Nevertheless, public opinion polls consistently show that Americans think English should be the official language. A 2006 Rasmussen Reports poll, for example, found 85 percent of Americans saying so.[72] Since 1981, over fifty bills have been introduced in Congress to make English the nation's official language. Five of these bills passed in one chamber but not in the other. As this book goes to press, similar legislation is again pending.

Unnecessary Action. Although proponents of English-only legislation claim that such action is essential to preserve a common language and provide a necessary bridge across a widening language barrier within the country, numerous polls and studies demonstrate that this action is unnecessary. For more than twenty-five years, public opinion polls have consistently shown that the large majority of foreign-born Americans believe learning English is important to become a part of U.S. society and to find a job.[73]

That attitude manifests itself in action. Today, first- and second-generation Americans are becoming fluent in English at a faster pace than did past immigrants. In the largest longitudinal study of second-generation Americans (5,200 immigrant children in Miami and San Diego), Rubén Rumbaut and Alejandro Portes found that 99 percent spoke fluent English and less than one-third maintained fluency in their parents' tongues by age 17.[74] Similarly, another study by Rumbaut revealed the preference by 73 percent of second-generation immigrants in Southern California with two foreign-born parents to speak English at home instead of their native tongue. By the third generation, more than 97 percent of these immigrants—Chinese Filipino, Guatemalan, Korean, Mexican, Salvadoran, and Vietnamese—preferred to speak only English at home.[75]

On a broader scale, the Census Bureau reports that, of those U.S. residents aged 18 to 64 who spoke an Asian or Pacific Islander language in 2000, 78 percent also spoke English "very well" or "well." Of the same age cohort who spoke Spanish in 2000, 68 percent also spoke English "very well" or "well."[76] Rumbaut reports that those who do not yet speak English well or at all are disproportionately the elderly (especially those in dense ethnic enclaves, such as among the Cubans in Miami), the most recently arrived, the undocumented, and the least educated.[77]

Multiculturalism

In its early phase, during the 1970s, **multiculturalism** meant including material in the school curriculum that related the contributions of non-European peoples to U.S. history. Next followed efforts to change all areas of the curriculum in elementary and secondary schools and colleges to reflect the diversity of U.S. society and to develop students' awareness of and appreciation for the impact of non-European civilizations on U.S. culture. The intent of this movement was to promote an expanded U.S. identity that recognized previously excluded groups as integral components of the whole, both in heritage and in present actuality (see the International Scene box on page 176).

Some multiculturalists subsequently moved away from an assimilationist or integrative approach, rejecting a common bond of identity among the distinct minority groups. The new multiculturalists advocate "minority nationalism" and "separatist pluralism," with a goal of specific, separate group identities, not of a collective national identity.[78]

To create a positive group identity, these multiculturalists go beyond advocacy for teaching and maintaining a group's own cultural customs, history, values, and festivals. They also deny the validity of the dominant culture's customs, history, values, and festivals. Two examples are Native Americans who object to Columbus Day parades and Afrocentrists who assert that Western culture was merely derived from Afro-Egyptian culture. Another striking example is the argument that only groups with power can be racist. This view holds that because Whites have power, they are intrinsically racist, whereas people of color lack power and so cannot be racist.[79]

Opponents counter that racism can and does exist within any group, regardless of how much power that group has. John J. Miller, a longtime pro-immigration advocate, argues that multiculturalism undermines the assimilation ethic, and the weaker our assimilation efforts, the fewer immigrants we can accept. His ten-point "Americanization Manifesto" includes ending ethnic-group preferences, bilingual education, and multilingual voting; strengthening the naturalization process; and reducing illegal immigration.[80]

Another battleground for multiculturalists involves offering or eliminating courses in Western civilization. Some institutions, such as Providence

The International Scene
Italy and Spain Struggle with Illegal Immigration

Italy and Spain own islands near the African coast that have become popular staging areas for migrants fleeing the poverty of their homelands. As a result, both countries are overwhelmed with the tens of thousands of illegal arrivals each year.

Italy's long coastline and close proximity to other countries make it especially vulnerable. The most popular clandestine sea route for Africans is from Libya or Tunisia to the Italian island of Lampedusa or to Sicily. The Spanish Canary Islands attract boatloads from Morocco and Mauritania. Despite the dangers of their rickety boats capsizing (hundreds have drowned), the overcrowded boats keep coming. Many are intercepted, but under cover of darkness, others get through.

Italy is also the destination by a second route: a sixty-mile speedboat ride by smugglers from Albania across the Adriatic Sea. Albanians, Afghans, Kurds, Turks, and Chinese are the most frequent arrivals this way. A third route brings in eastern Europeans by truck over the Slovenian border into Milan.

The Organization for Economic Cooperation and Development (OECD) reports that, in 2005, Italy's foreign-born population totaled 2.5 million, or 4.3 percent of the total population. Spain had 4.8 million foreign-born, 8.5 percent of its total population. With no border checks among European Union member nations, an illegal migrant reaching either country has essentially reached Europe as well, and so EU officials are attempting to persuade African nations to crack down on these illegal boatloads.

Italy and Spain enacted amnesty programs to cope with the great numbers not fully participating in their economic systems. These amnesties, however, did not solve the problem and instead tended more to attract new illegal migration than to drain the basin of illegality.

Africans and Asians are visible everywhere, selling cheap merchandise on the streets, trying to clean windshields at intersections, or pumping gas. The arrival of so many physically and culturally distinct newcomers in so short a period created an anti-immigrant backlash, transforming relatively open countries into closed ones. Racial incidents, including firebombings, became commonplace and the growing backlash resulted in increased popularity for anti-immigration political parties, forcing the ruling political parties to become more aggressive in their deportation efforts.

Critical thinking question: What patterns of similarity do you see between the United States and European experiences with undocumented migrants? What dissimilarities?

College in Rhode Island, expanded such course requirements and made them interdisciplinary; other institutions, such as Stanford University, questioned their inclusion at all. At many institutions, the proposals for curriculum change ranged from making all students take non-Western and women's studies courses as part of their degree requirements to excluding all Western history and culture courses from such requirements.

Regardless of their orientation, most multiculturalists are pluralists waging war with assimilationists. Neither side will vanquish the other, though, for both forces remain integral parts of U.S. society. The United States continues to offer a beacon of hope to immigrants everywhere, keeping the rich tradition of pluralism alive and well. And yet, as has been consistently demonstrated for centuries, assimilationist forces will remain strong, particularly for immigrant children and their descendants. Multiculturalism will no more weaken that process than did the many past manifestations of ethnic ingroup solidarity.

People who cite the Afrocentrist movement as divisive need to consider the reality of separate racial worlds within the United States, from colonial times to the revelations generated by the 1995 O. J. Simpson verdict. These separate worlds result not from multiculturalist teachings but from systemic racism. Only by breaking down the remaining racial barriers,

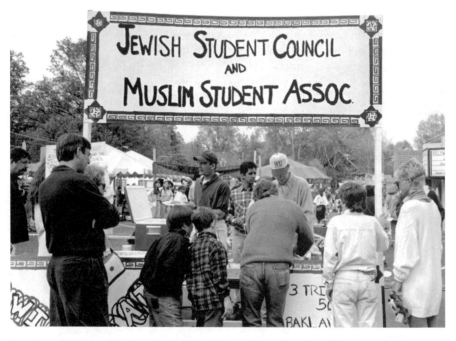

As the world's leading immigrant-receiving nation, the United States creates a social climate in which ethnic intergroup cooperation often exists in stark contrast to the ethnic hostilities in the same groups' homelands. Although visible in other U.S. settings as well, such scenes are especially commonplace on college campuses, which promote cultural diversity, such as this Washington University student fair.

eliminating institutional discrimination, and opening up paths to a good education and job opportunities for everyone can society improve racial integration. Afrocentrist schools do not undermine a cohesive U.S. society any
more than Catholic schools, yeshivas, or other religious schools do.

Racial and Ethnic Diversity in the Future

The Census Bureau, assuming that present demographic trends will continue, projects a dramatic change in the composition of U.S. society by the
mid-twenty-first century. Its estimates include an average of 1 million immigrants and 400,000 undocumented aliens entering the country each year for
the next five decades. Fertility rates, currently at 2.1, were adjusted by race
and factored into the population projections.[81]

However, the Census Bureau reports that the cumulative effects of immigration will be more important than births to people already living in the
United States. By the mid-twenty-first century, it said, 21 percent of the population—an estimated 82 million—will be either immigrants who arrived
after 1991 or children of those immigrants.

By 2050, Hispanics will number about 102.6 million, or 24.4 percent of
the total population. The Census Bureau projects that African Americans will
then number about 61.4 million, or 14.6 percent (Figure 7.6). All data reflect
midrange projections, not high or low estimates.

The nation's Asian and Pacific Islander population will grow to about
33.4 million, or 9 percent, by 2050. Native Americans will have increased to

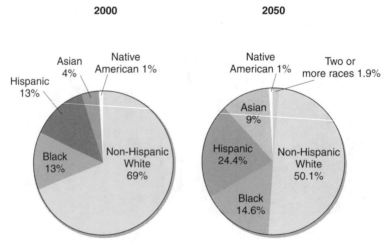

FIGURE 7.6   America's Growing Diversity

Source: U.S. Bureau of the Census middle-range projections.

about 4.4 million by then, slightly more than 1 percent of the total. The number of non-Hispanic Whites will be 210.3 million by 2050, or 50 percent of the population.

Some observers have reacted to these projections with alarm, using them to argue for immigration restrictions. Others relish the thought of U.S. society becoming more diverse. These projections, however, have some limitations, not the least of which is their assumption that conditions worldwide will remain constant 50 or more years into the future. Certainly, 50 years ago, no one would have predicted the current birth, death, and migration patterns that currently affect the United States. A forecast about the year 2050, then, is anything but certain.

Even more significant is the high probability that these Census Bureau projections will fall victim to the **Dillingham Flaw**. Who is to say that today's group categories will have the same meaning in the mid-twenty-first century? Fifty years ago, Italian, Polish, and Slavic Americans were still members of distinct minority groups that lacked economic, political, and social power. They displayed all the classic characteristics of minority groups: ascribed status, endogamy, unequal treatment, and visibility. Today, they are mostly in the mainstream, displaying traits of civic, marital, and structural assimilation. Like European Americans who intermarried earlier, those whose ancestry is Italian, Polish, and Slavic are now mostly a blend of other nationalities. Fifty years from now, the same may be true of other groups, such as Hispanics. Two generations from now, Americans will likely view one another very differently from how we do now.

Indicators of Ethnoreligious Change

Although the demographic patterns of fertility, mortality, and migration are helpful in making projections, other patterns give reason for caution in predicting the future.

Interethnic Marriages. Our expectation that Hispanic Americans will marry outside their ethnic group, as have European Americans, finds support in the process that is already under way. In 2005, nearly 2.2 million Hispanic Americans were married to someone of non-Hispanic origin, up 246 percent from 891,000 in 1980.[82] That is approximately 5 percent of the adult Hispanic American population, not an overwhelming proportion but nonetheless a growing one. The children born from these exogamous marriages are obviously of mixed ethnic heritage, which suggests that one day Hispanic American may be no more a separate ethnic category than Italian, Polish, or Slavic now is.

Interracial Marriages. So far, we have not succeeded in eliminating the racial barrier, and in 50 years that barrier may still exist. Nevertheless, one present-day trend suggests that our current simplistic racial categories are already obsolete. In 2005, 3.8 percent of all marriages in the continental United States were interracial, compared to 1.3 percent in 1980. By 2005, interracially married couples numbered about 2.3 million, almost one-fifth of them (422,000) Black–White couples—six times more than the 65,000 in 1970. Whites married to a non-White spouse of a race other than Black (most often, Asian) grew from 233,000 to 1.7 million. Couples consisting of Blacks married to a non-Black spouse of a race other than White increased from 12,000 to 145,000.[83]

Researchers are developing some interesting findings about interracial relationships. George and Sherelyn Yancey report that biracial relationships seem to form along the same lines as same-race relationships—that race is only an aesthetic factor, similar to others' preference of hair color or eye color.[84] They also suggested that, because interracial dating brings together individuals from different cultures, such relationships may increase appreciation for the partner's culture and promote healthy racial relations through marital assimilation.[85] Richard Lewis, Jr., George Yancey, and Siri S. Bletzer found that persons with a premarital history of biracial dating said cross-racial personal and sexual attractiveness, along with ease of talking, were important spouse selection factors.[86] An intriguing study by Adam Troy, Jamie Lewis-Smith, and Jean-Philippe Laurenceau found partners in interracial relationships reported significantly higher relationship satisfaction compared to those in intraracial relationships.[87]

Racial interracial marriage patterns vary if we control for ethnicity. For example, Suzanne Model and Gene Fisher found that West Indian men of any generation have lower exogamy rates than African American men, while exogamy rates are higher among West Indian women who arrived as children or were born in the United States than among African American women.[88] In this study, both gender and racial differences in interracial marriages occurred because of ethnicity.

As George Yancey suggests, interracial romantic relationships are a useful barometer of race relations and structural assimilation in U.S. society. In a study that separately analyzed African, Asian, European, and Hispanic Americans, he found similar demographic and social factors that predicted outdating across racial groups. Men were more likely to date interracially than women, particularly if they attended interracial schools. Neither religious preference nor geographic region were significant factors, nor did his findings support the notion that majority-group members use interracial dating relationships to "trade up" by dating racial minorities with higher economic and educational attainment.[89] It would appear, as also suggested by my social distance study discussed in Chapter 1, that the racial barrier is lowering when it comes to intimate social relations.

Over 3 million biracial children now live in the United States, and many adult Blacks and Whites also claim mixed racial ancestry. If we add to the biracial offspring from these marriages those Latinos, Filipinos, Native Americans, and Hawaiians with multiracial ancestry, we can readily understand why past Census Bureau single-race classifications were inadequate. Fortunately, the census in 2000 for the first time enabled people to identify themselves as members of more than one racial group, allowing the Bureau to report more accurately the multiracial reality that contributes to U.S. diversity and aiding demographers in making projections in this area. As a result, 6.8 million Americans said they belonged to more than one race in the 2000 census. As Kathleen Korgen reports:

> Biracial Americans today face choices in racial identity never available to preceding generations. Now the nation must adjust to their growing resolve to identify with both sides of their racial heritage.[90]

Religion and Migration   Earlier immigration waves transformed the United States from an almost exclusively Protestant country into a land of three major faiths: Catholic, Jewish, and Protestant. Because religion is often closely intertwined with ethnicity, current migration patterns offer clues about the religious preferences of future Americans if current trends continue.

Latino and Filipino migration may increase the Catholic population from the current 22 percent to 40 percent by 2050. Migration from Africa, Asia, and the Middle East may increase the Muslim population from 1 percent of the total to 5 percent. Other projections are that the Jewish population will decline from 2 percent to 1 percent and the Protestant population from 56 percent to 49 percent; the populations of other religions—including Buddhism, Hinduism, and Sikhism—will increase from 4 percent to 5 percent. Even if these predictions turn out to be somewhat inaccurate, the future will show greater religious diversity than the present does.

Caution is needed in accepting these predictions, of course, because the Dillingham Flaw of oversimplified generalizations and the imposition of present-day sensibilities may lead to a misreading of the eventual reality. Since religious intermarriage is now increasing among followers of all faiths, and since the nonreligious segment of society is also growing, we may find a very different future with respect to religion than we can accurately project.

Beyond Tomorrow

Diversity is the word that best describes the past, present, and future of the United States. United by a core culture and shared beliefs in certain ideals, the nation's peoples have not always understood their common bond or openly accepted one another as equals. As the dual realities of assimilation and pluralism continue to pull people seemingly in two directions at once, few people recognize that they are witnessing a recurring set of historical patterns. Instead, some voices cry out again against immigration, brand the newcomers as "unassimilable," and express fear for the character and cohesiveness of society.

Despite some progress, the United States has never fully resolved its race relations problems. As it becomes a more multiracial society than ever before, it may see a worsening of race relations. We've seen some indicators here: Black–Asian and Black–Latino conflicts in addition to Black–White conflicts, as well as polar-opposite perceptions between Blacks and Whites during the O. J. Simpson trial and verdict. Perhaps, though, the situation will improve with deconstruction of the rigid racial categories that presently promote greater social distance and with more sharing of power through the increased presence of non-White Americans in elective offices and other policymaking positions.

As we approach the future, we do so with the educational attainment of all Americans rising. If knowledge is power, perhaps that reality will lead us to greater appreciation and tolerance for one another. This book has been an attempt to enhance that understanding. We need to comprehend the larger context and patterns within which the dynamics of intergroup relations exist. We need to realize that pluralism has always been part of the U.S. experience and does not threaten either the assimilation process or the cohesiveness of society. We need to recognize that race and ethnicity are simply other people's humanity. When we reach that level of understanding, we will be able to acknowledge that diversity is the nation's strength, not its weakness; and when that happens, our society will be even stronger.

KEY TERMS

Bilingual education
Bilingualism
Dillingham Flaw
English as a Second Language (ESL)
  programs

English-plus programs
Multiculturalism
Segmented assimilation
Social capital
Spatial assimilation

REVIEW QUESTIONS

1. What are some of the explanations for ethnic consciousness? Which seems most plausible? Why?

2. Discuss ethnicity as a social process, applying the concepts of assimilation and pluralism to your discussion.

3. What do current immigration patterns indicate? Is immigration a problem for native-born U.S. residents? Explain.

4. What are the pros and cons of bilingual education?

5. Describe the varying viewpoints about multiculturalism and political correctness.

6. What is the future of ethnicity in the United States?

SUGGESTED READINGS

Bean, Frank D. and Gillian Stevens. *America's Newcomers and the Dynamics of Diversity.* New York: Russell Sage Foundation, 2005.

> A social scientific assessment of the impact of immigration on the United States and the country's trransformation into a multi-ethnic and multiracial society.

Graham, Otis L, Jr. *Unguarded Gates: A History of America's Immigration Crisis.* Rowman & Littlefield, 2006.

> A provocative examination of past restrictive immigration as a framework for addressing the current immigration crisis.

Hollinger, David A. *Postethnic America: Beyond Multiculturalism,* rev. ed. New York: Basic Books, 2006.

> A review of current issues in the multiculturalist–nativist debate from a historical perspective, advocating a middle-ground cosmopolitan approach and suggesting the need to find common ground, not just to tolerate one another.

Kivisto, Peter, and Georganne Rundblad (eds.). *Multiculturalism in the United States: Current Issues, Contemporary Voices.* Thousand Oaks, Calif.: Pine Forge Press, 2000.

> Anthology containing essays by many prominent scholars on contemporary racial and ethnic issues.

Lind, Michael. *The Next American Nation: The New Nationalism and the Fourth American Revolution,* reprint ed. New York: Free Press, 1996.

> A wide-ranging, thought-provoking proposal for a coherent, unified national identity based on recognition that the forces of nationalism and the ideal of a transracial melting pot need not conflict with one another.

Miller, John J. *The Unmaking of Americans: How Multiculturalism Has Undermined America's Assimilationist Ethic.* New York: Simon & Schuster, 1998.

> A history of Americanization from its organized beginnings around 1907 to the current controversy on multiculturalism and a call for renewed Americanization efforts to sustain higher immigration.

Mindel, Charles H., Robert W. Habenstein and Roosevelt, Jr. Wright (eds.). *Ethnic Families in America: Patterns and Variations,* 4th ed. New York: Prentice Hall, 1997.

> An excellent portrait of U.S. racial and ethnic groups, their family characteristics, and the impact of the feminist movement on ethnic family life.

Moen, Phyllis, Donna Dempster-McClain, and Henry A. Walker (eds.). *A Nation Divided: Diversity, Inequality, and Community in American Society.* Ithaca, NY: Cornell University Press, 1999.

> Leading social scientists explore persisting tensions and new sources of strain involving sexual and gender minorities, white and nonwhite immigrants, rich and poor.

Parrillo, Vincent N. *Diversity in America*, 2d ed. Thousand Oaks, Calif.: Pine Forge Press, 2005.

A brief look at our past, present, and future, with emphasis on immigration, multiculturalism, assimilation versus pluralism, and national identity. Includes a full discussion of the Dillingham Flaw.

Sowell, Thomas. *Ethnic America: A History*, reprinted. New York: Basic Books, 1983.

A fine comparative analysis of major racial and ethnic groups in the United States, with discussion of reasons for their varying success in U.S. society.

INTERNET RESOURCES

The Federation for American Immigration Reform is dedicated to reducing immigration and at its website (www.fairus.org) you will find extensive one-sided materials. However, here you will also find detailed immigration information about your state.

The League of United Latin American Citizens (LULAC) is another advocacy group, but one in favor of immigration. At its website (www.lulac.org/immigration.html) you will find many informative links about immigration.

Public Agenda is a nonpartisan opinion research and civic engagement organization. At its website (www.publicagenda.org), you will find discussion of both sides of the issues on immigration and race.

NOTES

Chapter 1

1. Aristotle, *The Rhetoric* (New York: Appleton, 1932), Book I, Chapter 11.
2. See, e.g., Theodore Newcomb, "The Acquaintance Process: Looking Mainly Backward," *Journal of Personality and Social Psychology* 36 (1978): 1075–83.
3. Donn Byrne et al., "The Ubiquitous Relationship: Attitude Similarity and Attraction. A Cross-Cultural Study," *Human Relations* 24 (1971): 201–7.
4. Emory S. Bogardus, "Comparing Racial Distances in Ethiopia, South Africa, and the United States," *Sociology and Social Research* 52 (1968): 149–56.
5. See Tom W. Smith and Glenn R. Dempsey, "The Polls: Ethnic Social Distance and Prejudice," *Public Opinion Quarterly* 47 (1983): 584–600.
6. Milton Kleg and Kaoru Yamamoto, "As the World Turns: Ethno-Racial Distances after 70 Years," *Social Science Journal* 35 (April 1998): 183–90.
7. Vincent N. Parrillo and Christopher Donoghue, "Updating the Bogardus Social Distance Studies: A New National Survey," *The Social Science Journal*, 42:2 (2005): 257–71.
8. James Dyer, Arnold Vedlitz, and Stephen Worchel, "Social Distance among Racial and Ethnic Groups in Texas: Some Demographic Correlates," *Social Science Quarterly* 70 (1989): 607–16.
9. Patricia Odell, Kathleen Korgen, and Gabe Wang, "Cross-Racial Friendships and Social Distance Between Racial Groups on a College Campus," *Innovative Higher Education* 29:4 (2005): 291–305.
10. Michael J. White, Ann H. Kim, and Jennifer E. Glick, "Mapping Social Distance: Ethnic Residential Segregation in a Multiethnic Metro," *Sociological Methods & Research* 34:2 (2005): 173–203.
11. Mark Fossett, "Ethnic Preferences, Social Distance Dynamics, and Residential Segregation: Theoretical Explorations Using Simulation Analysis," *Journal of Mathematical Sociology* 30 (2006): 185–273.
12. Lyn H. Lofland, *A World of Strangers* reprint ed. (Long Grove, Ill., 1985), p. 16.
13. Georg Simmel, "The Stranger," in Kurt H. Wolff, (ed.), *The Sociology of Georg Simmel* (New York: Free Press, 1950).
14. Alfred Schutz, "The Stranger," *American Sociological Review* 69 (May 1944): 449–507.
15. John Solomos and Les Back, "Marxism, Racism, and Ethnicity," *American Behavioral Scientist* 38 (1995): 407–20.

16. See Albert Szymanski, "Racial Discrimination and White Gain," *American Socio-logical Review* 41 (1976): 403–14; Sidney M. Willhelm, "Can Marxism Explain America's Racism?" *Social Problems* 28 (1980): 98–112.
17. Erving Goffman, *The Presentation of Self in Everyday Life* (Garden City, N.Y.: Doubleday, 1959).
18. Barbara Ballis Lal, "Symbolic Interaction Theories," *American Behavioral Scientist* 38 (1995): 421–41.
19. Peter L. Berger and Thomas Luckmann, *The Social Construction of Reality* (Garden City, N.Y.: Doubleday, 1963).
20. Donald Young, *American Minority Peoples* (New York: Harper, 1932), p. viii.
21. Louis Wirth, "The Problem of Minority Groups," in Ralph Linton (ed.), *The Science of Man in the World Crisis* (New York: Columbia University Press, 1945), pp. 347–72.
22. Richard Schermerhorn, *Comparative Ethnic Relations* (New York: Random House, 1970), p. 8.
23. Tamotsu Shibutani and Kian M. Kwan, *Ethnic Stratification* (New York: Macmillan, 1965).
24. Schermerhorn, *Comparative Ethnic Relations*, p. 12.
25. Charles Wagley and Marvin Harris, *Minorities in the New World* (New York: Columbia University Press, 1964).
26. See Ashley Montagu, *Man's Most Dangerous Myth: The Fallacy of Race*, 5th ed. (New York: Oxford University Press, 1974).
27. Michael J. Bamshad and Steve E. Olson, "Does Race Exist?" *Scientific American* 289 (December 2003): 78–85.
28. See Maria P. P. Root, (ed.), *Racially Mixed People in America* (Newbury Park, Calif.: Sage Publications, 1992). See also J. C. Brigham and L. W. Biesbrecht, "All in the Family: Racial Attitudes," *Journal of Communication* 26 (1976): 69–74.
29. Arab American Institute, "Arab Americans: Demographics." Accessed at http://www.aaiusa.org/arab-americans/22/demographics on December 28, 2006.
30. Brewton Berry and Henry L. Tischler, *Race and Ethnic Relations*, 4th ed. (Boston: Houghton Mifflin, 1978), pp. 30–32.
31. Milton Gordon, *Assimilation in American Life* (New York: Oxford University Press, 1964), p. 27; Shibutani and Kwan, *Ethnic Stratification*, p. 47; Jerry D. Rose, *Peoples: The Ethnic Dimension in Human Relations* (Chicago: Rand McNally, 1976), pp. 8–12.
32. William Graham Sumner, *Folkways* (Boston: Ginn, 1906), p. 13.
33. See Henri Taifel, *Human Groups and Social Categories* (Cambridge: Cambridge University Press, 1981).
34. See Marc J. Schwartz, "Negative Ethnocentrism," *Journal of Conflict Resolution* 5 (March 1961): 75–81.
35. Robin M. Williams, Jr., *Strangers Next Door* (Englewood Cliffs, N.J.: Prentice Hall, 1964), p. 23.
36. Robert A. Levine and Donald T. Campbell, *Ethnocentrism: Theories of Conflict, Ethnic Attitudes, and Group Behavior* (New York: Wiley, 1972), pp. 68, 202.
37. Kenneth E. Boulding, *Conflict and Defense: A General Theory* (New York: Harper, 1962), pp. 162–63; Lewis A. Coser (ed.), *Sociological Theory: A Book of Readings* (New York: Macmillan, 1957), pp. 87–110; P. C. Rosenblatt, "Origins and Effects of Group Ethnocentrism and Nationalism," *Journal of Conflict Resolution* 8 (1964):

131–46; M. Sherif and C. W. Sherif, *Groups in Harmony and Tension* (New York: Harper, 1953), p. 196.

38. Brewton Berry, *Race and Ethnic Relations*, 3d ed. (Boston: Houghton Mifflin, 1965), p. 55.
39. Morton Klass and Hal Hellman, *The Kinds of Mankind* (New York: Lippincott, 1971), p. 61.
40. Molefi Kete Asante, *The Afrocentric Idea*, rev ed. (Philadelphia: Temple University Press, 1998).
41. Martin E. Spencer, "Multiculturalism, 'Political Correctness,' and the Politics of Identity," *Sociological Forum* 9 (1994): 547–67.
42. See Vincent N. Parrillo, "Diversity in America: A Sociohistorical Analysis," *Sociological Form* 9 (1994): 523–35.
43. Vincent N. Parrillo, *Diversity in America*, 2d ed. (Thousand Oaks, Calif.: Pine Forge Press, 2005), p. 13.
44. C. Wright Mills, *The Sociological Imagination* (New York: Oxford University Press, 1959), p. 8.
45. Ibid., p. 9.
46. Ibid., p. 146.

Chapter 2

1. See, for example, Lee Cronk, *The Complex Whole: Culture and the Evolution of Human Behavior* (Boulder, Colo.: Westview Press, 1999).
2. The importance of symbols to social interaction has drawn much attention in sociology. See Benjamin Lee Whorf, *Language, Thought and Reality* (New York: Wiley, 1956); Gertrude Jaeger and Philip Selznick, "A Normative Theory of Culture," *American Sociological Review* 29 (1964): 653–59; Herbert Blumer, *Symbolic Interaction: Perspective and Method* (Englewood Cliffs, N.J.: Prentice Hall, 1969).
3. Center for the Study of Sport in Society, *2004 Racial and Gender Report Card*, available http://www.bus.ucf.edu/sport/public/downloads/2004_Racial_Gender_Report_Card.pdf [December 28, 2006].
4. Harry C. Bredemeier and Richard M. Stephenson, *The Analysis of Social Systems* (New York: Holt, Rinehart & Winston, 1962), p. 3.
5. Bear climbing a tree as seen from other side. Giraffe going past a second-story window. Hot dog on a hamburger roll.
6. This connection between Lippmann's comments, the Droodles, and human response to definitions of stimuli was originally made by Harry C. Bredemeier and Richard M. Stephenson, *The Analysis of Social Systems*, pp. 2–3.
7. Edward O. Wilson, *Sociobiology* reprint ed. (Cambridge, Mass.: Belknap Press, 2000), p. 550.
8. Desmond Morris, *Manwatching: A Field Guide to Human Behavior* (New York: Abrams, 1979).
9. William I. Thomas, "The Relation of Research to the Social Process," in *Essays on Research in the Social Sciences* (Washington, D.C.: Brookings Institution, 1931), p. 189.
10. See the discussion on p. 131.
11. Gregory Razran, "Ethnic Dislike and Stereotypes: A Laboratory Study," *Journal of Abnormal and Social Psychology* 45 (1950): 7–27.

12. Stanley Lieberson, "A Societal Theory of Race and Ethnic Relations," *American Sociological Review* 26 (December 1961): 902–10.
13. See Andrew M. Greeley, *The American Catholic: A Social Portrait* (New York: Basic Books, 1977), Chapter 1; see also Richard D. Alba, *Italian Americans: Into the Twilight of Ethnicity* (Englewood Cliffs, N.J.: Prentice Hall, 1985), pp. 9–12.
14. William M. Newman, *American Pluralism* (New York: Harper & Row, 1973), p. 53.
15. Barbara Solomon, *Ancestors and Immigrants* reprint ed. (Boston: Northeastern University Press, 1989), pp. 59–61.
16. John Higham, *Strangers in the Land* (New Brunswick, N.J.: Rutgers University Press, 2002), p. 248.
17. George R. Stewart, *American Ways of Life* (New York: Russell & Russell, 1971), pp. 23, 28.
18. Milton Gordon, *Assimilation in American Life* (New York: Oxford University Press, 1964), pp. 70–71.
19. Ibid., p. 81.
20. Richard D. Alba and Victor Nee, "Rethinking Assimilation Theory for a New Era of Immigration," *International Migration Review* 31 (1997): 826–74; Min Zhou, "Progress, Decline, Stagnation? The New Second Generation Comes of Age," pp. 272–302, in Roger Waldinger (ed.), *Strangers at the Gates: New Immigrants in Urban America* (Berkeley: University of California Press, 2001).
21. Louis Wirth, "The Problem of Minority Groups," in Ralph Linton (ed.), *The Science of Man in the World Crisis* (New York: Columbia University Press, 1945), pp. 347–72.
22. Solomon, *Ancestors and Immigrants*, pp. 59–81.
23. Newman, *American Pluralism*, p. 63.
24. J. Hector St. John de Crèvecoeur, *Letters from an American Farmer* (New York: Albert & Charles Boni, 1925), pp. 54–55. Reprinted from the original edition, London, 1782.
25. Frederick Jackson Turner, *The Frontier in American History* (New York: Henry Holt, 1920), p. 351.
26. Israel Zangwill, *The Melting-Pot: Drama in Four Acts* (New York: Macmillan, 1921), p. 33.
27. Actually, any student of Western civilizations would point out that centuries of invasions, conquests, boundary changes, and so on often resulted in crossbreeding and that truly distinct or pure ethnic types were virtually nonexistent long before the eighteenth century.
28. Gordon, *Assimilation in American Life*, pp. 109–10.
29. Ruby Jo Reeves Kennedy, "Single or Triple Melting Pot? Intermarriage Trends in New Haven, 1870–1940," *American Journal of Sociology* 49 (January 1944): 331–39; see also her follow-up study in *American Journal of Sociology* 58 (July 1952): 52–59.
30. See Herberg, *Protestant-Catholic-Jew*.
31. Henry Pratt Fairchild, *Immigration* (New York: Macmillan, 1925), p. 396.
32. Herberg, *Protestant-Catholic-Jew*, pp. 33–34.
33. Newman, *American Pluralism*, p. 67.
34. Horace M. Kallen, "Democracy Versus the Melting Pot," *The Nation* (February 18, 1915), pp. 190–94; (February 25, 1915), pp. 217–20.
35. Gordon, *Assimilation in American Life*, p. 135.
36. Richard D. Alba, "Assimilation's Quiet Tide," *Public Interest* (Spring 1995): 3–4.

37. Herbert J. Gans, "Toward a Reconciliation of 'Assimilation' and 'Pluralism': The Interplay of Acculturation and Ethnic Retention," *International Migration Review* 31 (Winter 1997): 875–92.
38. Richard D. Alba and Victor Nee, "Rethinking Assimilation Theory for a New Era of Immigration," *International Migration Review* 31 (Winter 1997): 826–74.
39. Jeff Hitchcock, *Lifting the White Veil: An Explanation of White Culture in a Multiracial Context* (Roselle, NJ: Crandall, Dostie, and Douglass Books, 2003), pp. 115–16.

Chapter 3

1. Mary C. Sengstock, "Social Change in the Country of Origin as a Factor in Immigrant Conceptions of Nationality," *Ethnicity* 4 (March 1977): 54–69.
2. W. Lloyd Warner and Paul S. Lunt, *The Social Life of a Modern Community*, Yankee City Series, Vol. 1 (New Haven, Conn.: Yale University Press, 1941).
3. Stephan Thernstrom, "Yankee City Revisited: The Perils of Historical Naiveté," *American Sociological Review* 30 (1965): 234–42.
4. W. Lloyd Warner and Leo Srole, *The Social System of American Ethnic Groups*, Yankee City Series, Vol. 3 (New Haven, Conn.: Yale University Press, 1945).
5. Alan C. Kerckhoff, *Socialization and Social Class* (Englewood Cliffs, N.J.: Prentice Hall, 1972), pp. 126–28.
6. John C. Leggett, "Economic Insecurity and Working Class Consciousness," *American Sociological Review* 29 (1964): 226–47.
7. Richard Centers, *The Psychology of Social Classes: A Study of Class Consciousness* (Princeton, N.J.: Princeton University Press, 1949); Oscar Glantz, "Class Consciousness and Political Solidarity," *American Sociological Review* 23 (August 1958): 375–82; Robert W. Hodge and Donald J. Treiman, "Class Identification in the U.S.," *American Journal of Sociology* 73 (March 1968): 535–47; Werner S. Landecker, "Class Crystallization and Class Consciousness," *American Sociological Review* 28 (April 1963): 219–29; Robert T. Morris and Raymond J. Murphy, "A Paradigm for the Study of Class Consciousness," *Sociology and Social Research* 50 (April 1966): 298–313.
8. Stephen Steinberg, *The Ethnic Myth: Race, Ethnicity, and Class in America*, 3d ed. (Boston: Beacon Press, 2001).
9. Thomas Sowell, *Ethnic America: A History* (New York: Basic Books, 1983).
10. Colin Greer (ed.), *Divided Society* (New York: Basic Books, 1974), p. 34.
11. Milton M. Gordon, *Assimilation in American Life* (New York: Oxford University Press, 1964).
12. William M. Newman, *American Pluralism* (New York: Harper & Row, 1973), p. 84.
13. Gordon, *Assimilation in American Life*, p. 47.
14. See Patricia L. McCall and Karen F. Parker, "A Dynamic Model of Racial Competition, Racial Inequality, and Interracial Violence," *Sociological Inquiry* 75 (2005): 273–93; Leo Kuper, *Race, Class, and Power: Ideology and Revolutionary Change* (Los Angeles: Aldine Transaction, 2005); Claire J. Kim, "Imagining Race and Nation in Multiculturalist America," *Ethnic and Racial Studies* 27:6 (2004): 987–1005.
15. Thomas M. Pettigrew, "The Changing but Not Declining Significance of Race," *Michigan Law Review* 77 (January–March 1979); 917–24; Charles V. Willie, "The Inclining Significance of Race," *Society* 15 (July–August 1978): 10–15.

16. E. Franklin Frazier, *The Negro Family in Chicago* (Chicago: University of Chicago Press, 1932); see also *The Negro Family in the United States*, rev. ed. (Chicago: University of Chicago Press, 1932).

17. Daniel P. Moynihan, *The Negro Family: The Case for National Action* (Washington, D.C.: U.S. Department of Labor, 1965).

18. Ibid., p. 5.

19. Ibid., p. 6.

20. Ibid., pp. 30, 47.

21. Bill Moyers, "The Vanishing Family: Crisis in Black America," CBS Special Report, Columbia Broadcasting System, 1986; for an analysis of both Moynihan's report and Moyers' documentary, see Patricia Hill Collins, "A Comparison of Two Works on Black Family Life," *Signs* 14 (1989): 875–84.

22. Daniel P. Moynihan, "Families Falling Apart," *Society* (July–August 1990): 21–22.

23. Originally in Daniel Patrick Moynihan, "A Family Policy for the Nation," *America* 113 (September 18, 1965): 280–83. See also Moynihan, "Families Falling Apart," p. 21; David Gergen, "A Few Candles in the Darkness," *U.S. News & World Report* (May 25, 1992), p. 44.

24. Oscar Lewis, *The Children of Sanchez* (New York: Random House, 1961); *La Vida*, (New York: Vintage, 1966), pp. xlii–lii.

25. Ibid., p. xlv.

26. See David L. Harvey and Michael H. Reed, "The Culture of Poverty: An Ideological Analysis," *Sociological Perspectives* 39 (Winter 1996): 465–95.

27. Edward C. Banfield, *The Unheavenly City: The Nature and Future of Our Urban Crisis* (Boston: Little, Brown, 1970), pp. 210–11.

28. Joe R. Feagin, "Poverty: We Still Believe That God Helps Those Who Help Themselves," *Psychology Today* 6 (November 1972), 101–10, 129; "Black and White: A *Newsweek* Poll," *Newsweek* (March 7, 1988), p. 23; James R. Kluegel and Eliot R. Smith, *Beliefs about Inequality* (New York: Aldine de Gruyter, 1986).

29. National Public Radio, Kaiser Family Foundation, and Harvard University, "Poverty and Welfare: People's Chief Concerns," 2001.

30. See, for example, William F. Spriggs, "Poverty in America: The Poor *Are* Getting Poorer," *Crisis* 113 (2006): 14–19.

31. William Ryan, *Blaming the Victim*, rev. ed. (New York: Vintage, 1976).

32. Charles A. Valentine, *Culture and Poverty* (Chicago: University of Chicago Press, 1968).

33. Ibid., p. 129.

34. Harvey and Reed, "The Culture of Poverty."

35. Michael Harrington, *The Other America: Poverty in the United States* (Baltimore: Penguin, 1963).

36. Ibid., p. 21.

37. Lola M. Irelan, Oliver C. Moles, and Robert M. O'Shea, "Ethnicity, Poverty, and Selected Attitudes: A Test of the 'Culture of Poverty' Hypothesis," *Social Forces* 47 (1969): 405–13.

38. Eliot Liebow, *Tally's Corner: A Study of Negro Streetcorner Men*, 2d ed. (Lanham, Md.: Rowman & Littlefield, 2003), pp. 222–23. See also Ulf Hannerz, *Soulside: Inquiries into Ghetto Culture and Community* (Chicago: University of Chicago Press, 2004).

39. Hyman Rodman, "The Lower Class Value Stretch," *Social Forces* 42 (1963): 205–15.
40. L. Richard Della Fave, "The Culture of Poverty Revisited: A Strategy for Research," *Social Problems* 21 (1974): 609–21.
41. David Steigerwald, "Our New Cultural Determinism," *Society* 42 (2005): 71–5; Richard G. Bagnall, "Lifelong Learning and the Limitations of Economic Determinism," *International Journal of Lifelong Education* 19 (2000): 20–35.
42. Robert E. Park, *Race and Culture* (Glencoe, Ill.: Free Press, 1949), p. 150.
43. Seymour M. Lipset, "Changing Social Status and Prejudice: The Race Theories of a Pioneering American Sociologist," *Commentary* 9 (May 1950): 479.
44. Stanford M. Lyman, *The Black American in Sociological Thought: A Failure of Perspective* (New York: Putnam, 1972), pp. 49–50.
45. Warner and Srole, *The Social System of American Ethnic Groups*, pp. 285–86.
46. Michael A. Zarate, Berenice Garcia, and Azenett A. Garza, "Cultural Threat and Perceived Realistic Group Conflict as Dual Predictors of Prejudice," *Journal of Experimental Social Psychology* 40 (2004): 99–105.
47. Peter Burns and James G. Gimpel, "Economic Insecurity, Prejudicial Stereotypes, and Public Opinion on Immigration Policy," *Political Science Quarterly* 115 (2000): 201–25.
48. Ashley W. Doane, Jr., "Dominant Group Ethnic Identity in the United States: The Role of 'Hidden' Ethnicity in Intergroup Relations," *The Sociological Quarterly* 38 (Summer 1997), 375–97.
49. Stanley Lieberson, "A Societal Theory of Race and Ethnic Relations," *American Sociological Review* 26 (1961): 902–10.
50. William J. Wilson, *Power, Racism, and Privilege* (New York: Free Press, 1973), pp. 47–65.
51. Robert Blauner, "Internal Colonialism and Ghetto Revolt," *Social Problems* 16 (Spring 1969): 393–406.
52. Ibid., p. 397.
53. Donald L. Noel, "A Theory of the Origin of Ethnic Stratification," *Social Problems* 16 (Fall 1968): 157–72.
54. Lewis A. Coser, "Conflict: Social Aspects," in David Sills (ed.), *International Encyclopedia of the Social Sciences* (New York: Macmillan, 1968), pp. 234–35.
55. Ralf Dahrendorf, *Class and Class Conflict in Industrial Society* (Stanford, Calif.: Stanford University Press, 1959), pp. 215–18.
56. Max Weber, "Class, Status, Party," 1922, in Hans Gerth and C. Wright Mills (trans. and ed.), *From Max Weber* (New York: Oxford University Press, 1946), pp. 193–94.
57. See Hubert M. Blalock, Jr., *Toward a Theory of Minority-Group Relations* (New York: Wiley, 1967), pp. 199–203.
58. James M. O'Kane, "Ethnic Mobility and the Lower-Income Negro: A Socio-Historical Perspective," *Social Problems* 16 (1969): 309–11; see also Leonard Reissman and Michael N. Halstead, "The Subject Is Class," *Sociology and Social Research* 54 (1970): 301–4.
59. Ibid., pp. 303–11.
60. Ibid., 397; See also Stuart L. Hills, "Negroes and Immigrants in America," *Sociological Focus* 3 (Summer 1970): 85–96; Nathan Glazer, "Blacks and Ethnic Groups," *Social Problems* 18 (1971): 444–61.

Chapter 4

1. See Hortense Powdermaker, *Probing Our Prejudices* (New York: Harper, 1941), p. 1.
2. Louis Wirth, "Race and Public Policy," *Scientific Monthly* 58 (1944): 303.
3. Ralph L. Rosnow, "Poultry and Prejudice," *Psychology Today* (March 1972): 53.
4. Reported by Daniel Wilner, Rosabelle Price Walkley, and Stuart W. Cook, "Residential Proximity and Intergroup Relations in Public Housing Projects," *Journal of Social Issues* 8 (1) (1952): 45. See also James W. Vander Zanden, *American Minority Relations*, 3d ed. (New York: Ronald Press, 1972), p. 21.
5. Gordon W. Allport, "Prejudice: Is It Societal or Personal?" *Journal of Social Issues* 18 (1962): 129–30.
6. Bernard M. Kramer, "Dimensions of Prejudice," *Journal of Psychology* 27 (April 1949): 389–451.
7. L. Perry Curtis, Jr., *Apes and Angels: The Irishman in Victorian Caricature*, rev. ed. (Washington, D.C.: Smithsonian Press, 1997).
8. See Marvin B. Scott and Stanford M. Lyman, "Accounts," *American Sociological Review* 33 (February 1968): 40–62.
9. Philip Mason, *Patterns of Dominance* (New York: Oxford University Press, 1970), p. 7. See also Philip Mason, *Race Relations* (New York: Oxford University Press, 1970), pp. 17–29.
10. T. W. Adorno, Else Frankel-Brunswik, Daniel J. Levinson, and R. Nevitt Sanford, *The Authoritarian Personality* (New York: Harper & Row, 1950).
11. H. H. Hyman and P. B. Sheatsley, "The Authoritarian Personality: A Methodological Critique," in R. Christie and M. Jahoda (eds.), *Studies in the Scope and Method of "The Authoritarian Personality"* (Glencoe, Ill.: Free Press, 1954).
12. Solomon E. Asch, *Social Psychology* (Englewood Cliffs, N.J.: Prentice Hall, 1952), p. 545.
13. E. A. Shils, "Authoritarianism: Right and Left," in *Studies in the Scope and Method of "The Authoritarian Personality."*
14. D. Stewart and T. Hoult, "A Social-Psychological Theory of 'The Authoritarian Personality.'" *American Journal of Sociology* 65 (1959): 274.
15. H. C. Kelman and Janet Barclay, "The F Scale as a Measure of Breadth of Perspective," *Journal of Abnormal and Social Psychology* 67 (1963): 608–15.
16. For an excellent summary of authoritarian studies and literature, see John P. Kirscht and Ronald C. Dillehay, *Dimensions of Authoritarianism: A Review of Research and Theory* (Lexington: University of Kentucky Press, 1967).
17. George E. Simpson and J. Milton Yinger, *Racial and Cultural Minorities: An Analysis of Prejudice and Discrimination* (New York: Harper & Row, 1953), p. 91.
18. Ibid., pp. 62–79.
19. Howard J. Ehrlich, *The Social Psychology of Prejudice* (New York: Wiley, 1974); G. Sherwood, "Self-Serving Biases in Person Perception," *Psychological Bulletin* 90 (1981): 445–59; T. A. Wills, "Downward Comparison Principles in Social Psychology," *Psychological Bulletin* 90 (1981): 245–71.
20. Jennifer Crocker and Ian Schwartz, "Prejudice and Ingroup Favoritism in a Minimal Intergroup Situation: Effects of Self-Esteem," *Personality and Social Psychology Bulletin* 11 (4) (December 1985): 379–86.
21. See Russell G. Geen, *Human Aggression*, 2d ed. (Berkshire, England: Open University Press, 2001).

22. Leviticus 16:5–22.
23. Gordon W. Allport, *The Nature of Prejudice* (Cambridge, Mass.: Addison-Wesley, (1961), pp. 13–14.
24. Carl I. Hovland and Robert R. Sears, "Minor Studies of Aggression: Correlation of Lynchings with Economic Indices," *Journal of Psychology* 9 (Winter 1940): 301–10.
25. Miller and Bugelski, "Minor Studies in Aggression," pp. 437–42.
26. Donald Weatherley, "Anti-Semitism and the Expression of Fantasy Aggression," *Journal of Abnormal and Social Psychology* 62 (1961): 454–57.
27. See Leonard Berkowitz, "Whatever Happened to the Frustration-Aggression Hypothesis?" *American Behavioral Scientist* 21 (1978): 691–708; L. Berkowitz, *Aggression: A Social Psychological Analysis* (New York: McGraw-Hill, 1962).
28. D. Zillman, *Hostility and Aggression* (Hillsdale, N.J.: Lawrence Erlbaum, 1979); R. A. Baron, *Human Aggression* (New York: Plenum Press, 1977); N. Pastore, "The Role of Arbitrariness in the Frustration-Aggression Hypothesis," *Journal of Abnormal and Social Psychology* 47 (1952): 728–31.
29. A. H. Buss, "Instrumentality of Aggression, Feedback, and Frustration as Determinants of Physical Aggression," *Journal of Personality and Social Psychology* 3 (1966): 153–62.
30. J. R. Averill, "Studies on Anger and Aggression: Implications for Theories of Emotion," *American Psychologist* 38 (1983): 1145–60.
31. Talcott Parsons, "Certain Primary Sources and Patterns of Aggression in the Social Structure of the Western World," in *Essays in Sociological Theory* (New York: Free Press, 1964), pp. 298–322.
32. For an excellent review of Parsonian theory in this area, see Stanford M. Lyman, *The Black American in Sociological Thought: A Failure of Perspective* (New York: Putnam, 1972), pp. 145–69.
33. Herbert Blumer, "Race Prejudice as a Sense of Group Position," *Pacific Sociological Review* 1 (1958): 3–7.
34. John Dollard, "Hostility and Fear in Social Life," *Social Forces* 17 (1938): 15–26.
35. Muzafer Sherif, O. J. Harvey, B. Jack White, William Hood, and Carolyn Sherif, *Intergroup Conflict and Cooperation: The Robbers Cave Experiment* (Norman: University of Oklahoma Institute of Intergroup Relations, 1961). See also M. Sherif, "Experiments in Group Conflict," *Scientific American* 195 (1956): 54–58.
36. Donald Young, *Research Memorandum on Minority Peoples in the Depression* (New York: Social Science Research Council, 1937), pp. 133–41.
37. Andrew Greeley and Paul Sheatsley, "The Acceptance of Desegregation Continues to Advance," *Scientific American* 210 (1971): 13–19; T. F. Pettigrew, "Three Issues in Ethnicity: Boundaries, Deprivations, and Perceptions," in M. Yinger and S. J. Cutler (eds.), *Major Social Issues: A Multidisciplinary View* (New York: Free Press, 1978); R. D. Vanneman and T. F. Pettigrew, "Race and Relative Deprivation in the United States," *Race* 13 (1972): 461–86.
38. See Harry H. L. Kitano, "Passive Discrimination in the Normal Person," *Journal of Social Psychology* 70 (1966): 23–31.
39. Thomas Pettigrew, "Regional Differences in Anti-Negro Prejudice," *Journal of Abnormal and Social Psychology* 59 (1959): 28–36.
40. Jeanne Watson, "Some Social and Psychological Situations Related to Change in Attitude," *Human Relations* 3 (1950): 15–56.

41. John Dollard, *Caste and Class in a Southern Town*, 3d ed. (Florence, Ky.: Routledge, 1998).

42. Joachim Krueger and Russell W. Clement, "The Truly False Consensus Effect: An Ineradicable and Egocentric Bias in Social Perception," *Journal of Personality and Social Psychology* 67 (1994): 596–610.

43. Michael R. Leippe and Donna Eisenstadt, "Generalization of Dissonance Reduction: Decreasing Prejudice through Induced Compliance," *Journal of Personality and Social Psychology* 67 (1994): 395–414.

44. William M. Newman, *American Pluralism* (New York: Harper & Row, 1973), p. 197.

45. Elliot Aronson, *The Social Animal*, 9th ed. (New York: Worth, 2003), p. 197.

46. David Katz and Kenneth Braly, "Racial Stereotypes of One Hundred College Students," *Journal of Abnormal and Social Psychology* 28 (1933): 280–90; G. M. Gilbert, "Stereotype Persistence and Change among College Students," *Journal of Abnormal and Social Psychology* 46 (1951): 245–54; Marvin Karlins, Thomas L. Coffman, and Gary Walters, "On the Fading of Social Stereotypes: Studies in Three Generations of College Students," *Journal of Personality and Social Psychology* 13 (1969): 1–16.

47. See, for example, Lee Jussim, Melvin Manis, Thomas E. Nelson, and Sonia Soffin, "Prejudice, Stereotypes, and Labeling Effects: Sources of Bias in Person Perception," *Journal of Personality and Social Psychology* 68 (1995): 228–46; Leonard Gordon, "College Student Stereotypes of Blacks and Jews on Two Campuses: Four Studies Spanning 50 Years," *Sociology and Social Research* 70 (1986): 200–201.

48. Ehrlich, *The Social Psychology of Prejudice*, p. 22.

49. Erdman Palmore, "Ethnophaulisms and Ethnocentrism," *American Journal of Sociology* 67 (1962): 442–45.

50. Irving Lewis Allen, *Unkind Words: Ethnic Labeling from Redskin to WASP* (New York: Bergin & Garvey, 1990), p. 3.

51. Brian Mullen, "Ethnophaulisms for Ethnic Immigrant Groups," *Journal of Social Issues* 57 (2001): 457–75.

52. See Jeffrey H. Goldstein, "Theoretical Notes on Humor," *Journal of Communication* 26 (1976): 102–12.

53. Lois Leveen, "Only When I Laugh: Textual Dynamics of Ethnic Humor," *MELUS* 21 (1996): 29–55.

54. U.S. Commission on Civil Rights, *Window Dressing on the Set: Women and Minorities in Television* (Washington, D.C.: U.S. Government Printing Office, 1977); *Window Dressing on the Set: An Update*, 1979.

55. George Gerbner, quoted in "Life According to TV," *Newsweek* (December 6, 1982), p. 136.

56. Ibid.

57. Dennis J. Ganahl, Thomas J. Prinsen, and Sara Baker Netzley, "A Content Analysis of Prime Time Commercials: A Contextual Framework of Gender Representation," *Sex Roles* 49 (2003): 545–51.

58. Shannon N. Davis, "Sex Stereotypes in Commercials Targeted toward Children: A Content Analysis," *Sociological Spectrum* 23 (2003): 407–25.

59. Jennifer J. Henderson and Gerald J. Baldasty, "Race, Advertising, and Prime-Time Television," *Howard Journal of Communications* 14 (2003): 97–112.

60. Children Now, "Why It Matters: Diversity on Television," *Media Now.* Available http://www.childrennow.org/media/medianow/mnsummer2002.htm [August 15, 2003].

61. Ed Palmer, K. Taylor Smith, and Kim S. Strawser, "Rubik's Tube: Developing a Child's Television World View." In Gordon L. Berry & Joy K. Asamen (eds.), *Children and Television in a Changing Socio-Cultural World* (pp. 143–54) (Newbury Park, Calif.: Sage Publications, 1993).

62. Nina Huntemann and Michael Morgan, "Mass Media and Identity Development," Chapter 15, in Dorothy G. Singer and Jerome L. Singer (eds.), *Handbook of Children and the Media* (Thousand Oaks, Calif.: Sage Publications, 2001).

63. For an overview of research on this program, see Stuart H. Surlin, "Five Years of 'All in the Family': A Summary of Empirical Research Generated by the Program," *Mass Communication Review* 3 (1976): 2–6. See also J. C. Brigham and L. W. Biesbrecht, "All in the Family: Racial Attitudes," *Journal of Communication* 26 (1976): 69–74.

64. Neil Vidmar and Milton Rokeach, "Archie Bunker's Bigotry," *Journal of Communication* 24 (1974): 36–47.

65. S. Robert Lichter and Linda S. Lichter, "Television's Impact on Ethnic and Racial Images" (New York: American Jewish Committee, 1988).

66. Scott Coltrane and Melinda Messineo, "The Perpetuation of Subtle Prejudice: Race and Gender Imagery in 1990s Television Advertising," *Sex Roles* 42 (2000): 363–89.

67. Dana E. Mastro and Susannah R. Stern, "Representations of Race in Television Commercials: A Content Analysis of Prime-Time Advertising," *Journal of Broadcasting & Electronic Media* 47 (2003): 638–47.

68. Jean Kilbourne, *Can't Buy My Love* (New York: Touchstone Books, 2000).

69. Gina M. Wingood, Ralph J. DiClemente, Jay M. Bernhardt, Kathy Harrington, Susan L. Davies, Allysa Robillard, and Edward W. Hook, III, "A Prospective Study of Exposure to Rap Music Videos and African American Female Adolescents' Health," *American Journal of Public Health* 93 (2003): 437–9.

70. See Allport, *The Nature of Prejudice*, p. 251; Robin M. Williams, Jr., *Strangers Next Door* (Englewood Cliffs, N.J.: Prentice Hall, 1964), p. 150; James W. Vander Zanden, *American Minority Relations*, 3d ed. (New York: Ronald Press, 1972), pp. 460–69.

71. Brewton Berry and Henry L. Tischler, *Race and Ethnic Relations*, 4th ed. (Boston: Houghton Mifflin, 1978), p. 250. See also David G. Myers, *Social Psychology*, 2d ed. (New York: McGraw-Hill, 1987), pp. 55–56.

72. Elliot Aronson and Neal Osherow, "Cooperation, Prosocial Behavior, and Academic Performance: Experiments in the Desegregated Classroom," *Applied Social Psychology Annual* 1 (1980): 163–96.

73. Iain Walker and Mary Crogan, "Academic Performance, Prejudice, and the Jigsaw Classroom: New Pieces to the Puzzle," *Journal of Community and Applied Social Psychology* 8 (1998): 381–93.

74. See the nine articles in the special issue, "Tolerance and Education: Can Schooling Promote Tolerance for Social and Political Diversity?" *Review of Education/Pedagogy/Cultural Studies* 16 (1994): 273–463.

75. Charles H. Stember, *Education and Attitude Change* (New York: Institute of Human Relations Press, 1961).
76. Blumer, "Race Prejudice as a Sense of Group Position," pp. 3–7.
77. Vincent N. Parrillo, *Diversity in America*, 2d ed. (Thousand Oaks, Calif.: Pine Forge Press, 2005), pp. 139–42.
78. U.S. Department of Defense, *2003 Demographics: Profile of the Military Community* (Arlington, Va.: Military Family Resource Center, 2003), p. v.

Chapter 5

1. Gordon W. Allport, *The Nature of Prejudice* (Cambridge, Mass.: Addison-Wesley, 1954).
2. The Prejudice Institute, "What Is Ethnoviolence?" Available http://www.prejudiceinstitute.org/ethnoviolenceFS.html [July 21, 2006].
3. Robin M. Williams, *Strangers Next Door* (Englewood Cliffs, N.J.: Prentice Hall, 1964), pp. 124–25.
4. Robert K. Merton, "Discrimination and the American Creed," in Robert M. MacIver (ed.), *Discrimination and National Welfare* (New York: Harper, 1949), pp. 99–126.
5. Stokely Carmichael and Charles Hamilton, *Black Power*, reprint ed. (New York: Vintage Books, 1992).
6. Hubert M. Blalock, Jr., *Toward a Theory of Minority Group Relationships* (New York: Perigee, 1973), pp. 204–7. For insight into the origin of this argument, see Stanford M. Lyman, "Cherished Values and Civil Rights," *The Crisis* 71 (December 1964): 645–54, 695.
7. William M. Newman, *American Pluralism* (New York: Harper & Row, 1973), p. 231.
8. John Rawls, *A Theory of Justice*, rev. ed. (Cambridge, Mass.: Belknap Press, 1999).
9. Joseph Tussman and Jacobus tenBroek, "The Equal Protection of the Laws," *California Law Review* 37 (September 1949): 341–81.
10. Ibid., p. 381.
11. Stanford M. Lyman, "Asians, Blacks, Hispanics: Confronting Vestiges of Slavery," paper presented at Eastern Sociological Society meeting, Boston, May 1, 1987.
12. John Leo, "Endgame for Affirmative Action," *U.S. News & World Report* (March 13, 1995), p. 18.
13. Gertrude Ezorsky, *Racism and Justice: The Case for Affirmative Action* (Ithaca, N.Y.: Cornell University Press, 1991).
14. Michael Wines, "How Affirmative Action Got So Hard to Sell," *New York Times* (July 23, 1995), p. E3.
15. Linda Greenhouse, "Justices Back Affirmative Action by 5 to 4, but Wider Vote Bans a Racial Point System," *New York Times* (June 24, 2003), p. A1.
16. Steven Greenhouse and Jonathan D. Glater, "Companies See Law School Ruling as a Way to Help Keep the Diversity Pipeline Open," *New York Times* (June 24, 2003), p. A25.
17. John Gpuhl and Susan Welch, "The Impact of the Bakke Decision on Black and Hispanic Enrollment in Medical and Law Schools," *Social Science Quarterly* 71 (1990): 458–73.

18. Evan Thomas and Bob Cohn, "Rethinking the Dream," *Newsweek* (June 26, 1995), p. 20.
19. See, for example, Troy Duster, "Individual Fairness, Group Preferences, and the California Strategy," pp. 111–134, in Robert Post and Michael Ragin (eds.), *Race and Representation: Affirmative Action*. Cambridge, Mass.: Zone Books, 1998.
20. Tim J. Wise, *Affirmative Action: Racial Preference in Black and White* (New York: Routledge, 2005), p. 164.
21. Linda Chavez, "Court Abandons Colorblind Society," *Human Events* 59 (June 30, 2003): 1–2; Thomas Sowell, "How 'Affirmative Action' Hurts Blacks," *Forbes* 160 (October 6, 1997): 64.
22. Wines, "How Affirmative Action Got So Hard to Sell."
23. CBS News (January 5–8, 2006). Available at www.pollingreport.com/race.htm (accessed December 28, 2006).
24. Sam Howe Verhovek, "In Poll, Americans Reject Means but Not Ends of Racial Diversity," *New York Times* (December 14, 1997), p. A1.
25. Associated Press, "Races Split on Achieving School Diversity" (March 10, 2003).
26. Department of Health and Human Services, *National Household Survey on Drug Use and Health: 2004* (Rockville, MD: U.S. Government Printing Office, 2005), Table 1.28A.
27. Department of Justice, *Racial Profiling Fact Sheet* (June 17, 2003), accessed online at www.usdoj.gov/opa/pr/2003/June/racial_profiling_fact_sheet.pdf [December 28, 2006].

Chapter 6

1. See Brent Simpson and Michael W. Macy, "Power, Identity, and Collective Action in Social Exchange," *Social Forces* 82 (2004): 1373–1409; Laura S. Billings et al., "Race-Based Social Judgment by Minority Perceivers," *Journal of Applied Social Psychology* 30 (February 2000): 221–40; Connie M. Kane, "Differences in Family of Origin Perceptions among African American, Asian American, and Hispanic American College Students," *Journal of Black Studies* 29 (September 1998): 93–105.
2. See, for example, A. E. Taslitz (ed.), "The New Data: Over-Representation of Minorities in the Criminal Justice System," *Law and Contemporary Problems* 66 (Summer 2003): 1–298; Rebecca A. Anderson and Amy L. Otto, "Perceptions of Fairness in the Justice System: A Cross-Cultural Comparison, *Social Behavior and Personality* 31 (2003): 557–63; Marvin D. Free, Jr., "Race and Presentencing Decisions in the United States: A Summary and Critique of the Research," *Criminal Justice Review* 27 (2002): 203–32; Jody Clay-Warner, "Perceiving Procedural Injustice: The Effects of Group Membership and Status," *Social Psychology Quarterly* 64 (2001); 224–38; Saundra D. Westervelt and John A. Humphrey (eds.), *Wrongly Convicted Perspectives on Failed Justice* (New Brunswick, N.J.: Rutgers University Press, 2001).
3. Clifford R. Shaw and Henry D. McKay, *Juvenile Delinquency and Urban Areas* (Chicago: University of Chicago Press, 1942).
4. J. Philippe Rushton et al., "Cross-National Variation in Violent Crime Rates: Race, R-K Theory, and Income," *Population and Environment* 23 (July 2002): 501–11; Per-Olof H. Wikstrom et al., "Do Disadvantaged Neighborhoods Cause Well-Adjusted Children to Become Adolescent Delinquents?" *Criminology* 38

(November 2000): 1109–42; Matthew R. Lee, "Community Cohesion and Violent Predatory Victimization," *Social Forces* 79 (December 2000): 683–706.

5. Ronald L. Simons and Phyllis A. Gray, "Perceived Blocked Opportunity as an Explanation of Delinquency among Lower-Class Black Males: A Research Note," *Journal of Research in Crime and Delinquency* 26 (1989): 90–101.

6. Paul R. Vowell and David C. May, "Another Look at Classic Strain Theory: Poverty Status, Perceived Blocked Opportunity, and Gang Membership as Predictors of Adolescent Violent Behavior: *Sociological Inquiry* 70 (2000): 42–60. See also Scott Cummings and Daniel J. Monti, *Gangs: The Origins and Impact of Contemporary Youth Gangs in the United States* (Albany: State University of New York Press, 1993).

7. Patricia H. Jenkins, "School Delinquency and School Commitment," *Sociology of Education* 68 (1995): 221–39.

8. See Donna K. Nagata and Yuzuru J. Takeshita, "Psychological Reactions to Redress: Diversity among Japanese Americans Interned during World War II," *Cultural Diversity & Ethnic Minority Psychology* 8 (2002): 41–59, for a study on acceptance by ex-internees decades later after government redress.

9. Kurt Lewin, *Resolving Social Conflicts* (New York: Harper & Row, 1948), pp. 186–200.

10. Gordon W. Allport, *The Nature of Prejudice* (New York: Perseus, 1988), pp. 152–53.

11. Jennifer Crocker, Kristin Voelkl, Maria Testa, and Brenda Major, "Social Stigma: The Affective Consequences of Attributional Ambiguity," *Journal of Personality and Social Psychology* 60 (1991): 218–28; Frances E. Aboud, "The Development of Ethnic Self-Identification and Attitudes," in Jean S. Phinney and Mary Jane Rotheram (eds.), *Children's Ethnic Socialization* (Newbury Park, Calif.: Sage Publications, 1987), pp. 32–55; Margaret Beale Spencer, "Black Children's Ethnic Identity Formation: Risk and Resilience of Castelike Minorities," in Ibid., pp. 103–16.

12. Gunnar Myrdal, *An American Dilemma* (New York: McGraw-Hill, 1964), pp. 25–28; originally published by Harper, 1944.

13. Gordon W. Allport, "The Role of Expectancy," in H. Cantril (ed.), *Tensions That Cause Wars* (Urbana: University of Illinois Press, 1950), chap. 2.

14. Allport, *The Nature of Prejudice*, p. 160.

15. Robert E. Park, "Human Migration and the Marginal Man," *American Journal of Sociology* 33 (May 1928): 891; see also Everett V. Stonequist, *The Marginal Man* (New York: Scribner, 1937).

16. See Debra Harley, Kristine Jolivette, and Katherine McCormick, "Race, Class, and Gender: A Constellation of Positionalities with Implications for Counseling," *Journal of Multicultural Counseling and Development* 30 (2002): 216–38.

17. See Adam Weisberger, "Marginality and Its Directions," *Sociological Forum* 7 (1992): 425–26.

18. Hubert M. Blalock, Jr., *Toward a Theory of Minority Group Relations* (New York: Perigee, 1973), pp. 79–84.

19. Edna Bonacich, "A Theory of Middleman Minorities," *American Sociological Review* 38 (1973): 583–94.

20. Edna Bonacich and John Modell, *The Economic Basis of Ethnic Solidarity* (Berkeley: University of California Press, 1981), p. 30.

21. See Lyn H. Lofland, *A World of Strangers* (Long Grove, Ill.: Waveland Press, 1985); Gideon Sjoberg, *The Preindustrial City: Past and Present* (New York: Free Press, 1965), p. 50.
22. See John J. Macionis and Vincent N. Parrillo, *Cities and Urban Life*, 4th ed. (Upper Saddle River, N.J.: Prentice Hall, 2007), pp. 43–46.
23. See Allport, *The Nature of Prejudice*, pp. 53–54.
24. Deuteronomy 2:32–35; 3:1, 3–4, 6–7.
25. Arnold J. Toynbee, *A Study of History*, reprint ed. (New York: Oxford University Press, 1987), p. 465.
26. See James Morris, "The Final Solution, Down Under," in Frank Chalk (ed.), *The History and Sociology of Genocide: Analyses and Case Studies* (New Haven, CT: Yale University Press, 1990), pp. 204–22.
27. See Winthrop D. Jordan, *White over Black: American Attitudes toward the Negro, 1550–1812*, reissue ed. (Chapel Hill: University of North Carolina Press, 1995).
28. See Joseph A. Page, *The Brazilians* (Boston: Addison-Wesley, 1996), p. 95.
29. For a discussion of Black lynchings and the media, see Richard M. Perloff, "The Press and Lynchings of African Americans," *Journal of Black Studies* 30 (January 2000): 315–30.
30. See Colin M. Tatz, *With Intent to Destroy: Reflections on Genocide* (New York: Norton, 2003).
31. Southern Poverty Law Center, "The Year in Hate, 2005," accessed online at http://www.splcenter.org/intel/intpro.jsp [December 27, 2006].
32. Federal Bureau of Investigation, "Hate Crime," *Crime in the United States 2004*, accessed online at http://www.fbi.gov/ucr/hc2005/incidentsoffenses.htm [December 27, 2006].
33. Edna Bonacich, "A Theory of Ethnic Antagonism: The Split Labor Market," *American Sociological Review* 37 (1972): 554.
34. Ibid.
35. Ibid., p. 550.
36. Cliff Brown, "The Role of Employers in Split Labor Markets: An Event-Structure Analysis of Racial Conflict and AFL Organizing, 1917–1919," *Social Forces* 79 (2000): 653–81.
37. Kathleen Auerhahn, "The Split Labor Market and the Origins of Antidrug Legislation in the United States," *Law and Social Inquiry* 24 (1999): 436.

Chapter 7

1. Mary C. Sengstock, "Social Change in the Country of Origin as a Factor in Immigrant Conceptions of Nationality," *Ethnicity* 4 (1977): 54–69.
2. Vincent N. Parrillo, "Asian Americans in American Politics," in Joseph S. Roucek and Bernard Eisenberg (eds.), *America's Ethnic Politics* (Westport, Conn.: Greenwood Press, 1982), pp. 89–112.
3. Jose Itzigsohn, "Immigration and the Boundaries of Citizenship: The Institutions of Immigrants' Political Transnationalism," *International Migration Review* 34 (2000): 1126–54.
4. Sheila E. Henry, "Ethnic Identity, Nationalism, and International Stratification: The Case of the African American," *Journal of Black Studies* 29 (1999): 438–54.

5. Sengstock, "Social Change in the Country of Origin as a Factor in Immigrant Conceptions of Nationality," pp. 56–57.
6. Ibid., pp. 61, 64.
7. Marcus L. Hansen, "The Third Generation in America," *Commentary* 14 (1952): 492–500.
8. Marcus L. Hansen, "The Third Generation," in Oscar Handlin (ed.), *Children of the Uprooted* (New York: Harper & Row, 1966), pp. 255–71.
9. Peter Skerry, "Do We Really Want Immigrants to Assimilate?" *Society* 37 (2000): 57–62.
10. Neil C. Sandberg, *Ethnic Identity and Assimilation: The Polish-American Community* (New York: Praeger, 1974).
11. John P. Roche, "Suburban Ethnicity: Ethnic Attitudes and Behavior Among Italian Americans in Two Suburban Communities," *Social Science Quarterly* 63 (1982): 145–53.
12. Sean Valentine "Self Esteem, Cultural Identity, and Generation Status as Determinants of Hispanic Acculturation," *Hispanic Journal of Behavioral Sciences* 23 (November 2001): 459–68.
13. Alejandro Portés and Dag MacLeod, "What Shall I Call Myself? Hispanic Identity Formation in the Second Generation," *Ethnic and Racial Studies* 19 (July 1996): 523–47.
14. Nazli Kibria, "The Construction of 'Asian American': Reflections on Intermarriage and Ethnic Identity among Second-Generation Chinese and Korean Americans," *Ethnic and Racial Studies* 20 (July 1997): 523–44.
15. See Reed Ueda, "American National Identity and Race in Immigrant Generations: Reconsidering Hansen's 'Law,'" *Journal of Interdisciplinary History* 22 (1992): 483–91.
16. Harold J. Abramson, "The Religioethnic Factor and the American Experience: Another Look at the Three-Generation Hypothesis," *Ethnicity* 2 (1975): 163–77.
17. Ibid., p. 173.
18. Thomas Sowell, *Ethnic America: A History* (New York: Basic Books, 1981).
19. Stephen Steinberg, *The Ethnic Myth: Race, Ethnicity, and Class in America* (New York: Atheneum, 1981).
20. See, for example, Vincent N. Parrillo, "Asian Americans in American Politics," op. cit.
21. Nina Glick Schiller, Linda Basch, and Cristina Blanc-Szanton, "Transnationalism: A New Analytic Framework for Understanding Migration," in N. Glick Schiller, L. Basch, and C. Blanc-Szanton (eds.), *Towards a Transnational Perspective on Migration: Race, Class, Ethnicity, and Nationalism Reconsidered* (New York: New York Academy of Sciences, 1992), pp. 1–24.
22. Thomas Faist, "Transnationalization in International Migration: Implications for the Study of Citizenship and Culture," *Ethnic & Racial Studies* 23 (2000): 189–222.
23. "Immigrant Temporalities: Transnationalism, the Diaspora, Exiles, and Refugees," National Center for English Language Acquisition, accessed at www.ncela.gwu.edu/pathways/immigration/transnationalism.htm [October 31, 2004].
24. Glick Schiller et al., chaps. 1 and 8.

25. Pierre Bourdieu and Loic Wacquant, *An Invitation to Reflexive Sociology* (Chicago: University of Chicago Press, 1992), p. 119.
26. Patricia M. Fernández-Kelly, "Social Capital and Cultural Capital in the Urban Ghetto: Implications for the Economic Sociology of Immigration," in Alejandro Portés (ed.), *Economic Sociology of Immigration* (New York: Russell Sage Foundation, 1998).
27. Alejandro Portés (ed.), *The Economic Sociology of Immigration*; Ivan Light and Stavros Karageorgis, "The Ethnic Economy," in Neil Smelser and Richard Swedberg (eds.), *Handbook of Economic Sociology* (Princeton, N.J.: Princeton University Press, 1994).
28. Alejandro Portés and Min Zhou, "The New Second Generation: Segmented Assimilation and Its Variants," *Annals of the American Political and Social Sciences* 530 (1993): 74–96.
29. Roger Waldinger and Cynthia Feliciano, "Will the New Second Generation Experience 'Downward Assimilation'? Segmented Assimilation Re-Assessed," *Ethnic & Racial Studies* 27 (2004): 376–402.
30. Charles Herschman, "The Educational Enrollment of Immigrant Youth: A Test of the Segmented-Assimilation Hypothesis," *Demography* 38 (2001): 317–36.
31. Reynolds Farley and Richard Alba, "The New Second Generation in the United States," *International Migration Review* 36 (2002): 669–90.
32. Herschman, "The Educational Enrollment of Immigrant Youth."
33. Min Zhou and Carl L. Bankston, "The Social Adjustment of Vietnamese American Adolescents: Evidence of a Segmented-Assimilation Approach," *Social Science Quarterly* 78 (1997): 508–13.
34. Mary C. Waters, *Black Identities: West Indian Immigrant Dreams and American Realities* (Cambridge, MA: Harvard University Press, 1999).
35. William L. Yancey, Eugene P. Ericksen, and Richard N. Juliani, "Emergent Ethnicity: A Review and Reformulation," *American Sociological Review* 41 (1976): 391–403.
36. Ibid., p. 393.
37. See Jose Itzigsohn, "Immigration and the Boundaries of Citizenship."
38. Stanley Lieberson and Mary C. Waters, "The Location of Ethnic and Racial Groups in the United States," *Sociological Forum* 2 (1987): 780–810.
39. Office of Immigration Statistics, "Legal Permanent Residents," *2005 Yearbook of Immigration Statistics* (Washington, DC: U.S. Government Printing Office, 2006), Table 3.
40. Marc J. Perry and Jason P. Schachter, "Migration of Natives and the Foreign Born: 1995 to 2000," *Census 2000 Special Reports* (August 2003).
41. Ibid., Table 1, p. 3.
42. Robert E. Park, "The Urban Community as a Spatial Pattern and a Moral Order," in Ernest W. Burgess (ed.), *The Urban Community* (Chicago: University of Chicago Press, 1926), pp. 3–18.
43. Douglas S. Massey and Nancy A. Denton, "Spatial Assimilation as a Socioeconomic Outcome," *American Sociological Review* 50 (1985): 94–105.
44. Richard D. Alba, *Ethnic Identity: The Transformation of White America* (New Haven, Conn.: Yale University Press, 1990).
45. Richard D. Alba, *Italian Americans: Into the Twilight of Ethnicity* (Englewood Cliffs, N.J.: Prentice Hall, 1985), pp. 159–75.

46. Yancey, Ericksen, and Juliani, "Emergent Ethnicity," p. 399.
47. See Herbert J. Gans, "Symbolic Ethnicity and Symbolic Religiosity: Towards a Comparison of Ethnic and Religious Acculturation," *Ethnic and Racial Studies* 17 (1994): 577–92.
48. Carl Haub, "Hispanics Account for Almost One-Half of U.S. Population Growth," *Population Bulletin* (February 2006): 1.
49. Steven A. Camarota, "Immigrant Job Gains and Native Job Losses 2000 to 2004," Center for Immigration Studies. Accessed online at www.cis.org/articles/2005/sactestimony050405.html [December 28, 2006].
50. George J. Borjas and Leonard F. Katz, "The Evolution of the Mexican-American Workforce in the United States," National Bureau of Economic Research, NBER Working Paper No. 11281 (April 2005).
51. Greg Anrig, Jr. and Tova A. Wang, "Immigration, Jobs, and the American Economy," The Century Foundation. Accessed online at www.immigrationonline.org/publications.asp?subjectID=1+pubid2491 [December 28, 2006].
52. National Research Council, *The New Americans: Economic, Demographic, and Fiscal Effects of Immigration*, ed. James P. Smith and Barry Edmonston (Washington, D.C.: National Academies Press, 1997), p. 337.
53. Ibid.
54. Greg Anrig, Jr. and Tova A. Wang, *op cit.*
55. Public Agenda, "Immigration: People's Chief Concerns." Accessed online at www.publicagenda.org/ [December 28, 2006].
56. Jeffrey Passel, "The Size and Characteristics of the Unauthorized Migrant Population in the United States," *Pew Hispanic Center Research Report* (2006).
57. Ibid.
58. U.S. Citizenship and Immigration Services, *This is USCIS*. Available at http://uscis.gov/graphics/aboutus/thisisimm.htm [August 4, 2006].
59. Philip Martin, "The Battle over Unauthorized Immigration to the United States," Population Reference Bureau (April 11, 2006): 1.
60. Quoted in W. C. Smith, *Americans in the Making* (New York: Appleton-Century, 1939), p. 394.
61. Maurice R. Davie, *World Immigration* (New York: Macmillan, 1936), p. 36.
62. Carl Wittke, *We Who Build America*, rev. ed. (Cleveland: Cast Western Reserve University Press, 1967), pp. 196–199; James S. Olson, *The Ethnic Dimension in American History* (New York: St. Martin's Press, 1979), pp. 103–6.
63. Hyon B. Shin and Rosalind Bruno, "Language Use and English-Speaking Ability: 2000," *Census 2000 Brief* [October 2003].
64. U.S. Department of Education, National Center for Education Statistics, *The Condition of Education: 2006* (Washington, DC: U.S. Government Printing Office, 2006), p. 34.
65. Michael Fix, "Immigrant Children, Urban Schools, and the No Child Left Behind Act," Migration Policy Institute (November 2005).
66. See Vickie W. Lewelling, "Official English and English Plus: An Update," *ERIC Digest*. Available at http://www.cal.org/resources/digest/lewell01.html [December 28, 2003].
67. Christine H. Rossell and Keith Baker, "The Educational Effectiveness of Bilingual Education," *Research in the Teaching of English* 30 (1996): 7–74.

68. Kendra Hamilton, "Bilingual or Immersion?" *Diverse Issues in Higher Education* 23 (2006): 23–6.
69. Alejandro Portés and Richard Schauffler, "Language and the Second Generation: Bilingualism Yesterday and Today," in Alejandro Portés (ed.), *The New Second Generation* (New York: Russell Sage Foundation, 1996), pp. 8–29.
70. Linda Chavez, "Hispanics vs. Their Leaders," *Commentary* (October 1991), pp. 47–49.
71. U.S. English, "Making English the Official language." Available at www.us-english.org/inc/ [December 28, 2006].
72. Rasmussen Reports, "85% Support English as Official Language of U.S." Accessed at www.rasmussenreports.com/2006/June%20Dailies/EnglishAs NationalLanguage.htm [December 28, 2006]. Nathan Kirkham, "Diversity and Dynamics of Opinion." Available http://web.utk.edu/nkirkham/podynamf99.html [December 28, 2006].
73. See Pew Hispanic Center, "Hispanic Attitudes Toward Learning English (2006). Accessed online at http://pewhispanic.org/files/factsheets/20.pdf [December 28, 2006]; Public Agenda, "Immigration: People's Chief Concerns." Accessed online at http://www.publicagenda.org/issues [December 28, 2006].
74. Rubén G. Rumbaut and Alejandro Portes, *Ethnicities: Children of Immigrants in America* (Berkeley: University of California Press, 2001).
75. Rubén G. Rumbaut, "A Language Graveyard? Immigration, Generation, and Linguistic Acculturation in the United States," paper presented to the International Conference on the Integration of Immigrants: Language and Educational Achievement, Social Science Research Center, Berlin, June 30–July 1, 2005.
76. U.S. Census Bureau, *Census 2000 Supplementary Survey*, Table PO35.
77. Rubén G. Rumbaut, "Origins and Destinies: Immigration to the United States since World War II," *Sociological Forum* 9 (1994): 615.
78. Martin E. Spencer, "Multiculturalism, Political Correctness and the Politics of Identity," *Sociological Forum* 9 (December 1994): 547–67.
79. Jacob Weisbergm, "Thin Skins," *New Republic* (February 18, 1991): 23.
80. John J. Miller, *The Unmaking of Americans: How Multiculturalism Has Undermined America's Assimilation Ethic* (New York: Simon & Schuster, 1998).
81. U.S. Bureau of the Census, *Projected Population by Race, and Hispanic Origin: 2000 to 2050* (March 18, 2004).
82. U.S. Bureau of the Census, *Statistical Abstract of the United States 2007* (Washington, D.C.: U.S. Government Printing Office, 2006), table 58, p. 51.
83. Ibid.
84. George A. Yancey and Sherelyn W. Yancey, "Black-White Differences in the Use of Personal Advertisements for Individuals Seeking Interracial Relationships," *Journal of Black Studies* 27 (May 1997): 650–67.
85. George A. Yancey and Sherelyn W. Yancey, "Interracial Dating: Evidence from Personal Advertisement," *Journal of Family Issues* 19 (May 1998): 334–48.
86. Richard Lewis, Jr., George Yancey, and Siri S. Bletzer, "Racial and Nonracial Factors That Influence Spouse Choice in Black/White Marriages," *Journal of Black Studies* 28 (September 1997): 60–78.
87. Adam B. Troy, Jamie Lewis-Smith, and Philippe Laurenceau, "Interracial and Intraracial Romantic Relationships: The Search for Differences in Satisfaction,

Conflict, and Attachment Style," *Journal of Social and Personal Relationships* 23 (2006): 665–80.

88. Suzanne Model and Gene Fisher, "Black-White Unions: West Indians and African Americans Compared," *Demography* 38 (2001): 177–85.

89. George Yancey, "Who Interracially Dates: An Examination of the Characteristics of Those Who Have Interracially Dated," *Journal of Comparative Family Studies* 33 (2002): 179–90.

90. Kathleen Odell Korgen, *From Black to Biracial: Transforming Racial Identity among Americans* (Westport, Conn.: Praeger, 1999).

APPENDIX

Immigration, 1820–2005

Immigration by Country, for Decades 1820–2005[a]

Countries	1820	1821–1830	1831–1840	1841–1850
All Countries[1]	**8,385**	**143,439**	**599,125**	**1,713,251**
Europe	7,690	98,797	495,681	1,597,442
Austria–Hungary[2]	—	—	—	—
Belgium	1	27	22	5,074
Denmark	20	169	1,063	539
France	371	8,497	45,575	77,262
Germany	968	6,761	152,454	434,626
Greece	—	20	49	16
Ireland[5]	3,614	50,724	207,381	780,719
Italy	30	409	2,253	1,870
Netherlands	49	1,078	1,412	8,251
Norway[6] ⎤ Sweden ⎦	3	91	1,201	13,903
Poland[23]	5	16	369	105
Portugal	35	145	829	550
Romania[7]	—	—	—	—
Soviet Union	14	75	277	551
Spain	139	2,477	2,125	2,209
Switzerland	31	3,226	4,821	4,644
United Kingdom[5,8]				
England	1,782	14,055	7,611	32,092
Scotland	268	2,912	2,667	3,712
Wales	—	170	185	1,261
Not specified	360	7,942	65,347	229,979
Other Europe	—	3	40	79
Asia	6	30	55	141
China[10]	1	2	8	35
India	1	8	39	36
Japan[14]	—	—	—	—
Turkey	1	20	7	59
Other Asia	3	—	1	11
Western Hemisphere	**387**	**11,564**	**33,424**	**62,469**
Canada and Newfoundland[17,18]	209	2,277	13,624	41,723
Mexico[18]	1	4,817	6,599	3,271
West Indies	164	3,834	12,301	13,528
Central America	2	105	44	368
South America	11	531	856	3,579

(continued)

See notes and source at end of appendix.

Immigration by Country, for Decades 1820–2005 *(Continued)*

Countries	1851–1860	1861–1870	1871–1880	1881–1890
All Countries[1]	**2,598,214**	**2,314,824**	**2,812,191**	**5,246,613**
Europe	2,452,577	2,065,141	2,271,925	4,735,484
Austria[2,3] ⎫				
Hungary ⎭	—	7,800	72,969	353,719
Belgium	4,738	6,734	7,221	20,177
Bulgaria	—	—	—	—
Czechoslovakia[4]	—	—	—	—
Denmark	3,749	17,094	31,771	88,132
Estonia	—	—	—	—
Finland	—	—	—	—
France	76,358	35,986	72,206	50,464
Germany	951,667	787,468	718,182	1,452,970
Greece	31	72	210	2,308
Ireland[5]	914,119	435,778	436,871	655,482
Italy	9,231	11,725	55,759	307,309
Latvia	—	—	—	—
Lithuania	—	—	—	—
Luxembourg	—	—	—	—
Netherlands	10,789	9,102	16,541	53,701
Norway[6]		71,631	95,323	176,586
Poland[23]	1,164	2,027	12,970	51,806
Portugal	1,055	2,658	14,082	16,978
Romania[7]	—	—	11	6,348
Soviet Union	457	2,512	39,284	213,282
Spain	9,298	6,697	5,266	4,419
Sweden[6]	20,931	37,667	115,922	391,776
Switzerland	25,011	23,286	28,293	81,988
United Kingdom[5,8]				
England	247,125	222,277	437,706	644,680
Scotland	38,331	38,769	87,564	149,869
Wales	6,319	4,313	6,631	12,640
Not specified	132,199	341,537	16,142	168
Yugoslavia[9]	—	—	—	—
Other Europe	5	8	1,001	682
Asia	**41,538**	**64,759**	**124,160**	**69,942**
China[10]	41,397	64,301	123,201	61,711
India	43	69	163	269
Japan[14]	—	186	149	2,270
Turkey	83	131	404	3,782
Other Asia	15	72	243	1,910
Western Hemisphere	**74,720**	**166,607**	**404,044**	**426,967**
Canada and Newfoundland[17,18]	59,309	153,878	383,640	393,304
Mexico[18]	3,078	2,191	5,162	1,913
West Indies	10,660	9,046	13,957	29,042
Central America	449	95	157	404
South America	1,224	1,397	1,128	2,304
Other America[22]	—	—	—	—

Immigration by Country, for Decades 1820–2005 *(Continued)*

Countries	1891–1900	1901–1910	1911–1920	1921–1930
All Countries[1]	3,687,564	8,795,386	5,735,811	4,107,209
Europe	3,555,352	8,056,040	4,321,887	2,463,194
Austria[2,3] ⎫			453,649	32,868
Hungary ⎭	529,707	2,145,266	442,693	30,680
Belgium	18,167	41,635	33,746	15,846
Bulgaria	160	39,280	22,533	2,945
Czechoslovakia[4]	—	—	3,426	102,194
Denmark	50,231	65,285	41,983	32,430
Estonia	—	—	—	—
Finland	—	—	756	16,691
France	30,770	73,379	61,897	49,610
Germany[2,3]	505,152	341,498	143,945	412,202
Greece	15,979	167,519	184,201	
Ireland[5]	388,416	339,065	146,181	157,420
Italy	651,893	2,045,877	1,109,524	159,731
Latvia	—	—	—	13,012
Lithuania	—	—	—	—
Luxembourg				51,084
Netherlands	26,758	48,262	43,718	220,591
Norway[6]	95,015	190,505	66,395	455,315
Poland[23]	96,720	—	4,813	—
Portugal	27,508	69,149	89,732	—
Romania[1]	12,750	53,008	13,311	—
Soviet Union[23]	505,290	1,597,306	921,201	26,948
Spain	8,731	27,935	68,611	68,531
Sweden[6]	226,266	249,534	95,074	227,734
Switzerland	31,179	34,922	23,091	29,994
United Kingdom[5,8]				67,646
England	216,726	388,017	249,944	61,742
Scotland	44,188	120,469	78,357	28,958
Wales	10,557	17,464	13,107	97,249
Not specified	67	—	—	29,676
Yugoslavia[9]	—	—	1,888	49,064
Other Europe	122	665	8,111	22,983
Asia	**74,862**	**323,543**	**247,236**	**112,059**
China[10]	14,799	20,605	21,278	29,907
India	68	4,713	2,082	1,886
Japan[14]	25,942	129,797	83,837	33,462
Turkey	30,425	157,369	134,066	33,824
Other Asia	3,628	11,059	5,973	12,980
Western Hemisphere	*38,972*	*361,888*	*1,143,671*	*1,516,716*
Canada and Newfoundland[17,18]	3,311	179,226	742,185	924,515
Mexico[18,19]	971	49,642	219,004	459,287
West Indies	33,066	107,548	123,424	74,899
Central America	549	8,192	17,159	15,769
South America	1,075	17,280	41,899	42,215
Other America[22]	—	—	—	31

(continued)

Immigration by Country, for Decades 1820–2005 *(Continued)*

Countries	1931–1940	1941–1950	1951–1960
All Countries[1]	528,431	1,035,039	2,515,479
Europe	347,552	621,124	1,325,640
Albania	2,040	85	—
Austria[24]	3,563	24,860	67,106
Hungary	7,861	3,469	36,637
Belgium	4,817	12,189	18,575
Bulgaria	938	375	—
Czechoslovakia[4]	14,393	8,347	918
Denmark	2,559	5,393	10,984
Estonia	506	212	—
Finland	2,146	2,503	—
France	12,623	38,809	51,121
Germany[24]	114,058	226,578	477,765
Greece	9,119	,973	47,608
Ireland	13,167	26,967	57,332
Italy	68,028	57,661	185,491
Latvia	1,192	361	—
Lithuania	2,201	683	—
Luxembourg	565	820	—
Netherlands	7,150	14,860	52,277
Norway	4,740	10,100	22,935
Poland[23]	17,026	7,571	9,985
Portugal	3,329	7,423	19,588
Romania	3,871	1,076	1,039
Soviet Union[23]	1,356	548	584
Spain	3,258	2,898	7,894
Sweden	3,960	10,665	21,697
Switzerland	5,512	10,547	17,675
United Kingdom[5,8]			204,468
England	21,756	112,252	—
Scotland	6,887	16,131	—
Wales	735	3,209	—
Not specified	—	—	—
Yugoslavia[9]	5,835	1,576	8,225
Other Europe	2,361	3,983	16,350
Asia	16,081	32,360	150,106
Cambodia	—	—	11
China[10]	4,928	16,709	9,657
India	496	1,761	1,973
Iran[12]	—	—	3,388
Israel[13]	—	—	25,476
Japan	1,948	1,555	46,250
Korea[15]	—	—	7,635
Philippines[16]	—	—	27,318
Turkey	1,065	798	3,519
Vietnam[11]	—	—	366
Other Asia	7,644	11,537	—

Countries	1931–1940	1941–1950	1951–1960
Western Hemisphere	**160,037**	**354,804**	**996,944**
Canada and Newfoundland[17,18]	108,527	171,718	377,952
Colombia[20]	—	—	18,048
Cuba[12]	—	—	78,948
Dominican Republic[20]	—	—	9,897
Ecuador[20]	—	—	9,841
El Salvador	—	—	5,895
Haiti[20]	—	—	4,442
Jamaica[21]	—	—	8,869
Mexico[18]	22,319	60,589	299,811
West Indies	15,502	49,725	—
Central America	5,861	21,665	—
South America	7,803	21,831	—
Other America[22]	25	29,276	—

Countries	1961–1970	1971–1980	1981–1990
All Countries[1]	**3,321,677**	**4,493,314**	**7,338,062**
Europe	**1,123,363**	**800,368**	**761,550**
Austria	20,621	9,478	18,340
Hungary	5,401	6,550	6,545
Belgium	9,192	5,329	7,066
Czechoslovakia	3,273	6,023	7,227
Denmark	9,201	2,609	5,370
France	45,237	25,069	32,353
Germany	190,796	43,986	91,961
Greece	85,969	92,369	38,377
Ireland[5]	37,461	44,731	31,969
Italy	214,111	129,368	67,254
Netherlands	30,606	10,492	12,238
Norway	15,484	3,941	4,164
Poland	53,539	37,234	83,252
Portugal	76,065	101,710	40,431
Romania	2,531	12,393	30,857
Soviet Union	2,336	38,961	57,677
Spain	44,659	39,141	20,433
Sweden	17,116	6,531	11,018
Switzerland	18,453	8,255	8,849
United Kingdom[5,8]	214,518	155,572	159,173
Yugoslavia	20,381	30,540	18,762
Other Europe	11,604	9,287	8,234
Asia	**427,771**	**1,507,178**	**2,738,157**
Cambodia	85	7,648	111,971
China[10]	34,764	124,326	346,747
India	27,189	164,134	250,786
Iran[12]	10,339	45,136	116,172
Israel[13]	29,602	37,713	44,273
Japan	39,988	49,775	47,085
Korea[15]	37,654	243,299	333,746

(continued)

Immigration by Country, for Decades 1820–2005 (Continued)

Countries	1961–1970	1971–1980	1981–1990
All Countries[1]	3,321,677	4,493,314	7,338,062
Philippines[16]	113,086	319,039	548,764
Turkey	10,142	13,399	23,233
Vietnam[11]	4,932	225,642	280,782
Western Hemisphere	1,716,374	1,982,529	3,615,225
Canada and Newfoundland[17,18]	413,310	249,560	156,938
Colombia[20]	72,028	77,347	122,849
Cuba[12]	208,536	264,863	144,578
Dominican Republic[20]	93,292	148,135	252,035
Ecuador[20]	36,780	50,077	56,315
El Salvador[20]	14,992	34,436	213,539
Haiti[20]	34,499	56,335	138,379
Jamaica[21]	74,906	137,577	208,1148
Mexico[18]	453,937	640,294	1,655,843

Countries	1991–2000	2001–2005	1820–2005
All Countries[1]	9,095,417	4,902,056	70,991,487
Europe	1,359,737	772,609	39,365,557
Austria	15,500	10,250	1,854,696[2,3]
Hungary	9,382	6,491	1,683,633[2,3]
Belgium	7,090	4,125	221,771
Czechoslovakia	9,816	9,290	164,907[4]
Denmark	6,079	3,100	379,591
France	35,820	22,116	845,523
Germany	92,606	74,164	7,250,235[23,24]
Greece	26,759	7,013	737,676
Ireland[5]	56,950	7,534	4,789,717
Italy	62,722	13,708	5,449,538
Netherlands	13,308	9,368	396,908
Norway	5,178	2,356	761,253[6]
Poland	163,747	65,471	835,554[23]
Portugal	22,916	5,866	530,043
Romania	51,203	24,535	280,579[7]
Soviet Union/Russia	462,874	246,075	4,152,655[23]
Spain	17,157	8,020	310,325
Sweden	12,715	8,061	1,267,584[6]
Switzerland	11,841	6,799	378,081
United Kingdom	151,866	87,849	5,358,865
Yugoslavia	66,557	90,637	293,465
Other Europe	57,651	36,848	276,473
Asia	2,795,672	1,598,969	10,413,821
China	419,114	259,121	1,592,511
Hong Kong	109,779	33,660	445,669[11]
India	363,060	323,996	1,142,772
Iran	68,556	33,587	278,994[12]
Israel	39,397	25,654	202,591[13]
Japan	67,942	44,816	575,002[14]

Countries	1991–2000	2001–2005	1820–2005
Korea	164,166	97,164	903,578[15]
Philippines	503,945	254,577	1,785,175[16]
Turkey	38,212	21,635	472,174
Vietnam	286,145	149,042	893,404[11]
Other Asia	735,356	268,116	2,034,190
Western Hemisphere	**4,486,806**	**2,095,813**	**19,650,167**
Argentina	26,644	22,027	179,789[20]
Canada and Newfoundland	191,987	125,949	4,613,521
Colombia	128,499	91,808	515,660[20]
Cuba	169,322	97,988	1,016,020[12]
Dominican Republic	335,251	127,066	972,453[20]
Ecuador	76,592	47,094	279,453[20]
El Salvador	215,798	139,390	629,855[20]
Haiti	179,644	80,736	495,137[20]
Jamaica	169,227	73,939	672,666[21]
Mexico	2,249,421	867,417	7,005,567[19]

Region	1820–1830	1831–1840	1841–1850	1851–1860	1861–1870	1871–1880	1881–1890
Africa	17	54	55	210	312	358	857
Caribbean	3,998	12,301	13,528	10,660	9,046	13,857	29,042
Central America	107	44	368	449	95	157	404
Oceania	3	9	29	158	214	10,914	12,574
South America	542	856	3,579	1,224	1,397	1,128	2,304
Not specified	33,330	69,902	53,145	29,011	17,791	790	789

Region	1891–1900	1901–1910	1911–1920	1921–1930	1931–1940	1941–1950	1951–1960
Africa	350	7,368	8,443	6,286	1,750	7,367	14,092
Caribbean	33,066	107,548	123,414	74,899	15,502	49,325	123,091
Central America	549	8,192	17,159	15,769	5,861	21,665	44,751
Oceania	3,965	13,024	13,427	8,726	2,483	14,551	12,976
South America	1,075	17,280	41,899	42,215	7,803	21,831	91,628
Not specified[22]	14,063	33,523	1,147	228	—	142	12,491

Region	1961–1970	1971–1980	1981–1990	1991–2000	2001–2005	Total Years 1820–2005
Africa	28,954	80,779	176,893	354,939	293,894	982,978
Caribbean	470,213	741,126	872,051	978,787	431,290	4,113,254
Central America	101,330	134,640	468,088	526,915	305,974	1,652,517
Oceania	25,122	41,242	45,205	55,845	33,158	293,625
South America	257,940	295,741	461,847	539,656	365,171	2,155,116
Not specified[22]	93	12	1,032	42,418	107,613	417,490
Total	883,652	1,343,540	2,025,116	2,498,560	1,537,100	9,614,980

[1] Data for years prior to 1906 relate to country whence alien came; data from 1906–79 and 1984–99 are for country of last permanent residence; and data for 1980–83 refer to country of birth. Because of changes in boundaries, changes in lists of countries, and lack of data for specified countries for various periods, data for certain countries, especially for the total period

1820–1999, are not comparable throughout. Data for specified countries are included with countries to which they belonged prior to World War I.

[2] Data for Austria–Hungary were not reported until 1861.

[3] Data for Austria and Hungary not reported separately for all years during the period.

[4] No data available for Czechoslovakia until 1920.

[5] Prior to 1926, data for Northern Ireland included in Ireland.

[6] Data for Norway and Sweden not reported separately until 1871.

[7] No data available for Romania until 1880.

[8] Since 1925, data for United Kingdom refer to England, Scotland, Wales, and Northern Ireland.

[9] In 1920, a separate enumeration was made for the Kingdom of Serbs, Croats, and Slovenes. Since 1922, the Serb, Croat, and Slovene Kingdom recorded as Yugoslavia.

[10] Beginning in 1957, China includes Taiwan. As of January 1, 1979, the United States has recognized the People's Republic of China.

[11] Data not reported separately until 1952.

[12] Data not reported separately until 1925.

[13] Data not reported separately until 1949.

[14] No data available for Japan until 1861.

[15] Data not reported separately until 1948.

[16] Prior to 1934, Philippines recorded as insular travel.

[17] Prior to 1920, Canada and Newfoundland recorded as British North America. From 1820 to 1898, figures include all British North America possessions.

[18] Land arrivals not completely enumerated until 1908.

[19] No data available for Mexico from 1886 to 1994.

[20] Data not reported separately until 1932.

[21] Data for Jamaica not collected until 1953. In prior years, consolidated under British West Indies, which is included in "Other Caribbean."

[22] Included in countries "Not specified" until 1925.

[23] From 1899 to 1919, data for Poland included in Austria-Hungary, Germany, and the Soviet Union.

[24] From 1938 to 1945, data for Austria included in Germany.

Source: Office of Immigration Statistics, *2004 Yearbook of Immigration Statistics*. Washington, DC: U.S. Government Printing Office, 2005, Table 2.

Photo Credits